# THE DEATH OF THE WEST

Also by Patrick J. Buchanan

*The New Majority*

*Conservative Votes, Liberal Victories*

*Right from the Beginning*

*The Great Betrayal*

*A Republic, Not an Empire*

· PATRICK J. BUCHANAN ·

# THE DEATH
# OF THE WEST

HOW DYING POPULATIONS AND
IMMIGRANT INVASIONS IMPERIL OUR
COUNTRY AND CIVILIZATION

Thomas Dunne Books

ST. MARTIN'S GRIFFIN    NEW YORK

THOMAS DUNNE BOOKS.
An imprint of St. Martin's Press.

www.stmartins.com

Production Editor: David Stanford Burr

Library of Congress Cataloging-in-Publication Data

Buchanan, Patrick J.
       The death of the West : how dying populations and immigrant invasions imperil our
   country and civilization / Patrick J. Buchanan.
       p. cm.
   Includes bibliographical references.
   ISBN 0-312-28548-5 (hc)
   ISBN 0-312-30259-2 (pbk)
       1. Civilization, Western—Forecasting. 2. Social prediction—United States. 3. Social
   prediction—Europe. 4. United States—Social conditions—1980—Forecasting. 5.
   Europe—Social conditions—Forecasting. 6. United States—Population—Forecasting. 7.
   Europe—Population—Forecasting. 8. United States—Emigration and immigration—Social
   aspects. 9. Europe—Emigration and immigration—Social aspects. I. Title.

   CB245 .B83 2002
   306'.0973'01—dc21

                                                                             2001051289

First St. Martin's Griffin Edition: October 2002

10  9  8  7  6  5  4  3  2  1

# CONTENTS

This is the way the world ends

This is the way the world ends

This is the way the world ends

Not with a bang but a whimper.

—T. S. Eliot,

"The Hollow Men"

Some withered nerve in her brain twitched slightly, she softened, smiled, and told him a story about her grandfather who had been a page at Queen Victoria's coronation.

"That was another world," he said.

"Another civilisation," she corrected him, "the one I was born into. It has died. I say: died, not vanished, because it was a living organism. A civilisation based on the family. What has taken its place is not alive; an atomised society, without security, without warmth, a chaos of fragmented mechanical relationships. O, I know as well as you do, that in my world all was not well, there was ignorance and poverty. But the right way was not to tear that world down and replace it by anarchy. The family base should have been extended, cherished, encouraged."

—Storm Jameson, 1966,
*The Early Life of Stephen Hind*

# INTRODUCTION

"**P**at, we're losing the country we grew up in."

Again and again in the endless campaign of 2000 I heard that lament from men and women across America. But what did they mean by it?

WHY SHOULD SADNESS or melancholy—as though one's father were dying and there were nothing to be done—have crept into the hearts of Americans on the cusp of the "Second American Century"? Were these not, as Mr. Clinton constantly reminded us, the best of times in America, with the lowest unemployment and inflation in thirty years, crime rates falling, and incomes soaring? Are we not, as Madeleine Albright never ceased to boast, "the indispensable nation"? Was this not, as Mr. Bush trumpeted, our time "of unrivaled military power, economic promise, and cultural influence"?[1] We had won the Cold War. Our ideas were winning all over the world. What were they talking about? What was their problem?

It is this: America has undergone a cultural and social revolution. We are not the same country that we were in 1970 or even 1980.

We are not the same people. After the 2000 election, pollster William McInturf told the *Washington Post:* "We have two massive colliding forces. One is rural, Christian, religiously conservative. [The other] is socially tolerant, pro-choice, secular, living in New England and the Pacific Coast . . ."[2]

Disraeli said Victorian England was "two nations," rich and poor.[3] Novelist John Dos Passos wrote after the trial and execution of Sacco and Vanzetti, "All right, we are two nations."[4] As I listened to the Inaugural address, a line struck home. President Bush seemed to have heard what I had heard and found what I had found. "And sometimes," he said, "our differences run so deep, it seems we share a continent, but not a country."[5]

While the awful events of September 11 created a national unity unseen since Pearl Harbor—behind President Bush and his resolve to punish the perpetrators of the massacres of three thousand Americans—they also exposed a new divide. This chasm in our country is not one of income, ideology, or faith, but of ethnicity and loyalty. Suddenly, we awoke to the realization that among our thirty-one million foreign-born, a third are here illegally, tens of thousands are loyal to regimes with which we could be at war, and some are trained terrorists sent here to murder Americans. For the first time since Andrew Jackson drove the British out of Louisiana in 1815, a foreign enemy is inside the gates, and the American people are at risk in their own country. In those days after September 11, many suddenly saw how the face of America had changed in their own lifetimes.

When Richard Nixon took his oath of office in 1969, there were 9 million foreign-born in the United States. When President Bush raised his hand, the number was nearing 30 million. Almost a million immigrants enter every year; half a million illegal aliens come in with them. The adjusted census of 2000 puts the number of illegals in the United States at 9 million. Northeastern University estimates 11 million, as many illegal aliens as there are people in Alabama, Mississippi, and Louisiana.[6] There are more foreign-born in California—8.4 million—than people in New Jersey, more foreign-born in New York

State than people in South Carolina. Even the Great Wave of immigration from 1890 to 1920 was nothing like this.

"America is God's Crucible, the great Melting-Pot where all the races of Europe are melting and reforming," wrote Israel Zangwill, the Russian-Jewish playwright, in his famous 1908 play *The Melting Pot*.[7] But the immigration tsunami rolling over America is not coming from "all the races of Europe." The largest population transfer in history is coming from all the races of Asia, Africa, and Latin America, and they are not "melting and reforming."

In 1960, only sixteen million Americans did not trace their ancestors to Europe. Today, the number is eighty million. No nation has ever undergone so rapid and radical a transformation. At Portland State in 1998, Mr. Clinton rhapsodized to a cheering student audience about a day when Americans of European descent will be a minority.

> Today, largely because of immigration, there is no majority race in Hawaii or Houston or New York City. Within five years there will be no majority race in our largest state, California. In a little more than fifty years there will be no majority race in the United States. No other nation in history has gone through demographic change of this magnitude in so short a time.[8]

Correction: no nation in history has gone through a demographic change of this magnitude in so short a time, and remained the same nation. Mr. Clinton assured us that it will be a better America when we are all minorities and realize true "diversity." Well, those students are going to find out, for they will spend their golden years in a Third World America.

Uncontrolled immigration threatens to deconstruct the nation we grew up in and convert America into a conglomeration of peoples with almost nothing in common—not history, heroes, language, culture, faith, or ancestors. Balkanization beckons. "The strongest tendency of the late [twentieth century]," writes Jacques Barzun in his history of the West, *From Dawn to Decadence*, "was Separatism. . . .

It affected all forms of unity. . . . The ideal of Pluralism had disintegrated and Separatism took its place; as one partisan of the new goal put it, 'Salad Bowl is better than melting pot.' "⁹ The great nations of Europe have begun to break apart. Writes Barzun:

> If one surveyed the Occident . . . one could see that the greatest political creation of the West, the nation-state, was stricken. In Great Britain the former kingdoms of Scotland and Wales won autonomous parliaments; in France the Bretons, Basques, and Alsatians cried out for regional power. Corsica wanted independence and a language of its own, Italy harbored a League that would cut off the North from the South, and Venice produced a small party wanting their city a separate state . . . ¹⁰

As people return their allegiance to the lands whence they came, transnational elites pull us in the opposite direction. The final surrender of national sovereignty to world government is now openly advocated. From Walter Cronkite to Strobe Talbott, from the World Federalist Association to the UN Millennium Summit, the chorus swells.

At Maastricht in 1991, fifteen European nations, including France, Italy, Germany, and Great Britain, decided to begin converting their free-trade zone into a political union and transferring their sovereign powers to a socialist superstate. In 2000, the president-elect of Mexico came here to propose a North American Union of Canada, Mexico, and the United States. Though the erasure of our borders would mean the end of our nation, Vicente Fox was hailed in the U.S. media as a visionary, and President Clinton expressed his regret that he might not be around to see it happen: "I think over the long run, our countries will become more interdependent. . . . It will be the way of the world. . . . I regret that I won't be around for a lot of it. But I think it's a good thing."¹¹

Nor is America immune to the forces of separatism. A sense that America, too, is pulling apart along the seams of ethnicity and race is spreading. Moreover, America has just undergone a cultural revolution, with a new elite now occupying the commanding heights. Through its capture of the institutions that shape and transmit ideas, opinions, beliefs, and values—TV, the arts, entertainment, education—this elite is creating a new people. Not only ethnically and racially, but culturally and morally, we are no longer one people or "one nation under God."

Millions have begun to feel like strangers in their own land. They recoil from a popular culture that is saturated with raw sex and trumpets hedonistic values. They see old holidays disappear and old heroes degraded. They see the art and artifacts of a glorious past removed from their museums and replaced by the depressing, the ugly, the abstract, the anti-American. They watch as books they cherished disappear from the schools they attended, to be replaced by authors and titles they never heard of. The moral code that they were raised to live by has been overthrown. The culture they grew up with is dying inside the country they grew up in.

In half a lifetime, many Americans have seen their God dethroned, their heroes defiled, their culture polluted, their values assaulted, their country invaded, and themselves demonized as extremists and bigots for holding on to beliefs Americans have held for generations. "To make us love our country, our country ought to be lovely," said Burke.[12] In too many ways America is no longer lovely. Though she remains a great country, many wonder if she is still a *good* country. Some feel that she is no longer their country. We did not leave America, they say, she left us. As Euripides wrote, "There is no greater sorrow on earth, than the loss of one's native land."[13]

When Cornwallis's army marched out of Yorktown, the fife and drums played "The World Turned Upside Down." Now *our* world has been turned upside down. What was right and true yesterday is wrong and false today. What was immoral and shameful—promiscuity, abortion, euthanasia, suicide—has become progressive and praiseworthy. Nietzsche called it the transvaluation of all values; the old virtues become sins, and the old sins become virtues.

Every few years, a storm erupts when some public figure blurts out, "America is a Christian nation!" She was once, and a majority yet call themselves Christians. But our dominant culture should more accu-

rately be called post-Christian, or anti-Christian, for the values it cel-
ebrates are the antithesis of what it used to mean to be a Christian.

"I am the Lord thy God; thou shalt not have strange gods before
me" was the the first commandment Moses brought down from
Mount Sinai. But the new culture rejects the God of the Old Testament and burns its incense at the altars of the global economy.
Kipling's "Gods of the Market Place" have shouldered aside the God
of the Gospels. Sex, fame, money, power—those are what our new
America is all about.

We are two countries, two peoples. An older America is passing
away, and a new America is coming into its own. The new Americans
who grew up in the 1960s and the years since did not like the old
America. They thought it a bigoted, reactionary, repressive, stodgy
country. So they kicked the dust from their heels and set out to build
a new America, and they have succeeded. To its acolytes the cultural
revolution has been a glorious revolution. But to millions, they have
replaced the good country we grew up in with a cultural wasteland
and a moral sewer that are not worth living in and not worth fighting
for—their country, not ours.

In the election of 2000, the political differences between the Beltway
parties were inconsequential. Mr. Bush wanted a larger tax cut than
Mr. Gore, who wanted to spend more for prescription drugs. Why then
the bile and bitterness of the Florida recount? Writes Terry Teachout
in his postelection assessment of a polarized America, "The rancorous
intensity with which the Bush and Gore camps disputed the outcome of
the 2000 election all too clearly reflected the magnitude of their culture
differences, and it may be that the tone of that dispute will characterize
American politics for the foreseeable future."[14]

Exactly. The savagery of our politics reflects the depth of the moral
divide that separates us as Americans. A hundred times in the campaign of 2000, a voter would come up and say that he or she believed
in me and agreed with me, but could not vote for me. These people
had to vote for Bush, because only Bush could keep Gore out of the
White House, and, "We must stop Gore!" It was not that they dis-

agreed with Clinton and Gore. They detested them. The cultural revolution has poisoned American politics, and we have not begun to see the worst of it.

In the hours after that awful morning of September 11, Americans did come together again—in grief and sorrow over our terrible losses, in admiration and awe of the heroic firemen who ran into the World Trade Center as others ran out to safety, in our rage and resolution to do justice to those who did this to our countrymen. But by the new year, that unity had begun to fade. It did not long survive our first victory over the Taliban anymore than the first President Bush's 90-percent support survived his victory in Desert Storm. For our divisions are rooted in our deepest beliefs, and upon those beliefs Americans are as divided as we were when General Beauregard gave the order to fire on Fort Sumter.

Once again, we are seceding from one another; only this time, it is a secession of the heart.

In one of the more controversial addresses of the twentieth century, I told the 1992 Republican National Convention at Houston:

> My friends, this election is about more than who gets what. It is about who we are. It is about what we believe, it is about what we stand for as Americans. There is a religious war going on in our country for the soul of America. It is a cultural war, as critical to the kind of nation we shall one day be as was the Cold War itself. And in that struggle for the soul of America, Clinton and Clinton are on the other side, and George Bush is on our side. And, so, we have to come home—and stand beside him.[15]

The words ignited a firestorm that blazed on through 1992 and has not yet burnt itself out. My words were called divisive and hateful. They were not. They were divisive and truthful. Let others judge, after eight years, whether I spoke the truth about Bill and Hillary Clinton.

But Mr. Clinton was rescued from certain impeachment because he personified the other side of that culture war, and his removal would have imperiled the gains of a decade. That not a single Democrat voted to convict Mr. Clinton testifies to the success of the revolution in overthrowing the old moral order and its objective standards of truth, morality, and justice. To the new elite, what advances the revolution is moral, and what threatens it is immoral. Between Senate Democrats and the O.J. jury there is a moral equivalence: truth, justice, and morality triumphed in both cases, because our side won and our man got off.

THE BOLSHEVIK REVOLUTION that began with the storming of the Winter Palace in 1917 died with the fall of the Berlin Wall in 1989. The dream of its true believers was to create a new socialist man. But police terror, the camps of the Gulag, and seventy years of indoctrinating children in hatred of the West and the moral superiority of Marx and Lenin did not work. Communism was *The God That Failed*. When the mighty structure built on a foundation of lies came crashing down, the peoples of Eastern Europe and Russia threw the statues of Stalin and Lenin and the books of Marx and Engels onto the landfill of history without looking back.

But where Lenin's revolution failed, the one that erupted on the campuses in the sixties succeeded. It put down roots in society, and it created a new America. By 2000, the adversary culture of the sixties had become our dominant culture, its victory conceded when the political base camp of traditionalism raised a white flag in Philadelphia. On the moral and social issues—the fight for the sanctity of human life and the return of God to the public square of this land we used to call "God's Country"—the Republican party raised its gloves and pleaded, *"No más."*

In *The Death of the West* I hope to describe this revolution—what it stands for, where it came from, how it went about dethroning our God, vandalizing our temples, altering our beliefs, and capturing the young, and what its triumph portends. For this revolution is not unique to us; it has captured all the nations of the West. A civilization, a culture, a faith, and a moral order rooted in that faith are passing away and are being replaced by a new civilization, culture, faith, and moral order.

But the title of this book is *The Death of the West*. And though our culture war has divided us, and mass immigration risks the balkanization of America, a graver, more immediate, crisis is at hand.

The West is dying. Its nations have ceased to reproduce, and their populations have stopped growing and begun to shrink. Not since the Black Death carried off a third of Europe in the fourteenth century has there been a graver threat to the survival of Western civilization. Today, in seventeen European countries, there are more burials than births, more coffins than cradles. The countries are Belgium, Bulgaria, Croatia, the Czech Republic, Denmark, Estonia, Germany, Hungary, Italy, Latvia, Lithuania, Portugal, Romania, Slovakia, Slovenia, Spain, and Russia.[16] Catholic, Protestant, Orthodox—all the Christian faiths are represented in the great death march of the West.

The new hedonism seems unable to give people a reason to go on living. Its earliest fruits appear to be poisonous. Will this new "liberating" culture that our young have so enthusiastically embraced prove the deadliest carcinogen of them all? And if the West is in the grip of a "culture of death," as the pope contends and the statistics seem to show, is Western civilization about to follow Lenin's empire to the same inglorious end?

A century ago, Gustave Le Bon wrote in his classic *The Crowd:*

> The real cause of the great upheavals which precede changes of civilisations, such as the fall of the Roman Empire and the rise of the Arabian Empire, is a profound modification in the ideas of the peoples. . . . The memorable events of history are the visible effects of the invisible changes of human thought. . . . The present epoch is one of these critical moments in which the thought of mankind is undergoing a process of transformation.[17]

Le Bon was speaking of his own time, the end of the nineteenth century, but what he wrote is truer of ours.

For it is this cultural revolution that has led to just such a "profound modification in the ideas" of peoples. And those ideas have made Western elites apparently indifferent to the death of their civilization. They do not seem to care if the end of the West comes by depopulation, by a surrender of nationhood, or by drowning in waves of Third World immigration. Now that all the Western empires are gone, Western Man, relieved of his duty to civilize and Christianize mankind, reveling in luxury in our age of self-indulgence, seems to have lost his will to live and reconciled himself to his impending death. Are we in the twilight of the West? Is the Death of the West irreversible? Let us review the pathologist's report.

# ENDANGERED SPECIES

Europeans are a vanishing species.[1]
>                                     —*London Times*

The most important single new certainty—if only because there is no precedent for it in all of history—is
the collapsing birthrate in the developed world.[2]
>                                     —Peter F. Drucker

As a growing population has long been a mark of healthy nations
and rising civilizations, falling populations have been a sign of nations
and civilizations in decline. If that holds true, Western civilization,
power and wealth aside, is in critical condition. For, like the Cheshire
Cat, the people of the West have begun to fade away.

As late as 1960, European people, including Americans, Austra-
lians, and Canadians, numbered 750 million, one-fourth of the 3
billion people alive. Western nations were in the baby boom of the
century. Shorn of their empires, the wounds of war healed, they
seemed alive with vitality. Indeed, neo-Malthusians were bewailing the
population explosion, warning darkly that the earth's resources and
land were running out. They were laughed at. By 2000, however, no
one was laughing.

While world population had doubled to six billion in forty years,
the European peoples had stopped reproducing. Their populations
had begun to stagnate and, in many countries, had already begun to

fall. Of Europe's forty-seven nations, only one, Muslim Albania, was, by 2000, maintaining a birthrate sufficient to keep it alive indefinitely. Europe had begun to die.

The prognosis is grim. Between 2000 and 2050, world population will grow by more than three billion to over nine billion people, but this 50 percent increase in global population will come entirely in Asia, Africa, and Latin America, as one hundred million people of European stock vanish from the earth.

In 1960, people of European ancestry were one-fourth of the world's population; in 2000, they were one-sixth; in 2050, they will be one-tenth. These are the statistics of a vanishing race. A growing awareness of what they portend has induced a sense of foreboding, even panic, in Europe.

## EUROPE

In 2000, the total population of Europe, from Iceland to Russia, was 728 million. At present birthrates, however, without new immigration, her population will crash to 600 million by 2050. That is the projection of *World Population Prospects: The 2000 Revision Highlights* released by the authoritative UN Population Division on February 28, 2001. Another study has Europe's population plummeting to 556 million by midcentury.[3] The last time Europe's population showed a drop of this magnitude was during the Black Plague of 1347–52. Economics professor Jacqueline Kasun of Humboldt State University in California, author of *War Against Population,* considers today's birth dearth an even graver crisis:

> With a plague like the [fourteenth-century] Black Death, maybe a third of Europe died, but it took the elderly as well as the young. . . . But this plunging fertility takes only the young. A couple still has parents and grandparents to support, directly or through their taxes. Since they've got fewer or no

siblings to share that burden, having children seems even more
unaffordable. So how do you dig your way out of a hole like a
shrinking population?[4]

Excellent question, and if Europe does not find the answer soon,
Europe dies. How bleak is the situation? Of the twenty nations with
the lowest birthrates in the world, eighteen are in Europe. The average
fertility rate of a European woman has fallen to 1.4 children, with
2.1 needed just to replace the existing population. Says columnist Ben
Wattenberg: This does not mean ZPG (Zero Population Growth), this
means ZP—Zero Population.[5]

Americans in NATO will soon be defending a vast Leisure World.

If the present fertility rates hold, Europe's population will decline
to 207 million by the end of the twenty-first century, less than 30
percent of today's. The cradle of Western civilization will have become
its grave.

Why is this happening? Socialism, the beatific vision of European
intellectuals for generations, is one reason. "If everyone has the promise of a state pension, children are no longer a vital insurance policy
against want in old age," argues Dr. John Wallace of Bologna's Johns
Hopkins University: "If women can earn more than enough to be
financially independent, a husband is no longer essential. And if you
can also have sex and not babies—and this seems to be true now of
Catholic Italy as it is of secular Britain—why marry?"[6]

By freeing husbands, wives, and children of family responsibilities,
European socialists have eliminated the need for families. Conse-
quently, families have begun to disappear. When they are gone, Europe goes with them. But as Europe is dying, the Third World adds
one hundred million people—one new Mexico—every fifteen months.
Forty new Mexicos in the Third World by 2050, while Europe will
have lost the equivalent of the entire population of Belgium, Holland,
Denmark, Sweden, Norway—and Germany! Absent divine intervention, or a sudden desire on the part of Western women to begin
having the same-size families as their grandmothers, the future be-

longs to the Third World. As T. S. Eliot wrote in "The Hollow Men": "This is the way the world ends / Not with a bang but a whimper."[7]

## CLEMENCEAU'S REVENGE

"There are twenty million Germans too many!" muttered Georges Clemenceau, the "Tiger of France" and the statesman most responsible for the Versailles Treaty, which stripped Germany of her colonies, a tenth of her land, and an eighth of her people.[8] Clemenceau's hatred is understandable. As Alistair Horne writes in his history of the fall of the Third Republic, "Clemenceau had been one of the deputies to protest against the surrender of Alsace-Lorraine in 1871, and had narrowly escaped being lynched in the civil war that followed with the Commune."[9] He had witnessed the dethronement of his emperor and seen a German kaiser crowned at Versailles. In the Great War, he had seen his beloved France ravaged by the armies of Hindenburg and Ludendorff which had left behind the bodies of 1.5 million Frenchmen when they marched home to the Reich.

In fifty years, the Tiger will have his revenge, for German women are refusing to have children. For ten years, Germany's birthrate has stood at 1.3 children per woman, far below the 2.1 needed to replace the present population. Here is the future that is now hard upon the German nation. By 2050:

- Twenty-three million Germans will have disappeared.
- Germany's eighty-two million people will have fallen to fifty-nine million.
- The number of German children under fifteen will have dropped to 7.3 million.
- A third of Germany's population will be over sixty-five. These seniors will outnumber German children more than two to one.
- Germany's total population will be two-thirds of 1 percent of the world's population, and only 1 of every 150 people on earth will

be a German. And Germans will be among the oldest people on
earth.

At the request of the author, Joseph Chamie, director of the UN's
Population Division, projected the population of several European
nations out to 2100. If the present German birthrate is sustained and
immigration is zero, Germany's population will fall from 82 million
to 38.5 million by century's end, a drop of 53 percent.[10]

The Bavarian conservative and potential chancellor Edmund
Stoiber considers Germany's birthrate a "ticking time bomb."[11] He
urges a tripling of the child allowance for the first three years of life.
Today, Germany pays monthly subsidies of $140 a child for the first
two, more for a third. Stoiber's idea is called radical today; it will not
be tomorrow.

"My reason for not having kids is that I like to sleep. I read a lot,
and I can sleep throughout the night," says Gabrielle Thanheiser,
thirty-four, a banker in Berlin vacationing in Rome with her live-in
boyfriend.[12] "We are DINKS," confirmed Andreas Gerhmann, thirty-
seven, using the acronym popular even in Germany for "double income, no kids" couples.[13] In the long run, the self-indulgence of
DINKS like Gerhmann and Thanheiser may prove more fateful for
the German people than the Third Reich.

With the fall of the Berlin Wall, West German chancellor Helmut
Kohl sought to reunify his country after forty-five years of Cold War
division. In Britain, Russia, France, even in the United States, were
heard anguished cries that the world could not trust a united Germany. Twice, Germany had tried to conquer Europe, it was protested.
What guarantee have we that a united Germany will not march again
on Europe?

This is one worry the West can lay to rest. With the German people
aging and dying, with five million fewer German children expected in
2050 than are alive in 2000, Germany, like the old soldier of General
MacArthur's ballad, is about to "just slowly fade away."

## ITALY, A THEME PARK

Prospects for the Italian race, which gave us Rome and all its glory, St. Peter's and the Sistine Chapel, Dante and Michelangelo, Columbus and Galileo, are even more dire. Italy's birthrate has been below replacement levels for twenty-five years and is down to 1.2 children per woman. At this rate, Italy's fifty-seven million people will fall to forty-one million by 2050. Writes population researcher Nicholas Eberstadt of American Enterprise Institute: "Barely 2 percent of the [Italian] population in 2050 would be under five years old, but more than 40 percent would be 65 or older."[14] The birthrate in "that most Catholic and romantic of nations," adds *New Republic*'s Greg Easterbrook, "means that Italy will be a theme park in a few generations."[15]

A recent survey in the popular "semifeminist" magazine *Noi Donne* found that 52 percent of Italian women between sixteen and twenty-four planned to have no children.[16] "Career" was their principal reason for not wanting any kids. University of Rome demographer Antonio Golini says that the nation is already dependent upon immigrants to bear the load of its deeply indebted pension system. But now Italian culture is at risk. Golini believes, "Italy will no longer be Italian. . . . It will be the end of society as we know it."[17]

Golini was called a "demographic terrorist" twenty years ago, when he first warned of Italy's impending population crisis.[18] He is called that no longer, though Dr. Golini remains deeply pessimistic about his country: "In an increasingly globalized labor market, Italy must compete with France, with the United States, with India. How can we, with such an aged society and so few young people?"[19]

Cardinal Giacomo Biffi of Bologna has called on Rome to restrict immigration to Catholics to "save the nation's identity," raising eyebrows with his remark that Muslims have "different food, festivals, and family morals."[20] But where does His Eminence propose to find these Catholics?

Certainly not in Spain, where in the days of the Caudillo, Gen.

Francisco Franco, big families were sacred and received medals and gifts from the state. The Spanish birthrate is the lowest in all Europe, lower than that of Italy, the Czech Republic, or Romania, all of which have fallen to 1.2 children per woman. In Spain, the birthrate is down to 1.07 children per woman, and the population is projected to fall by 25 percent in fifty years as the number of Spaniards over sixty-five soars by 117 percent. "In one generation we have gone from a society in which families of eight or even 12 children were not unusual to one in which childless couples are common, or people think long and hard about having a second child," says Madrid sociologist Victor Perez Diaz.[21] By 2050, the median age in Italy will be fifty-four and in Spain fifty-five, fourteen years *above* the median age of Japan, the oldest nation on earth today.

"Prosperity has strangled us," says Dr. Pierpaolo Donati, a leading Catholic intellectual and professor of sociology at the University of Bologna. "Comfort is now the only thing anybody believes in. The ethic of sacrifice for a family—one of the basic ideas of human societies—has become a historical notion. It is astonishing."[22]

In 1950, Spain had three times as many people as Morocco across the Strait of Gibraltar. By 2050, Morocco's population will be 50 percent larger. If one hundred Spanish young people marry today, they can expect to have fifty-eight children, thirty-three grandchildren, but only nineteen great-grandchildren.

## RUSSIA

What of the late command post of a Soviet Empire that shook the world for seventy years? With a birthrate of 1.35 children per woman, Russia's 147 million people will fall to 114 million by 2050, a greater loss than the 30 million dead attributed to Stalin. The number of children in Russia under fifteen will have fallen from 26 to 16 million, while today's 18 million seniors will have grown to 28 million.

In December 2000, however, more ominous news came in. Russia's birthrate had already plummeted to 1.17 children, below Italy's. Its population had fallen to 145 million; one estimate had it headed to 123 million by 2015. "If you believe the forecasts made by serious people who have devoted their whole lives to studying this question," warns President Putin, "in 15 years' time there will be 22 million fewer Russians. Just think about that figure—it's a seventh of [Russia's] population."[23] A loss of 22 million Russians in fifteen years would be greater than all the Soviet Union's losses in the Hitler-Stalin war. Putin went on to add ominously, "If the present tendency continues, there will be a threat to the survival of the nation."

Life expectancy for Russian men is now fifty-nine, and two of every three pregnancies in Russia are terminated before birth. Russian women average 2.5 to 4 abortions each, and Russia's death rate is now 70 percent higher than the birthrate.[24] Even the return of millions of Russians from the former Soviet republics cannot offset the dying. Most ominous for the largest nation on earth, the population of vast, vacant Siberia is in a steep decline as China's enormous population swells inexorably.

When the deputy speaker of the state duma, the rabid nationalist Vladimir Zhirinovsky, advanced such ideas as polygamy, allowing every Russian male to have five wives, plus a ten-year ban on abortion and a prohibition on Russian women traveling abroad, his ideas were ridiculed and his population bills hooted down.[25] But the life crisis of Russia cannot be dismissed, and the geostrategic implications for America are ominous.

Mr. Chamie projected Russia's population, at present birthrates with zero immigration, out to the century's end, and came up with fewer than eighty million Russians in 2100, roughly the population of the United States when Theodore Roosevelt left office in 1909.[26]

## GREAT BRITAIN

What does the future hold for the cousins?

"Demographers have calculated that by the end of this century the English people will be a minority in their homeland. The English are not having enough children to reproduce themselves," writes the syndicated columnist Paul Craig Roberts.[27] This is the first time in history, says the *London Observer,* "that a major indigenous population has voluntarily become a minority, rather than through war, famine or disease."[28]

The *Observer* is mistaken. The honor of being the first nation to voluntarily turn its majority indigenous population into a minority will go to the United States. President Clinton predicted it would happen by 2050, half a century before Great Britain. But the British are clearly heading in the same direction. Ethnic minorities already constitute 40 percent of London's population, and, as Lee Jasper, the race relations adviser to the mayor of London, states, "The demographics show that white people in London will become a minority by 2010."[29]

Among the reasons is the steadily falling birthrate among native-born British. In 2000, there were 17,400 fewer births in England and Wales than in 1999, a drop of almost 3 percent, and the fertility rate fell to 1.66 births per woman, the lowest since statistics began to be kept in 1924.[30]

## JAPAN

Of the twenty-two nations with the lowest birthrates, only two are outside Europe—Armenia and Japan, the first Asian nation to enter the modern era.

Not until 1868 did Japan break out of her isolation. But within thirty years this dynamic nation was a rival of the Western powers. Japan had defeated China, colonized Taiwan, and in 1900 sent her soldiers to march beside Europeans and Americans to relieve the diplomatic legations in Peking besieged by the Chinese rebels known as "the Boxers." The Russo-Japanese War (1904–5) was the first in which an Asian people defeated a great Western power. Begun with a surprise attack on the Russian naval squadron at Port Arthur, the war ended in one of the most decisive battles in history, the sinking of the czar's Baltic fleet in the Straits of Tsushima in thirty-six hours by Admiral Togo.

In World War I, Japan was an Allied power whose contribution to the war effort was to roll up the kaiser's colonies in China and the Pacific, defend Europe's imperial possessions in Asia, and escort the troops of Australia and New Zealand to Gallipoli. Japan also sent a naval squadron to the Mediterranean. But when President Harding and Secretary of State Charles Evans Hughes pressured London to break its twenty-year alliance with Japan at the Washington Naval Conference, the Japanese felt betrayed, humiliated, isolated. The die was cast. Twenty years later came Pearl Harbor and the total destruction of Japan and an empire constructed over sixty years at an immense cost in blood and treasure.

But with American assistance and by copying American methods and ideas, postwar Japan became the most dynamic nation on earth. By 1990, her economy was the second largest, half the size of the United States economy, though Japan occupied an area smaller than Montana—an extraordinary achievement of an extraordinary people.

But something has happened to Japan. She, too, has begun to die. Japan's birthrate is half what it was in 1950. Her population is projected to crest soon at 127 million, but fall to 104 million by 2050, when there will be fewer than half as many Japanese children as there were in 1950 but eight times as many seniors as in 1950. Her dynamism will be dead, her Asian role diminished, for there will be fifteen Chinese for every single Japanese. Even the Philippines, which had only a fourth of Japan's population in 1950, will have 25 million more people by 2050.

The reason for Japan's baby bust? More than half of all Japanese women now remain single by thirty years of age. Known as "Parasite Singles," they live at home with their parents and pursue careers, and many have abandoned any idea of marrying and having children.[31] "Live for myself and enjoy life" is their motto. With Japan's elementary schools in 2000 taking in the smallest class in recorded history, Tokyo has raised the child allowance to $2,400 a year per child for six years. Some conservatives want to multiply that tenfold.

One pioneering Japanese female journalist in her sixties, Mitsuko Shimomura, told the *New York Times's* Peggy Orenstein that Japan is getting what it deserves for not granting full equality to women:

> I don't regret the decline in the birth rate. . . . I think it's a good thing. The Parasites have unintentionally created an interesting movement. Politicians now have to beg women to have babies. Unless they create a society where women feel comfortable having children and working, Japan will be destroyed in a matter of 50 or 100 years. And children's subsidies aren't going to do it. Only equality is.[32]

These women are deciding the fate and future of the Japanese nation.

Japan's Asian Empire was smashed in 1945; but something happened more recently to sap her vitality and will to live, grow, and expand and conquer in industry, technology, trade, and finance. Observers call it a loss of what famed economist J. M. Keynes described as "animal spirits."

But perhaps there is another, simpler explanation: age. Of the 190 nations on earth, Japan is the oldest, with a median age of forty-one— for Japan was the first modern nation to legalize abortion (1948), and her baby boom ended soon afterward, long before the end of the baby booms in the West.

Is there a parallel between a dying Christianity in the West and the death of Japan's prewar and wartime faith? When nations lose their sense of mission, their mandate of heaven, the faith that brought them into this world as unique countries and cultures, is that when they die? Is that when civilizations perish? So it would seem.

LET US LOOK again at the population projections for 2050, and try to visualize what our world will look like.

In Africa, there will be 1.5 billion people. From Morocco to the Persian Gulf will be an Arab-Turkic-Islamic sea of 500 million. In South Asia will live 700 million Iranians, Afghans, Pakistanis, and Bangladeshis, and 1.5 billion Indians. There will be 300 million Indonesians, and China, with 1.5 billion people, will brood over Asia.

Russia, with a shrinking population of only 114 million, will have largely disappeared from Asia. Almost all Russians will be west of the Urals, back in Europe. Western Man, who dominated Africa and Asia in the first half of the twentieth century, will have disappeared from Africa and Asia by the middle of the twenty-first except perhaps for tiny enclaves in South Africa and Israel. In Australia, a nation of only 19 million, where the white birthrate is now below replacement levels, the European population will have begun to disappear.

There is a terrible dilemma confronting the First World nations:

At present birthrates, Europe must bring in 169 million immigrants by 2050 if it wishes to keep its population aged fifteen to sixty-four at today's level. But if Europe wishes to keep its present *ratio* of 4.8 workers (fifteen–sixty-four) for every senior, Europe must bring in *1.4 billion* emigrants from Africa and the Middle East. Put another way: Either Europe raises taxes and radically downsizes pensions and health benefits for the elderly, or Europe becomes a Third World continent. There is no third way.

If Europe's fertility rate does not rise, European children under fifteen will fall by 40 percent to 87 million by 2050, as the number of seniors rises 50 percent to 169 million. The median age of a European will be fifty, the highest in history, nine years older than the present median age in Japan. Writes French demographer Alfred Sauvy, Europe is about to become a continent of "old people in old houses with old ideas."[33]

IS THE DEATH of the West inevitable? Or, like all previous predictions of Western decline and demise, will this cup, too, pass away and expose as fools all who said we must drink it?

After all, Malthus was wrong. Marx was wrong. Democracy did not die during the Great Depression as the Communists predicted. And Khrushchev did not "bury" us. We buried him. Neville Chute's *On the Beach* proved as fanciful as *Dr. Strangelove* and *Seven Days in May*. Paul Ehrlich's *Population Bomb* never exploded. It fizzled. *The Crash of '79* produced Ronald Reagan and an era of good feelings. The Club of Rome notwithstanding, we did not run out of oil. The world did not end at the close of the second millenium, as some prophesied and others hoped. Who predicted the disappearance of the Soviet Empire or disintegration of the Soviet Union? Is it not possible that today's most populous nations—China, India, and Indonesia—could break into pieces as well? Why do predictions of the Death of the West not belong on the same back shelf as the predictions of "nuclear winter" and "global warming"?

Answer: the Death of the West is not a prediction of what is going to happen, it is a depiction of what is happening now. First World nations are dying. They face a mortal crisis, not because of something happening in the Third World, but because of what is *not* happening at home and in the homes of the First World. Western fertility rates have been falling for decades. Outside of Muslim Albania, no European nation is producing enough babies to replace its population. As years slip by, that birthrate is not stabilizing; it is falling. In a score of countries, the old are already dying off faster than the young are being born. There is no sign of a turnaround. Now the absolute numbers of Europeans have begun to fall.

This is not a matter of prophecy, but of mathematics. The steeper and longer the dive, the more difficult it is to pull out. The First World has to turn this around, and soon, or it will be overwhelmed by a Third World that is five times as populous and will be ten times as populous in 2050. The ability to pull out of this dive diminishes each year. No end of the birth dearth is in sight, and all the social and cultural indicators show that more and more Western women are converting to the idea of having no children.

Moreover, there is an arithmetical certitude about some aspects of demography. Italy cannot have more young adults of childbearing age in 2020 than it has teenagers, children, tots, and infants today. No existing population cohort can be added to, except by immigration. Only the mass reconversion of Western women to an idea that they seem to have given up—that the good life lies in bearing and raising children and sending them out into the world to continue the family and nation—can prevent the Death of the West.

Why are Western women having fewer children than their mothers or none at all? Why have so many enlisted in what Mother Teresa called "the war against the child"?[34] Western women have long had access to the methods and means of birth control but chose not to use them to the extent they do today. For thirty years, American women have had easy access to abortion, but, unlike the women of China, they are also free to choose life. No federal judge forces any woman to have an abortion.

Yet, Western women are terminating their pregnancies at a rate that represents autogenocide for peoples of European ancestry and an end of their nations. "Cherishing children is the mark of a civilized society," said Joan Ganz Cooney.[35] Why are children no longer cherished as they once were? What caused the sea change in the hearts and minds of Western women, and men? And is it reversible? For if it is not, we can begin to write the final chapters of the history of our civilization and the last will and testament of the West.

# "WHERE HAVE ALL THE CHILDREN GONE?"

And ye shall be left few in numbers, whereas ye were as
the stars of heaven for multitude; because thou wouldst
not obey the voice of the Lord thy God.
                                         —Deuteronomy XXVIII: 28
                                         Holy Bible, King James Version

Why have Europe's nations and peoples stopped having babies and
begun to accept their disappearance from this earth with such seeming
indifference? Did the wounds of wars or the loss of empire kill the
will to live? From the evidence, neither appears to be the case.

The Great War left Imperial Germany defeated and dismem-
bered, with two million dead and millions crippled. Yet the German
population grew so quickly after 1919 that France, which had been
among the victors, was alarmed. After World War II, baby booms
exploded among the vanquished Japanese and Germans as well as
the victorious Americans. From studying the birth charts, we find
that something happened in the mid-1960s, in the midst of the
postwar prosperity, that changed the hearts and minds of Western
women and killed in them the desire to live as their mothers had.
But if the reason Western women stopped having babies remains in
dispute, how they did so is not. Contraception halted the population growth of the West, with abortion as the second line of defense against the unwanted child.

FIRST, A LITTLE history: Only once had the U.S. birthrate fallen below population replacement, during the Depression, when the economy shrank by half and a fourth of America's breadwinners were out of work, many of them out on the streets. Pessimism, a sense of despair that the good times are over and may never come again, can apparently impact national fertility. The Silent Generation was born in the 1930s, a relatively small cohort and the only generation of the twentieth century never to have produced a president.

The postwar baby boom began in 1946, peaked in 1957, and fizzled out in 1964. But just as the World War II generation was about done having babies, and the baby boomers themselves were about to begin, a new and more convenient way to prevent pregnancies was discovered.

Historians may one day call "the pill" the suicide tablet of the West. It was first licensed in 1960. By 1963, 6 percent of American married women were using Dr. Rock's invention; by 1970, 43 percent were "on the pill."[1] As Catholics furiously debated the morality of contraception and Pope Paul VI issued his encyclical *Humanae Vitae*—which declared all artificial birth control to be immoral for Catholics, the pill included—suddenly a graver issue arose.

Arizona TV personality Sherry Finkbine, a married mother of four who had taken thalidomide, the drug that had caused deformities in babies in Europe, learned that she was pregnant. Mrs. Finkbine did not want a deformed child and confided to friends that she desired an abortion. When the news leaked out, Mrs. Finkbine was subjected to threats from some and offers from others to raise the child if only she would carry it to term. As abortion was still against the law, a blazing national debate ensued. But Mrs. Finkbine mooted the issue by flying to Sweden and having the child aborted.

By 1966, however, the Finkbine affair was ancient history, for 6,000 abortions were being done every year. By 1970, that figure had leapt to 200,000 as Governors Rockefeller of New York and Reagan of

California signed the most liberal abortion laws in America.² By 1973, 600,000 abortions were being done.³ That year, the Supreme Court, with three of President Nixon's four nominees concurring, declared that a woman's right to an abortion was protected by the Constitution. Within a decade, the number of abortions had soared to 1.5 million a year, and abortions had replaced tonsillectomies as the most common surgical procedure in America. Since Justice Blackmun's decision, 40 million abortions have been performed in the United States. Thirty percent of all pregnancies now end on a tabletop in an abortionist's clinic.

In 2000, the Food and Drug Administration approved RU-486, a do-it-yourself abortion drug for use in the first seven weeks of pregnancy. As no U.S. firm wished to be associated with RU-486, a China-based company began quietly to produce the drug. Cynics might characterize China's role in producing RU-486 for America as an act of assisted suicide for the one nation blocking Beijing's path to Asian hegemony and world power.

ROE V. WADE put a constitutional canopy over a woman's right to an abortion. Yet that decision does not of itself explain the sea change in the attitudes of American and Western women. What was it that made them so hostile to the idea of pregnancy and motherhood that they would prefer to have an abortion, an act their own grandparents would have considered a monstrous offense against God and man? In the 1950s, abortion was not only a crime, but a shameful act. There was no national clamor for its legalization. Yet, fifteen years later, a Supreme Court decision declaring abortion a constitutional right was hailed as a milestone of social progress. A revolutionary transformation had taken place in the beliefs of tens of millions of Americans. One of two things had happened: Either the sixties drove a moral wedge between us, or the sixties exposed a moral fracture that had existed, but that we had failed to recognize. I believe the former is true. In that pivotal de-

cade of the last century, a large slice of young America was converted to a new way of thinking, believing, and living.

FROM 1945 TO 1965, America passed through what sociologists call
"the golden age of marriage," when the average age of first marriages
fell to record lows for both men and women, and the proportion of
adults who were married reached an astronomical 95 percent. The
America of Eisenhower and John F. Kennedy was a vibrant, dynamic
nation. But, as Allan Carlson, president of The Howard Center for
Family, Religion, and Society, writes:

> All the indicators of family well-being abruptly turned in these
> places [Western nations] during the short 1963–1965 period.
> Fertility resumed its fall, tumbling well below zero-growth lev-
> els; a massive retreat from marriage commenced; and Western
> societies seemed to lose all sense of inherited family order.[4]

Dutch demographer Dirk van de Kaa traces the phenomenon to
four transformations: (A) A shift from the golden age of marriage to
the dawn of a new age of cohabitation. (B) A shift from a time of
"king-child" with parents to that of king-parents with one child. (C)
A shift from preventive contraception, to benefit early children, to
self-fulfilling contraception, to benefit parents. (D) A shift from a
uniform family system to a pluralistic system of families and households, including single-parent families.[5]

As the drop-off in the birthrate began in the mid-1960s, this is the
site to excavate to discover the causes of this tectonic shift in attitude
of American and Western women away from having children. What
ideas did the boomers bring to maturity? What ideas did they absorb
in college?

———

THE BOOMERS ARRIVED on campus in the fall of 1964. They were the first American generation with the freedom and the means to choose how they wanted to live their lives. In the 1930s, college had been a privilege only a few could afford. Family decisions were imposed by family hardships. If the breadwinner lost his job, sons and daughters could forget about college; they had to quit school and find work. Tens of millions still lived in small towns in rural America, where the Depression had hit the farms long before the 1929 Crash hit Wall Street. After Pearl Harbor, the war and war economy made the career decisions for America's young. The Silent Generation of the fifties grew up with parents, teachers, and clergy still as authority figures. Not until 1957 did Professor Galbraith discover that we were all living in *The Affluent Society*.

But the parents who had gone through the Depression and the war were determined that "my kid's not going to have it as rough as I did." So the baby boomers were raised differently, spending almost as many hours in front of a television as in school. By the mid-1950s, parents had a serious rival for their children's attention, and youngsters had an entertaining and witty ally, and a privileged sanctuary to retreat to, in the age-old struggle against parents. The message that came from TV, especially the ads, was instant gratification.

By 1964, the year of Mario Savio and the Free Speech movement at Berkeley, when the first wave of boomers hit the campuses, never having known hardship or war, it was ready to rock. And though the student riots and rebellions were blamed on LBJ, Nixon, Agnew, and Vietnam, this will not do. For student rebellions were not confined to America. They broke out across Europe and even in Japan. As the 1968 Days of Rage tore apart the Democratic party in the streets of Chicago, Czech students who made the Prague Spring were facing Russian tanks, Mexican students were being shot down in the streets of the capital, and French students almost seized Paris from President de Gaulle.

What baby boomers had in common with contemporaries abroad was not Vietnam, but their numbers, affluence, security, and freedom, and the televised example of their peers all over the world. In childhood, they had all had the same baby-sitter, TV—a baby-sitter more entertaining than the parents. Its incessant ad message was the same: "Kids! You need this—now!"

WITH MILLIONS OF young women "liberated" from parents, teachers, and preachers, with money to burn, and with the in loco parentis authority of dons and deans crumbling, the revolutions rolled over the campuses: the antiwar movement ("Hey, hey, LBJ, / How many kids did you kill today?" and "Ho, Ho, Ho Chi Minh / The NLF is going to win!"); the drug revolution ("turn on, tune in, and drop out"); and the sexual revolution ("make love, not war").

Then came the women's movement, modeled on the civil rights movement; it won converts even in Middle America. As blacks had demanded equal rights with whites, women demanded the same rights as men. Nothing less than full equality. If the boys can sow their wild oats in frat houses and singles bars and with one-night stands, why not us? But as nature did not design the sexes that way, and the consequences of promiscuity are unequally borne by women, in the form of babies, solutions had to be found. The magic of the marketplace did the rest. If you forgot to take the pill, or the contraceptive didn't work, the local abortionist would not fail.

The old sanctions against promiscuity collapsed. Nature's sanctions—unwanted pregnancy and fear of disease—were taken care of by the pill, available abortion, and the new miracle drugs. No need for shotgun marriages. One teary-eyed trip to the Center for Reproductive Rights gets the job done. The fear of social stigma—loss of reputation—was lifted by a popular culture that celebrated the sexual revolution and applauded as "swingers" girls who in the 1940s and 1950s might have been called less attractive names. The moral sanctions—the sense of shame and sin, of violating God's law, of risking one's immortal soul—were eased by a new breed of "Are-You-Running-with-Me-Jesus?" priests and pastors who won huge popularity by explaining that He (or She) was just not that kind of "judgmental" God and, hey, "Hell is only a metaphor!"

Not only did the old sanctions collapse, a new way of measuring morality emerged to justify and even to sanctify "doing one's own thing." Under the new code, morality was now to be determined not by who slept with whom or who inhaled what—trivial matters of personal preference—but by who went South for civil rights, who protested apartheid, who had marched against the "dirty, immoral war" in Vietnam. As has often been true in history, a new moral code was crafted to justify the new lifestyle already adopted. As they indulged themselves in sex, drugs, riots, and rock and roll, the young Jacobins had the reassurance of their indulgent and pandering elders that, yes, indeed, "This is the finest young generation we have ever produced." Has it not ever been so with revolutions? "Bliss was it in that dawn to be alive / But to be young, very heaven!" burbled the great Wordsworth of an earlier revolution that turned out rather badly.

IN THE 1960S, both a student rebellion and a cultural revolution rolled over the campuses. When the rebels graduated, got jobs, and got married, they ceased to be rebels, taking their place in the country of their parents and voting for Ronald Reagan; though it took some— our president comes to mind—perhaps longer than others to "break away."

The sixties' rebels, however, were not the revolutionaries. Converts to the revolution came to college thinking and believing one way and left thinking and believing an entirely different way that changed their whole lives. Hillary Rodham, the Goldwater Girl who came to Wellesley in 1965 and left as a social radical in 1969, with new values, a new moral code, and a steely resolve to change the corrupt society in which she had been raised, is as good an example of the revolutionary as Mr. Bush is of the rebel.

The cultural revolution that swept America's campuses was a true revolution. In a third of a century the Judeo-Christian moral order it defied has been rejected by millions. Its hostility to Ozzie-and-Harriet America has been internalized by our cultural elites, and through their domination of our opinion- and value-shaping institutions— film, TV, the theater, magazines, music—these evangelists of revolution have spread their gospel all over the world and converted scores of millions.

We are two Americas: Mother Angelica and the Sunday sermon compete with Ally McBeal and *Sex and the City*. And the message the dominant culture emits, day and night, reacts with mocking laughter to the old idea that the good life for a woman means a husband and a houseful of kids. And there are now powerful collateral forces in society that are also pulling American women away from the maternity ward forever.

(A) *The New Economy.* In an agricultural economy, the workplace was the home where husband and wife labored together and lived together. In the industrial economy, the man left the home to work in a factory, while his wife stayed home to look after the children. The agricultural economy gave us the extended family; the industrial economy, the nuclear family. But in the postindustrial economy, husband and wife both work at the office, and no one stays home with the children. Indeed, there may be no children. As political science professor James Kurth of Swarthmore writes:

> The greatest movement of the second half of the nineteenth century was the movement of men from farm to the factory. . . . The greatest movement of the second half of the twentieth century has been the movement of women from the home to the office. . . . [This] movement separates the parents from the

children, as well as enabling the wife to separate herself from her husband. By splitting the nuclear family, it is helping to bring about the replacement of the nuclear family with the non-family.[6]

As men's jobs in manufacturing, mining, farming, and fishing are no longer needed, or are shipped overseas, the skills and talents of women are now more desirable. There are also opportunities in government, education, and the professions open to women today that their mothers and grandmothers never had. Businesses, large and small, offer packages of pay and benefits to lure talented women out of the home and keep them out of the maternity ward, where they are "no good to the company."

It is working. In the scores of millions, American women have left the home for the office to work beside and compete with men. By the tens of millions, women college graduates have put off marriage, many forever. "You can have it all!" the modern woman is told—baby and a career. With nannies, courtesy of open borders, with equal-pay-for-equal work, maternity leave, and daycare, courtesy of government and the company, the lure is not a lie. What you can't have is a brood of kids back home while keeping pace with the competition at the office.

Forced to choose, women are choosing career, or career and the joy of motherhood, once. The Global Economy works hand in hand with the New Economy, transferring manufacturing jobs from high-wage Western nations to the low-wage, newly industrializing nations of Asia and Latin America. With Working America's yellow brick road to the middle class down to one lane, wives must work to keep up with the Joneses next door. So children are put off, sometimes for good. In 1950, 88 percent of women with children under six stayed home, where they often had more kids. Today, 64 percent of American women with children under six are in the labor force.[7]

"How you gonna keep 'em down on the farm, after they've seen Paree?" was said of the World War I soldiers who went off to Europe. Well, how you gonna get 'em back in the 'burbs, after they've seen

D.C., one might ask of the talented women lawyers, journalists, PR specialists, and political aides who have enjoyed the great game in an exciting city.

Writing in the *Spectator,* Eleanor Mills is an authentic voice of her generation: "The fact is that girls like me—i.e., healthy, hearty, middle-class women in their 20s—are just not breeding."[8] Why not? Because, she writes, "my generation's twin preoccupations are, unfortunately, looks and money."[9] She quotes one of her many childless contemporaries:

> "If I had a kid," said Jane, an advertising executive, thoughtfully, "I wouldn't be able to do half the things I take for granted. Every Saturday at 10:30 A.M. when we are still in bed, my husband and I look at each other and just say, 'Thank God we weren't up at 5 A.M. caring for a brat.' We have such a great time just the two of us; who knows if it would work if we introduced another person into the equation?"[10]

"The rich are different from us," said F. Scott Fitzgerald. To which Hemingway replied, "Yes, they have more money." But the rich also have fewer children. Using Occam's razor—the simplest explanation is usually the right one—the best explanation for the sinking birthrate in the West may be the simplest. As America's poor enter the middle class, and the middle class becomes affluent, and the affluent become rich, each adopts the style of the class they have lately entered. All begin to downsize their families; all begin to have fewer children. A corollary follows: The richer a nation becomes, the fewer its children, and the sooner it begins to die. Societies organized to ensure the maximum pleasure, freedom, and happiness for all their members are, at the same time, advancing the date of their own funerals. Fate may compensate the Chinese, Islamic, and Latin peoples for their hardships and poverty in this century with the domination of the earth in the next. Indeed, do we not have it on high authority that "Blessed are the meek . . . they shall inherit the earth"?

(B) *End of the "Family Wage."* In the 1830s, as America's industrial revolution was about to begin, the Philadelphia Trade Union warned its members about the hidden agenda of what it called "cormorant capital":

> Oppose [employment of our women folks] with all your minds and with all your strength for it will prove our ruin. We must strive to obtain sufficient remuneration for our labor to keep the wives and daughters and sisters of our people at home. . . . That cormorant *capital* will have every man, woman, and child to toil; but let us exert our families to oppose its designs.[11]

In 1848, the year of Karl Marx's *Communist Manifesto,* the labor publication *Ten Hour Advocate* editorialized: "We hope the day is not distant when the husband will be able to provide for his wife and family, without sending [the wife] to endure the drudgery of a cotton mill."[12]

This vision of American free labor was at war with the view being espoused by Marx and his patron and collaborator, Friedrich Engels, who wrote in *The Origin of the Family, Private Property, and the State:* "The first condition for the liberation of the wife is to bring the whole female sex into public industry and . . . this in turn demands the abolition of the monogamous family as the economic unit of society."[13] Is it not a remarkable coincidence how global capitalism's view of women—as units of production, liberated from husbands, home, and family—conforms so precisely to the view of the fathers of global communism?

As Allan Carlson, who also publishes *The Family in America,* writes, there was a consensus in America, not so long ago, that employers should pay fathers a "family wage" sufficient to support their wives and children in dignity without their having to leave the home to go to work.[14] That was considered one of the defining characteristics of a good society.

The idea is enshrined in Pope Leo XIII's 1891 encyclical *Rerum*

*Novarum.* In books such as *A Living Wage,* Catholic social critic Fr. John Ryan championed the idea and stressed the need to "moralize" the wage contract to protect the home. "The State has both the right and the duty to compel all employers to pay a living wage," wrote Father Ryan.[15]

This idea was widely accepted. Carlson notes that the "wage gap" between men and women actually widened after World War II. In 1939, women earned 59.3 percent of men's pay; by 1966, that had fallen to 53.6 percent.[16] In the 1940s and 1950s, the culture, with a good conscience, separated men and women in the workplace. In newspapers, the "Men Wanted" ads were run separate from the "Women Wanted" ads. Only rarely could working women be found outside such occupations as clerk-typist, secretary, nurse, school-teacher, or salesgirl. Carlson writes:

> To an observer from the Year 2000, the most amazing thing about this system was that it was both understood by the average people and popularly supported. In opinion polls, large majorities of Americans (85 percent or more), women and men, agreed that fathers deserved an income that would support their wives and children at home and that the labor of mothers was second-ary or supplemental. This was seen as simple justice.[17]

This system fell apart in the 1960s, when feminists managed to add "sex" to the discriminations forbidden by the sweeping Civil Rights Act of 1964, which had been written to protect the rights of African Americans. This turned the new Equal Employment Opportunity Commission (EEOC) into a siege gun against the family wage. "Men Wanted" ads were declared discriminatory and outlawed. Gender equality replaced "moral contract." The rights of individuals took precedence over the requirements of family. Women's pay soared, and as women began moving into occupations that had been largely restricted to men—medicine, law, the media, the academy, the upper bureaucracy, and business—families began to crumble.

Between 1973 and 1996, writes Dr. Carlson, "the [real] median income of men, aged 15 and above, working full-time, *fell 24 percent,* from $37,200 to $30,000."[18] Marching under feminist banners— equal pay for equal work, and equal pay for comparable work—women moved into direct competition with men. Millions succeeded, shouldering men aside with superior performance. Their pay rose steadily, and the absolute and relative pay of married men stagnated or fell. With their families under pressure, married men began to yield to wives' insistence that they "go back to work." Young men found they no longer earned enough in their late teens or early twenties to start a family, even if that had been their hope and dream. Stripped of the duties of fatherhood and family, many of these young men wound up in trouble—and even in prison.

America's young women found they could achieve independence on their own. They need not get married, certainly not yet. More and more did not marry. In 1970, only 36 percent of women aged twenty to twenty-four were unmarried. By 1995, 68 percent were in the "never married" category. Among women twenty-five to twenty-nine, the "never marrieds" had soared from 10 percent to 35 percent.[19]

The young family with a batch of kids is now an endangered species. Only the young rich can afford that "lifestyle," and they are uninterested. With the Democratic party so beholden to feminism that it cannot even oppose partial birth abortions, and the GOP in thrall to libertarian ideology and controlled by corporate interests, the call of the gods of the marketplace for more women workers prevails over the command of the God of Genesis: "Be fruitful and multiply, and replenish the earth."

Many conservatives have succumbed to the heresy of *Economism,* a mirror-Marxism that holds that man is an economic animal, that free trade and free markets are the path to peace, prosperity, and happiness, that if we can only get the marginal tax rates right and the capital gains tax abolished, Paradise—*Dow 36,000!*—is at hand. But when the income tax rate for the wealthiest was above 90 percent in the 1950s, America, by every moral and social indicator, was a better country.

The reformed radical and Christian convert Orestes Brownson saw this new idolatry of "Mammon worship" rising in the America of the nineteenth century: "Mammonism has become the religion of Sax-ondom, and God is not in all our thoughts. We have lost our faith in the noble, the beautiful and the just."[20] A century later, another convert from a failed materialistic faith would remind us again. Wrote Whittaker Chambers, "Economics is not the central problem of our age, faith is."[21]

(C) *The "Population Bomb" Hysteria.* Then there was the antipeo-ple movement of the 1960s and 1970s, the elite's backlash against the baby boom. Paul Ehrlich, a Stanford University biologist, was its guru, and his bestseller, *The Population Bomb,* did for population con-trol what Rachel Carson's *Silent Spring* had done for environmental-ism. Ehrlich was a twentieth-century reincarnation of Thomas Robert Malthus, the British demographer whose prediction of world starva-tion proved so spectacularly wrong in the nineteenth century. Malthus had written: "It may be safely asserted . . . that population, when un-checked, increases in geometrical progression of such a nature as to double itself every twenty-five years."[22] As the world's food production could not double every twenty-five years, said the gloomy parson, mass starvation was dead ahead.

Malthus proved as wrong about food production as Ehrlich did about the world's resources, which he assured us were running out. Today, the six billion on earth live in far greater freedom and pros-perity than did the three billion in 1960, the two billion in 1927, or the one billion in 1830. Political incompetence and criminality, foolish ideas and insane ideologies, are the causes of starvation and misery, not people.

Published by the Sierra Club, Ehrlich's book became required read-ing in many high schools. By 1977, former secretary of defense and World Bank president Robert McNamara was playing Henny Penny to Ehrlich's Chicken Little, warning that "continued population growth would cause 'poverty, hunger, stress, crowding, and frustration,' that would threaten social, economic and military stability."²³

In 1978, a congressional select committee on population announced that the "major biological systems that humanity depends upon . . . are being strained by rapid population growth . . . [and] in some cases, they are . . . losing productive capacity."²⁴ As Jacqueline Kasun, author of *The War Against Population,* writes, about this time the Smithsonian Institution created a "traveling exhibit for schoolchildren called 'Population: The Problem Is Us,' [that] featured a picture of a dead rat on a dinner plate as an example of 'future food sources.' "²⁵

As a result of this antipopulation propaganda from America's elite institutions of politics and ideas, the public funding for population control here and abroad exploded. But though the message was taken to heart by the First World wealthy and middle class, it was largely ignored by the Third World poor, at whom it had been targeted. We can see the results today: a birth dearth among the affluent nations, and baby booms across the Third World.

(D) *Feminism.* To be "pro-choice" on abortion is today almost a defining mark of the "modern woman." To many feminists, the phrase "women's liberation" means liberation from the traditional and, in their view, narrow and constricting roles of wife, mother, and homemaker. But among the founding mothers of feminism it was not always so. Writing on the Supreme Court's *Roe v. Wade* decision in *The New Oxford Review,* Catholic columnist Joseph Collison observed:

> Early feminists had been fiercely antiabortion. Elizabeth Cady Stanton, organizer of the first women's rights convention in 1848, called abortion "a disgusting and degrading crime." . . . And Susan B. Anthony, early crusader for the women's vote, wrote that "No matter what the motive . . . the woman is awfully guilty who commits the deed. It will burden her conscience in life; it will burden her soul in death." It was in fact the 19th century feminists who campaigned to pass the laws that criminalized abortion.²⁶

Collison adds that in early editions of *The Feminist Mystique,* Betty Friedan's seminal work, abortion went unmentioned. It was not a feminist issue in the early 1960s.

Back before World War II, when Margaret Sanger, birth mother of Planned Parenthood, wrote that "the most merciful thing a large family can do to one of its infant members is to kill it," she was a radical socialist far outside the American mainstream.[27] But the Sanger animus against big families has since become a central feature of the new American feminism that was mainstreamed in the 1960s and 1970s. Today, the perception that marriage is human bondage has become a hallmark of movement militants.

Marriage, writes Andrea Dworkin in *Pornography: Men Possessing Women,* is "an institution [that] developed from rape as a practice. Rape, originally defined as abduction, became marriage by capture. Marriage meant the taking was to extend in time, to be not only use but possession of ownership."[28] Pure Marx. And a logical conclusion follows. "The nuclear family must be destroyed," said the feminist Linda Gordon. "Families have supported oppression by separating people into small, isolated units, unable to join together to fight for common interests."[29]

In 1970, Robin Morgan, now the nanny of Gloria Steinem's love child, *Ms.* magazine, called marriage "a slavery-like practice. We can't destroy the inequities between men and women until we destroy marriage."[30] That same year, Ms. Morgan edited *Sisterhood Is Powerful,* containing an essay by Valerie Solanis, president of the Society for Cutting Up Men. "It is now technically possible to reproduce without the aid of males . . . and to produce only females," wrote Ms. Solanis. "We must begin immediately to do so. The male is a biological accident. . . . The male has made the world a shitpile."[31] Not a lady to be trifled with, Ms. Solanis established her bona fides by going out and shooting Andy Warhol.

By late 1973, Nancy Lehmann and Helen Sullinger had circulated a new manifesto of the movement they titled *Declaration of Feminism,* which was broadly reproduced and widely praised:

Marriage has existed for the benefit of men; and has been a legally sanctioned method of control over women. . . . We must work to destroy it. . . . The end of the institution of marriage is a necessary condition for the liberation of women. Therefore it is important for us to encourage women to leave their husbands and not to live individually with men. . . . All of history must be rewritten in terms of oppression of women. We must go back to ancient female religions like witchcraft.[32]

Among feminists, the slavery simile competes with the prostitution metaphor. "Being a housewife is an illegitimate profession," wrote Vivian Gornick, Penn State professor and author, in 1980. "The choice to serve and be protected and plan toward being a family-member is a choice that shouldn't be. The heart of radical feminism is to change that."[33]

"I can't mate in captivity," Gloria Steinem told a *Newsweek* reporter in 1984.[34] In a 1991 *Wall Street Journal* piece, Christina Sommers quotes legal scholar Catherine MacKinnon as saying: "Feminism stresses the indistinguishability of prostitution, marriage and sexual harassment."[35]

To the militant feminist, marriage is prostitution, and the family is at best a failed institution and at worst a prison or slave quarters. A decade ago, novelist Toni Morrison told *Time*, "The little nuclear family is a paradigm that doesn't work."[36] In 1994, the *Chicago Tribune* quoted Judith Stacey: "The belief that married-couple families are superior is probably the most pervasive prejudice in the Western world."[37] In the *Jewish World Review* in February 2000, in a piece titled "NOW: Pro-Fatherhood Funding Is Unconstitutional," Sheila Cronin was quoted: "Since marriage constitutes slavery for women, it is clear that the women's movement must concentrate on attacking this institution. Freedom for women cannot be won without the abolition of marriage."[38]

Now, most American women do not harbor so bitter and hostile a view of marriage and family. If they did, there would be even fewer children and the Death of the West would be imminent. But millions are influenced by feminist ideology and its equation of marriage with prostitution and slavery, and that ideology has persuaded many to put off marriage and not to have children. If the preservation of peoples of European ancestry, and of the Western civilization they have created, were up to the feminists, Western Man would have no future.

*Ideas Have Consequences* is the title of the late conservative Richard Weaver's famous little book, and the success of feminist ideas has had consequences for our country. They may be seen in the 1,000 percent increase in the number of unmarried couples living together in the United States, from 523,000 in 1970 to 5.5 million today.[39] The 2000 census also reports that, for the first time in our history, nuclear families account for fewer than one in four households, while single Americans who live alone are now 26 percent of all households.[40] Marriage is out of fashion.

Back in 1990, Katarina Runske, an author far less famous than the American feminists, published in Britain a book called *Empty Hearts and Empty Homes,* in which she addressed the inevitable result of all this antimale, antimarriage rhetoric. Feminism, she said, is

> a Darwinian blind alley. In biological terms, there is nothing that identifies a maladaptive pattern so quickly as a below-replacement level of reproduction; an immediate consequence of feminism is what appears to be an irreversible decline in the birth rate. Nations pursue feminist policies at their peril.[41]

In short, the rise of feminism spells the death of the nation and the end of the West. Oddly, that most politically incorrect of poets, Rudyard Kipling, saw it all coming back in 1919:

> On the first Feminian Sandstones, we were promised the Fuller Life
> (Which started by loving our neighbor, and ended by loving his wife)
> Till our women had no more children and the men lost reason and
> faith
> And the Gods of the Copybook Headings said: "THE WAGES OF SIN IS
> DEATH."[42]

(E) *The Popular Culture,* in its hierarchy of values, puts the joys of sex far above the happiness of motherhood. The women's magazines, the soaps, romance novels, and prime-time TV all celebrate career, sex, and the single woman. "Taking care of baby" is for Grandma. Marriage and monogamy are about as exciting as a mashed-potato sandwich. That old triumvirate "the world, the flesh, and the devil," not only has all the best tunes, but all the best ad agencies. How many TV shows today tout motherhood? How long ago did *The Brady Bunch* go off the air? Paul Anka's signature song, "You're Having My Baby," is now "We're Having Our Baby," but "I Am Woman" is still around. It is a sign of the times that *Ozzie and Harriet* is not just behind the times. Like *Amos 'n' Andy,* it has become a metaphor for what was wrong with the times.

"Any human society," wrote anthropologist J. D. Unwin, "is free to choose either to display great energy or to enjoy sexual freedom. The evidence is that it cannot do both for more than one generation."[43] What is now called the Greatest Generation came of age in the Depression and World War II. It displayed great energy and gave America a position of unrivaled preeminence. The baby boomers and Gen-Xers, by and large, opted for "sexual freedom." Soon we shall see if Unwin was right. The early returns suggest that he was, that the West will not survive its experiment in sexual liberation in recognizable form. As the conservative columnist Jenkin Lloyd Jones observed, "Great civilizations and animal standards of behavior coexist only for short periods."[44]

(F) *The Collapse of the Moral Order.* What people truly believe about right and wrong can better be determined by how they live their lives than by what they tell the pollsters. If so, the old moral order is dying. As late as the 1950s, divorce was a scandal, "shacking up" was how "white trash" lived, abortion was an abomination, and homosexuality the "love that dare not speak its name." Today, half of all marriages end in divorce, "relationships" are what life is about, and "the love that dare not speak its name" will not shut up. The collapse of marriage and marital fertility, says Belgian demographer Ron Lesthaeghe, is due to a long-term "shift in the Western ideational system" away from values affirmed by Christianity—sacrifice, altruism, the sanctity of commitment—and toward a militant "secular individualism" focused on the self.[45]

When, in 1968, Pope Paul VI issued his encyclical against contraception, *Humanae Vitae,* the almost universal hostility with which it was received, even among many Catholics, bore witness to the sea change in society. Yet the late pope has proved prophetic. As Archbishop Charles J. Chaput of Denver writes, in *Humanae Vitae* Pope Paul predicted four consequences of man's embrace of a contraceptive mind-set: (1) Widespread "conjugal infidelity and the general lowering of morality." (2) Women would no longer be man's "respected and beloved companion," but serve as a "mere instrument of selfish enjoyment." (3) It would "put a dangerous weapon in the hands of public authorities who take no heed of moral exigencies." (4) The treatment of men and women as objects, and unborn children as a disease to be prevented, would result in the dehumanization of the species.[46]

With rampant promiscuity and wholesale divorce, the explosion of pornography and the mainstreaming of the *Playboy* philosophy, taxpayer funding of abortion, and a day in America when we can read about teenage girls throwing newborn infants into dumpsters and leaving them out in the snow, the world Paul VI predicted is upon us. Indeed, the new world takes on the aspect of the old world of pagan Rome, where unwanted babies were left on hillsides to die of exposure. Life is no longer respected as it was by the Greatest Generation, which came home after seeing how life had been so disrespected in a world at war. As the pope predicted, the beneficiaries of contraception and abortion have turned out to be selfish men who use women and toss them away like Kleenex.

Nowhere is the overthrow of the old moral order more evident than in how homosexuality is seen today, and yesterday. In World War II, Undersecretary of State Sumner Welles, who wore the "old school tie" of FDR, was forced out of office for propositioning a sleeping car porter. LBJ feared that the arrest of aide Walter Jenkins, caught in a police sting in a men's room at the YMCA, might cost him millions of votes. Rising GOP star Bob Bauman lost his House seat when caught soliciting teenagers in the tenderloin district of D.C. That was then; now is now.

The turning point came when Gerry Studds, who seduced a sixteen-year-old male page, defied House sanctions and was reelected in Massachusetts, a Catholic state. Barney Frank easily survived House chastisement for fixing parking tickets for a live-in male lover who was running a full-service whorehouse out of Barney's basement, and, in the Clinton era, he began to bring his boyfriend to White House socials. In 2001, John Ashcroft was lacerated during his confirmation hearings by former Senate colleagues for having opposed the nomination of homosexual James Hormel as ambassador to Luxembourg. Hormel, broadcasting the San Francisco gay pride parade, had laughingly welcomed the transvestite "Sisters of Perpetual Indulgence," who mock the pope and Catholic nuns. Truly, the world is turned upside down.

When America's most public lesbian couple, actresses Anne Heche and Ellen DeGeneres, broke up, the president of the United States called to offer his sympathy. Hillary Clinton became the first First Lady to march in the New York City gay pride parade. Did the *New York Times,* the good Gray Lady of Forty-third Street, editorially question the wisdom of America's First Lady parading with drag queens and men in thongs? Not at all. As *Times* national political correspondent Richard Berke told colleagues at the tenth-anniversary reception of the National Lesbian and Gay Journalists Association, "Three quarters of the people who decide what goes on the front page [of the *Times*] are 'not-so-closeted' homosexuals."[47]

Nine months after marching for gay pride, Mrs. Clinton refused to march in the 240th St. Patrick's Day parade, once a must for all New York City politicians. The Ancient Order of Hibernians, the fraternal Roman Catholic group that runs the parade, does not permit the Irish Lesbian and Gay Organization to march as a unit; and Mrs. Clinton had been chastised by gay rights groups for marching on St. Patrick's Day in 2000. That Senator Clinton would appease the homosexuals, even if it meant affronting Irish Catholics, testifies to the new balance of power in the Democratic party and the new correlation of forces in the culture war.

Were she a real rather than a fictional character, Hawthorne's Hester Prynne, instead of being up on that scaffold having a scarlet "A" pinned to her blouse, would be on *Rosie,* exposing Dimmesdale as a deadbeat dad and telling a cheering audience what Dr. Laura could do with her advice.

Even the children of Middle America now do tours of duty in the sexual revolution. "Do your own thing!" is now a moral norm. Every American woman of childbearing age has had abortion as a fallback, and millions will not give it up. They want it there for themselves and their daughters and will vote against any politician or party that threatens to take it away.

Euthanasia has come to Europe and is coming to America. Upon what moral ground do we any longer stand to stop it? Dr. Kevorkian, a ghoul in an earlier age, some of whose victims were just depressed, not dying, gets a sympathetic profile on *Sixty Minutes*. In the Age of the Individual, people believe in this life, not the next; in the quality of life, not the sanctity of life; and no one wants to be told how he should live his life. "Americans are not going to lead 21st-century lives based on 18th- and 19th-century moral ideals," writes sociologist and public intellectual Alan Wolfe: "Any form of higher authority has to tailor its demands to the needs of real people."[48] After a millennium and a half, paganism is the "comeback kid."

THE AMERICA MANY of us grew up in is gone. The cultural revolution has triumphed in the minds of millions and is beyond the power of politicians to overturn, even had they the courage to try. Half a nation has converted. The party of working-class Catholics is almost 100 percent "pro-choice" and pro–gay rights. The party of the Moral Majority and Christian Coalition has thrown in the towel on the social issues—to go out and do the Lord's work growing the Department of Education. Young people are not concerned about their souls; they're worried about the Nasdaq. Most of the intellectual and media elite are fighting allies of the revolution or fellow travelers, and many conservatives are trolling for the terms of armistice.

What a tiny band of secular humanists declared in a manifesto in 1973 has become the moral compass of America and is becoming the law of the land. Americans have listened, absorbed, and embraced the values of a revolution that scandalized their parents and grandparents, calling to mind the insight of Alexander Pope:

> Vice is a monster of so frightful mien,
> As to be hated needs but to be seen;
> Yet seen too oft, familiar with her face,
> We first endure, then pity, then embrace.[49]

Only a social counterrevolution or a religious awakening can turn the West around before a falling birthrate closes off the last exit ramp and rings down the curtain on Western Man's long-running play. But not a sign of either can be seen on the horizon.

What force can resist the siren's song of a hedonistic culture that is so alluring and appealing and is promoted by almost all who speak to the young—Hollywood, MTV, the soaps, prime-time TV, the hot mags and the hot music, romance novels and bestsellers? How do parents compete when even teachers and preachers are handing out condoms? What is going to convert American women to wanting what their mothers wanted and grandmothers prayed for: a good man, a home in the suburbs, and a passel of kids? Sounds almost quaint.

In *Caesar and Christ,* Book III of his *Story of Civilization,* historian Will Durant argues that "biological factors" were "fundamental" to the fall of the Roman Empire:

A serious decline of population appears in the West after Ha-
drian. . . . A law of Septimus Severus speaks of a *penuria
hominum*—a shortage of men. In Greece the depopulation had
been going on for centuries. In Alexandria, which had boasted
of its numbers, Bishop Dionysius calculated that the population had in his time [250 A.D.] been halved. He mourned to
see "the human race diminishing and constantly wasting away."
Only the barbarians and Orientals were increasing, outside the
Empire and within.[50]

How did Rome reduce its population? "Though branded as a crime,
infanticide flourished. . . . Sexual excesses may have reduced human
fertility; the avoidance or deferment of marriage had a like effect."[51]
Adds Durant: "Perhaps the operation of contraception, abortion and
infanticide . . . had a dysgenic as well as a numerical effect. The ablest
men married latest, bred least and died soonest."[52] Christians were
having children, the pagans were not: "Abortion and infanticide,
which were decimating pagan society, were forbidden to Christians as
the equivalents to murder; in many instances Christians rescued exposed infants, baptized them, and brought them up with the aid of
the community fund."[53]

Irony of ironies. Today, an aging, dying Christian West is pressing
the Third World and the Islamic world to accept contraception, abortion, and sterilization as the West has done. But why should they
enter a suicide pact with us when they stand to inherit the earth
when we are gone?

WHEN SURRENDER OF his forces was demanded at Waterloo,
General Cambronne replied, "The Old Guard dies; but it does not
surrender."[54] A splendid motto for those holed up in our own Cor-
regidor of the culture war. Yet a cold appraisal of the battlefield—
who has the big guns? who holds the high ground?—suggests that
the Old Guard is going to die. For the decisions women are making

today will determine if Western nations will even be around in a century, and Western women are voting no.

But where did this revolution come from that so swiftly captured so vast a slice of the most Christianized and "churched" people of the West? And what are its dogmas and doctrines?

# CATECHISM OF A REVOLUTION

When the Round Table is broken every man must follow Galahad or Modred: middle things are gone.[1]
—C. S. Lewis

Wwhat does this new religion, this new faith that came on the wings
of the revolution, hold and teach? How does it differ from the old?

First, this new faith is of, by, and for this world alone. It refuses
to recognize any higher moral order or moral authority. As for the
next world, it will happily yield that to Christianity and traditional
faiths, so long as they stay out of the public square and public schools.
As for the old biblical stories of creation, Adam and Eve, the serpent
in the garden, original sin, the expulsion from Eden, Moses on Mount
Sinai, and the Ten Commandments being written in stone and binding on all men—believe all that if you wish, but it is never again to
be taught as truth. For the truth, as discovered by Darwin and confirmed by science, is that our species and world are the remarkable
results of eons of evolution. "Science affirms that the human species
is an emergence from natural evolutionary forces," declares the second
*Humanist Manifesto,* written in 1973.[2] That picture on the wall in
biology class of the apes walking on four legs, then on two, then
evolving into *Homo erectus*—that is how it happened.

The new gospel has as its governing axioms: there is no God; there
are no absolute values in the universe; the supernatural is superstition.
All life begins here and ends here; its object is human happiness in

this, the only world we shall ever know. Each society establishes its own moral code for its own time, and each man and woman has a right to do the same. As happiness is life's end and we are rational beings, we have a right to decide when the pain of living outweighs the pleasure of living and to end this life, either by ourselves or with the assistance of family and doctors.

In the moral realm the first commandment is "All lifestyles are equal." Love and its natural concomitant, sex, are healthy and good. All voluntary sexual relations are permissible, and all are morally equal—no one's business but one's own, and certainly not the business of the state to prohibit. This principle—all lifestyles are equal—is to be written into law, and those who refuse to respect the new laws are to be punished. To disrespect an alternative lifestyle marks one as a bigot. Discrimination against those who adopt an alternative lifestyle is a crime. Homophobia, not homosexuality, is the evil that must be eradicated.

"Thou shalt not be judgmental" is the second commandment. But the revolution is not only judgmental; it is severe on those who violate its first commandment. How defend this apparent double standard?

According to the catechism of the revolution, the old Christian moral code that condemned sex outside of marriage and held homosexuality to be unnatural and immoral was rooted in prejudice, biblical bigotry, religious dogma, and barbaric tradition. That repressive and cruel Christian code was an impediment to human fulfillment and happiness and responsible for the ruin of countless lives, especially those of gay men and women.

The new moral code is based on enlightened reason and respect for all. When the state wrote the Christian moral code into law, it codified bigotry. But when we write our moral code into law, we advance the frontiers of freedom and protect the rights of persecuted minorities.

A corollary to the new moral code that enshrines sexual freedom logically follows: As condoms and abortion are necessary to prevent the unwanted and undesirable consequences of free love—from herpes to HIV to pregnancy—these must be made available to anyone who is sexually active, down to the fifth grade if need be.

UNDER THE NEW catechism, the use of public schools to indoctrinate children in Judeo-Christian beliefs is strictly forbidden. But public schools can and should be used to indoctrinate children in a tolerance of all lifestyles, an appreciation of reproductive freedom, respect for all cultures, and the desirability of racial, ethnic, and religious diversity. In the new schools, the holy days of Easter Week, commemorating the Passion, Crucifixion, and Resurrection of Christ, are out as holidays. Earth Day, where the children are taught to love, preserve, and protect Mother Earth, is our day of atonement and reflection, from which no child is exempt. Environmentalism, wrote the conservative scholar Robert Nisbet, is "well on its way to being the third great wave of redemptive struggle in Western history, the first being Christianity, the second modern socialism."[3]

The cultural revolution is not about creating a level playing field for all faiths; it is about a new moral hegemony. After all the Bibles, books, symbols, pictures, commandments, and holidays have been purged from the public schools, these schools shall be converted into learning centers of the new religion. Here is John Dunphy writing with refreshing candor in 1983 in *The Humanist* about the new role of America's public schools:

> The battle for humankind's future must be fought and won in the public school classroom by teachers who correctly perceive their role as proselytizers of a new faith, a religion of humanity. . . . These teachers must embody the same selfless dedication as the most rabid fundamentalist preachers, for they will be ministers of another sort, utilizing a classroom instead of a pulpit to convey humanist values in whatever subject they teach. . . . The classroom must and will become an arena of conflict between the old and the new—the rotting corpse of Christianity, together with all its adjacent evils and misery, and the

new faith of humanism, resplendent in its promise of a world in which the never-realized Christian ideal of "love they neighbor" will be finally achieved.[4]

The new secularism is no milk-and-water faith.

IN POLITICS, THE new faith is globalist and skeptical of patriotism, for an excessive love of country too often leads to suspicion of neighbors and thence to war. The history of nations is a history of wars, and the new faith intends an end of nations. Support for the UN, foreign aid, treaties to ban land mines, abolish nuclear weapons, punish war crimes, and forgive the debts of poor nations are the marks of progressive men and women. Whenever a new supranational institution is formed—the World Trade Organization, the Kyoto Protocol to prevent global warming, the new UN International Criminal Court—the revolution will support the transfer of authority and sovereignty from nations to the new institutions of global governance.

Shelley once called poets the "unacknowledged legislators of the world."[5] In modern times, songwriters have replaced poets in the consciousness of the young, and in the 1960s, the Beatles were the most famous, with John Lennon the poet laureate to a generation. In his song "Imagine," Lennon lays out in a few stanzas the heaven on earth that is envisioned in the post-Christian dispensation:

> Imagine there's no heaven
> It's easy if you try
> No hell below us
> Above us only sky
> Imagine all the people living for today.
>
> Imagine there's no countries
> It isn't hard to do
> Nothing to kill or die for
> And no religion too

> Imagine all the people
> Living life in peace.[6]

A self-described "instinctive socialist," Lennon went on to imagine a world of "no possessions," where everyone shares everything. Yet, on his death, at forty, the world would learn that Lennon had coolly managed to acquire $275 million worth of possessions, making him one of the richest men on earth.[7] And though the world of John Lennon's imagination, and that of fellow Beatle Paul McCartney and Bob Dylan, was utopian, that did not diminish its attraction for the young. For these songwriters offered a new faith to believe in, with its own beatific vision of life here on earth, to replace the Christian faith that had shriveled in their souls. As David Noebel, author of *The Legacy of John Lennon,* wrote, the poet-songwriter knew exactly what he was about. In a statement that stunned the America of the mid-1960s, Lennon predicted: "Christianity will go. It will vanish and shrink. I needn't argue about that. I'm right and will be proven right. We're more popular than Jesus now."[8]

## "THE CANCER OF HUMAN HISTORY"

But a religion needs devils as well as angels. And much of what the new faith teaches stems from a hatred of what it views as a shameful, wicked, criminal past. To the revolution, Western history is a catalog of crimes—slavery, genocide, colonialism, imperialism, atrocities, massacres—committed by nations that professed to be Christian. "The white race is the cancer of human history," wrote Susan Sontag, a birth mother of the revolution, in 1967. "The white race and it alone . . . eradicates autonomous civilizations wherever it spreads."[9]

> America was founded on a genocide. . . . This is a passionately racist country. . . . The truth is that Mozart, Pascal, Boolean Algebra, Shakespeare, parliamentary government, baroque

churches, Newton, the emancipation of women, Kant, Marx, and Balanchine ballets don't redeem what this particular civilization has wrought upon the world.[10]

Like Rubashov in *Darkness at Noon,* our elites have come to accept Sontag's indictment of their civilization and have volunteered, pro bono, to assist the prosecution in making its case. If many Americans look back on their history with disgust, who can blame them? For, as Myron Magnet writes in *The Dream and the Nightmare:*

> Campus after campus [has] jettisoned traditional Western civilization great books and great ideas courses as obsolete. . . . An alternative canon, supposed to be adequate to the new reality, emerged: Paul Goodman, Norman O. Brown, Herbert Marcuse, Franz Fanon, Michel Foucault, James Baldwin, Malcolm X, later even the lyrics of Bob Dylan, shouldered aside Plato and Montaigne. The relevant message was Western Society's oppressiveness, stifling the instinctual satisfactions for the privileged and tyrannically exploiting the poor and nonwhite at home and in the Third World.[11]

What was novelist James Baldwin's view of his country at the end of his life? There is not in American history, he wrote, "nor is there now, a single American institution which is not a racist institution."[12] In her text *Progressive Constitutionalism,* Robin West adds, "The political history of the United States . . . is in large measure a history of almost unthinkable brutality toward slaves, genocidal hatred of Native Americans, racist devaluation of nonwhites and nonwhite cultures, sexual devaluation of women. . . ."[13] Deconstructionalist Jonathan Culler says that the Bible must be understood "not as poetry or narrative but as a powerfully influential racist and sexist text."[14] Such sentiments are no longer rarities, but more and more the rule in higher education in the United States.

In 1990, Tulane announced a new program, "Initiatives for the

Race and Gender Enrichment of Tulane University." University president Eamon Kelly explained the urgency: "Racism and sexism are pervasive in America and are fundamentally present in all American institutions. . . . We are all the progeny of a racist and sexist America."[15] A recent New York State Regents Report on curriculum reform underscores the need for a fresh look at American history: "African Americans, Asian Americans, Puerto Ricans/Latinos, and Native Americans have all been victims of a cultural oppression and stereotyping that has characterized institutions . . . of the European American world for centuries."[16]

This is the message children receive in college and even in high school: Europeans and Americans are guilty of genocide against the native peoples of this continent. Our ancestors transported millions of Africans in death ships to the New World, enslaved them to do the hard labor that our forefathers would not do, and maimed and killed millions. Europe's nations imposed racist regimes on peoples of color, especially in Africa, and robbed them of their wealth. Christianity coexisted with and condoned slavery, imperialism, racism, and sexism for four hundred years.

"After such knowledge, what forgiveness?" asks the old man in Eliot's "Gerontion."[17] "We are used to hearing the Founders charged with being racists, murderers of Indians, representatives of class interests," wrote Allan Bloom in *The Closing of the American Mind;* these slanders are "weakening our convictions of the truth or superiority of American principles and our heroes."[18] Indeed they are, for that is their purpose.

Before the bar of history, America and the West have been indicted on the Nuremberg charge of "crimes against humanity." And all too often Western intellectuals, who should be conducting the defense of the greatest and most beneficent civilization in history, are aiding the prosecution or entering a plea of *nolo contendere*. Too many can only offer the stammering defense of the "good Germans"—"But we did not know."

In moving this indictment, the revolution has complementary goals: to deepen a sense of guilt, to morally disarm and paralyze the West, and to extract endless apologies and reparations until the wealth of the West is transferred to its accusers. It is moral extortion of epic proportions, the shakedown of the millennium. If the West permits its enemies to pull this off, we deserve to be robbed of our inheritance.

Why are so many Western leaders unable to refute the accusations? Because in their hearts, Clinton, Jospin, and Schroeder believe the charges are true, and that the West is guilty. Why else would Mr. Clinton have traveled to Africa to apologize for slavery to the heirs of the tribal chiefs who captured and sold the slaves? Slavery existed, even before Arkansas. And the West did not invent slavery; the West ended slavery.

IN THE CATECHISM of the revolution, why did the West perpetrate history's greatest horrors? Because Western nations believed that their civilization and culture were superior and that they had the right to impose their rule on "inferior" civilizations, cultures, and peoples. This is the *radix malorum,* the root of all evil, the belief that one culture is superior to another, which leads to the murder of the other. Eradication of the idea of superior cultures and civilizations is thus a first order of business of the revolution.

Equality is the first principle. Who sins against equality is *extra ecclesiam,* outside the church. In the new dispensation, no religion is superior, no culture is superior, no civilization is superior. All are equal. It is "diversity," the representation in society of all creeds, colors, and cultures in the multiethnic, multicultural nation that we should aspire to and, prayerfully, are headed for. Logically it follows that any candidate who would rally a constituency on the idea that Western civilization and culture are superior and Christianity is the one true faith is a heretic and a menace.

How crucial is this conviction to our new cultural establishment?

IN 1994, THE culture war came to Lake County, Florida, when the school board voted three to two to require that children be taught that America's heritage and culture were "superior to other foreign or historic cultures."[19] Board chair Pat Hart, a self-described patriot and a Christian, said the idea was adopted in response to Florida's multicultural education policy. It is fine, said Mrs. Hart, for students to learn about other nations and cultures, but they should be taught that America's is "unquestionably superior."[20]

A stunned teachers' union called the proposal jingoistic. "People don't understand the purpose and point of this," Keith Mullins of People for Mainstream Values told the *New York Times*.[21]

Nonsense. The blazing controversy that ensued showed that people knew exactly what "the purpose and point" were. School board member Judy Pearson made it clear: "We need to reinforce that we should be teaching America first."[22] Otherwise, said Ms. Pearson, young people, "if they felt our land was inferior or equal to others, would have no motivation to go to war and defend our society."[23]

One dissenter charged the school board majority with "undermining our school system."[24] The Associated Press reported, "Some teachers and parents say what's really being taught is bigotry."[25] The spokesman for the national School Boards Association, Jay Butler, warned that " 'values' in education . . . is something we hear more about with the rise of the religious right wing."[26]

The local teachers' union president, Gail Burry, accused the board of violating the First Amendment: "The board's majority wants to start from a conclusion—that America is superior to all other nations—and then work backwards from it. . . . That's not education. That's indoctrination."[27] But isn't starting from the conclusion that America is simply equal to all other nations also "indoctrination"?

At the heart of the dispute is Pilate's question "What is truth?" To the revolution, Lake County was contradicting the truth, i.e., all cultures are equal; none is superior. By claiming America's culture was superior, Mrs. Hart's board had committed heresy. The revolution could not permit open defiance of a core dogma to be taught as truth to children in Lake County. So it went to battle stations. In the fall election, in a huge turnout, all supporters of the "America first" policy were defeated.

"The people turned out the extremists," said Mr. Mullins.[28]

The episode exposes the true character of our new dominant culture. About its core beliefs, it is deeply intolerant and will not abide challenge or contradiction. Anyone who would teach children that America's culture is superior is an "extremist" teaching a lie, who has no business in the public schools of the new America.

AS EQUALITY IS its core principle, the cultural revolution teaches that the real heroes of history are not the conquerors, soldiers, and statesmen who built the Western nations and created the great empires, but those who advanced the higher cause—the equality of peoples. Thus, the end of segregation in the South and of apartheid in South Africa are triumphs greater than the defeat of communism, and Mandela and Gandhi are the true moral heroes of the twentieth century. Thus, Martin Luther King stands tallest in the American pantheon, and any state that refuses to set aside a holiday to celebrate his birth is to be boycotted. As for George Washington, if his name is removed from schools, so be it. Was he not an owner of slaves? Did he not participate in America's most egregious violation of human equality?

As equality is a first principle, one-person, one-vote democracy is the highest form of government and the only truly legitimate form. It alone may be imposed by force, as it was upon Germany and Japan, and should have been upon Iraq. Military intervention for national interests is selfish and ignoble, but moral intervention that sheds blood in the cause of democracy, as in Somalia, Haiti, and the Balkans—nothing is more pure.

By this standard, the revolution judges the morality of America's wars. The War of 1812, the Mexican-American War, the Indian wars, and the Spanish-American War may have secured a continent at a tiny cost in lives, but these wars are forever sullied by the annexationist and chauvinist spirit of the America that fought them. And though Korea and Vietnam were fought to save small nations from murderous Asian communism, they were unwise or unjust wars. For we were allied with corrupt regimes and fought to keep those countries in our camp in a Cold War that never had the moral clarity of the war against fascism.

President Nixon's support for General Pinochet's overthrow of the Castroite Salvador Allende in Chile was an outrage. So, too, was Ronald Reagan's assistance to the Nicaraguan Contras fighting to recapture their country from the pro-Soviet Sandinistas. As for Reagan's invasion of Grenada, to rescue that tiny island from the Stalinist thugs who murdered its Marxist ruler, Maurice Bishop—that was American aggression. But Clinton's invasion of Haiti to restore to power the Marxist defrocked priest, Father Aristide—that was intervention on behalf of democracy and fully justified.

And so long as it is a "good war," the end justifies the means in the catechism of the revolution. That Mr. Lincoln made himself an absolute dictator, trampled on the Constitution, imprisoned dissidents without trial, and unleashed Generals Sherman and Sheridan to burn the South to ashes was fine. The eradication of slavery justified the means employed, even if fellow Americans suffered terribly. As for "the Good War," World War II, allying ourselves with the mass murderer Stalin and firebombing cities like Nagasaki, killing scores of thousands of women and children in hours, were acceptable, because our hearts were pure and our enemy was evil.

Richard Nixon is denounced for the "murder bombing" of Hanoi to free our POWs, bombing that North Vietnam said killed 1,900 people over thirteen days. Yet, Harry Truman is forever a hero even though he ordered the atomic bombing of Hiroshima and Nagasaki, killing 140,000 civilians, and sent 2 million Russian prisoners of war back to be tortured and murdered by Stalin in Operation Keelhaul.

FOR THE CULTURAL revolution the enemy is always on the Right, and the revolution does not forgive or forget. Compare the remorseless pursuit to his grave of General Pinochet, the dictator who crushed Castroism in Chile, with the expressions of sorrow at the deaths of Mao's partners in murder, Chou En-lai and Deng Xiaoping.

Byron De La Beckwith, charged with assassinating NAACP leader Medgar Evers in Mississippi in 1963, is tried, retried, and tried a third time, thirty years later, and dies in prison, as the revolution demands, even as it pleads for clemency for Leonard Peltier, who murdered two wounded FBI agents after a 1975 shootout on Pine Ridge Reservation. The latest cultural icon is Mumia Abu-Jamal, who is on death row for murdering a policeman in Philadelphia in 1981 by emptying his gun into the wounded officer, who lay bleeding. One hundred academic historians have urged that Mumia be given a new trial and that the killing of that policeman be "viewed in the light of history."[29] As Peltier is an Indian and Mumia is black, they qualify as members of a victim class. But two dead FBI agents and a dead cop— three white males—do not.

THE EQUALITY THE revolution preaches is a corruption of Jefferson's idea "All men are created equal." Jefferson meant that all were endowed by their Creator with the same right to life, liberty, and property, and all must be equal under the law. He rejected egalitarianism. As he wrote John Adams in 1813: "I agree with you that there is a natural aristocracy among men. The grounds of this are virtue and talent."[30]

Measured by virtues and talents, it is more true to say that "no two men were ever created equal." What America is about is not equality of condition or equality of result, but freedom, so a "natural aristocracy" of ability, achievement, virtue, and excellence—from athletics to the arts to the academy—can rise to lead, inspire, and set an example for us all to follow and a mark for us all to aim at. Hierarchies are as natural as they are essential. Consider the American institutions of excellence, from Microsoft to the New York Yankees, from the U.S. Marine Corps to the Mayo Clinic. How many are run on a one-person, one-vote principle?

As history demonstrates, all peoples, cultures, and civilizations are not equal. Some have achieved greatness often, others never. All life-styles are not equal. All religions are not equal. All ideas are not equal. Indeed, what is true martyrdom but that most eloquent and compelling of all testimonies that all ideas are *not* equal.

While all ideas have a right to be heard, none has an automatic right to be respected. The First Amendment requires that we tolerate the false as well as the true, the foolish as well as the wise; but nations and societies advance by separating the wheat from the chaff, and discarding the chaff. The revolution's idea of equality is ideological, utopian, absurd, and ultimately ruinous. Only a society adrift would award the black berets of rangers, who have volunteered to take the gravest risks and gone through the most arduous training, to every clerk, cook, and bottle washer in the army. Was it not Lord Acton who said that if democracy dies it is always equality that kills it?

THIS DEBASED FORM of equality traces its paternity to the French, not the American, Revolution; to nineteenth-century socialists, not to the eighteenth-century American patriots. Indeed, as all men are endowed differently with gifts, talents, and virtues, the only way to achieve equality of result is tyranny. And that is not America. Those who endlessly revise scholastic aptitude tests, because the results collide with their preconceptions, then give extra points to students based on ethnicity, then throw the tests out because they still do not yield the desired results, are hopeless ideologues whose false ideas about human nature will never survive their first collision with reality.

The equality the revolution teaches may be found in the final results of the "Caucus race" in *Alice's Adventures in Wonderland*. After all the participants had all run around in circles for half an hour, they asked, "But who has won?"

And the Dodo said, "Everybody has won and all shall have prizes."[31]


MERE TOLERANCE, SAID G. K. Chesterton, "is the virtue of men who no longer believe in anything." But our new faith is tolerant only about what it considers inconsequential: sex, pornography, filthy language, boorish manners, slovenly dress, and obscene art. It has no tolerance for those who defy its secularist dogmas.

In the new dispensation you can make a movie depicting Jesus Christ as a wimp who lusts after Mary Magdalene, as in *The Last Temptation of Christ*. But suggest a link between heredity and intelligence, as Charles Murray did in *The Bell Curve,* and you will learn what it means to cross the revolution. A local druggist may sell condoms to thirteen-year-olds, but sell cigarettes to the same kids and you will be prosecuted for endangering their health and imperiling their morals. Books that proclaim that "God is dead," or that St. Paul was a homosexual, or that celibacy is crippling, or that Pius XII was "Hitler's Pope" will attract warm reviews for "boldness," "creativity," and "irreverence." But slip and use a racial slur, as Senator Byrd did, or a vulgarism about homosexuals, as Rep. Dick Armey famously did in his malapropism "Barney Fag," and you will not escape the whipping post.

In the nineteenth century, blasphemy was a crime in many states. Today, blasphemy, vulgarity, and obscenities are acceptable, even on prime time, but ethnic humor is "hate speech" that must be punished severely. We can "save the Baptists," says Darwinist David Dennett, but "not if it means tolerating the deliberate misinforming of children about the natural world."[32] Dennett warns Creationists: "You are free to preserve or create any religious creed you wish, so long as it does not become a public nuisance. . . . Those who will not accommodate, who will not temper, who insist on keeping only the purest and wildest strains of their heritage alive, we shall be obliged, reluctantly, to cage or disarm."[33]

There is the militant spirit of the modernist orthodoxy.

## HATE CRIMES

Like any religion, the new dispensation has its own catalog of moral crimes. The most odious are "hate crimes," assaults motivated by hatred of a victim's color, creed, national origin, or sexual orientation.

Now, clearly, the murders of James Byrd and Matthew Shepard were cowardly and contemptible acts that merit the maximum punishment. But why were these two murders, of the fifteen thousand committed each year, made a cause of special denunciation by our political and cultural elites? After all, the killers were nobodies. In the case of Byrd, ex-cons high on drugs; in the case of Shepard, thugs, nonentities.

True, the killing of Byrd, tied to a truck and dragged to his death, was particularly gruesome, but that did not qualify it as a hate crime. It was a hate crime because Byrd was black and his killers chose him because he was black. Shepard was beaten unconscious and chained to a fence in a freezing countryside after he made sexual advances to one of two thugs, who then decided to rob and kill him. His murder was a hate crime because Shepard was homosexual and his killers were white heterosexuals, enraged that one of them had been propositioned. Had Shepard been murdered in the same brutal fashion by ex-lovers, his killing would not have qualified as a hate crime, nor would his death have gotten presidential notice.

All of us have biases, so let the author concede his. Had the killers of Matthew Shepard chosen a sixteen-year-old girl rather than a twenty-one-year-old gay man, her rape-murder would have been to me an even greater evil. But the killers in both cases should suffer the same penalty. And if the killers of James Byrd had been black, or Byrd white, his dragging-death would have been an equally vicious atrocity, justifying the same penalty.

Why were these two cruel murders singled out by the president and the press? Because they fit the profile perfectly. In the catechism of the revolution, the murder of homosexuals because they are gay, and of blacks because they are black, are the worst of crimes, worse even than the rape-murder of a child. How do we know?

Less than a year after Shepard's murder, two men in Arkansas were charged in the murder of thirteen-year-old Jesse Dirkhising. Here are the details, as reported by the Associated Press:

> According to police, Davis Carpenter Jr., 38, and Joshua Brown, 22, drugged and blindfolded Jesse Dirkhising, gagged him with underwear, and strapped him to a mattress face down with duct tape and belts. Then the boy was repeatedly raped and sodomized with various objects before he suffocated because of the position he was in, investigators said.
>
> At the apartment the police found handwritten instructions and a diagram of how to position the boy. Other notes described apparently unfulfilled fantasies of molesting other children . . .
>
> On the night of Jesse's death, Brown repeatedly raped the boy while Carpenter watched, police said. Brown took a break to eat a sandwich and noticed the boy had stopped breathing.[34]

Carpenter and Brown were lovers, and the former masturbated as Brown raped the boy. Yet this torture-rape-murder got almost no national press. Why? Because this was a "sex crime," not a "hate crime," and because to show homosexuals in acts of sadistic barbarism does not fit the villain-victim script of our cultural elite. To spotlight the brutality of Carpenter and Brown would have set back the cause. Writes media critic Brent Bozell:

> Had Jesse Dirkhising been shot inside his Arkansas school he would have been an immediate national story. Had he been openly gay and his attackers heterosexual, the crime would have led all the networks. But no liberal media outlet would dare to be the first to tell a grisly murder story which has as its villains two gay men.[35]

When Brown's trial was held, the *Washington Times,* almost alone among national newspapers, reported the proceedings. "The discrepancy [in national coverage of the Shepard and Dirkhising murders] isn't just real," wrote Andrew Sullivan, a homosexual and columnist for the *New Republic,* "it's staggering."[36] Sullivan found three thousand stories on Shepard's murder in a search of the Nexis database the first month after the killing, but only forty-six stories on the slaying of Jesse Dirkhising. FOX NEWS was the only network to report on Brown's murder trial and conviction. The Big Media have been converted into a communications arm of the revolution.

SOON AFTER BYRD'S dragging death, six-year-old Jake Robel died the same horrible way. As his mother Christy went into a take-out sandwich shop in Independence, Missouri, Jake was left strapped in his seat belt in the back of her Chevy Blazer. Christy left the keys in the ignition. Kim Davis, thirty-four, just out of jail, watched her go into the sandwich shop and jumped in the driver's seat. Christy Robel ran to rescue her son, opening the back door to pull him out. Davis shoved the boy out, still tied to his seat belt. Christy Robel screamed hysterically for him to stop. Davis looked into the backseat, then into the rearview mirror, and sped off, dragging the boy five miles until stopped by motorists who spotted the boy's body being dragged along the highway. Why did this crime not get national attention? Because Jake Robel was white and Davis is black. Hate crimes are the cultural elite's way of racially profiling white males.

TEN DAYS BEFORE Christmas of 2000, an atrocity more evil than what was done to Matthew Shepard or James Byrd was committed in Wichita.

Five young people were at a party when their home was invaded by brothers, ages twenty-three and twenty. The five were put into a car, driven to an ATM machine, forced to withdraw their money, and taken onto a soccer field. The two women were forced to strip and were raped. Then the victims were forced to have sex with each other at gunpoint. All were made to kneel down. Each was shot in the head. The three young men and one woman died. The other woman, left for dead, ran bleeding and naked for a mile in the cold to find help, as the brothers drove back to ransack the house.

Heather Muller, twenty-five, was remembered for her singing voice. Aaron Sander had just returned from Mount St. Mary's College and Seminary in Emmitsburg, Maryland, where he had decided to become a priest. Bradley Herman, twenty-seven, was Aaron's friend. Jason Befort, twenty-six, was a science teacher and coach at Augusta High. He had planned to propose to the woman who survived and had bought a ring and a book on how to go about it. "Jason didn't get the chance to make the proposal or give her the ring," writes Frank Morriss in the *Wanderer*. "The Catholic church in his hometown of Pratt wasn't big enough for his funeral; so, it was moved to the larger Methodist Church."[37] In the minutes before he died, Jason Befort was forced to watch as the woman he hoped to marry was raped.

What Morriss did not mention was that all the victims were white and the killers black. Had the races been reversed, this would have been the hate crime of the decade. Yet this atrocity never made Brokaw, never made Rather, never made Jennings, never made page one of the national press. Why not? "The story did not fit the politically correct national melodrama of black victimhood, white oppression," writes columnist and author David Horowitz.[38]

Mr. Horowitz seems to have a point. According to the 1999 *Index of Leading Cultural Indicators,* African Americans, though only 13 percent of our population, are responsible for 42 percent of all violent crimes and over half of the murders in the United States.[39] The statistics on interracial crimes show an even more shocking pattern of prejudice.

In 1990, Prof. William Wilbanks of the Department of Criminal Justice at Florida International University was angered by a campaign to reduce black-on-black crime, as it seemed to treat assaults on whites as less worthy of condemnation. After an in-depth study of the 1987 Justice Department figures on victims of crime, Wilbanks discovered and reported the following:

- In 1987, white criminals chose black victims in 3 percent of violent crimes, while black criminals chose white victims fifty percent of the time.
- When the crime was rape, white criminals chose black women in 0 percent of their assaults, while black criminals chose white women in 28 percent of assaults. Of eighty-three thousand cases of rape, Wilbanks could not find any in which the rapist was white and the victim was black.
- White criminals chose black victims in 2 percent of their robberies; but black criminals chose white victims in 73 percent of their robberies.[40]

When Professor Wilbanks's startling and depressing figures were first reported, there was no refutation, no challenge, no contradiction, simply silence. Ten years later, in 1999, the *Washington Times* published the findings of a study on interracial crime by the New Century Foundation, which relied on the 1994 Justice Department statistics. The NCF study supported Wilbanks's findings.

- Blacks had committed 90 percent of interracial violent crimes in 1994.
- As blacks were 12 percent of the population, these figures meant they were fifty times as likely to commit acts of interracial violence as whites.
- Blacks were 100 to 250 times more likely than whites to commit interracial gang rapes and gang assaults.
- Even in the "hate crimes" category—less than 1 percent of interracial crimes—blacks were twice as likely to be the assailant as the victim.[41]

The NCF study found Asian Americans to be the least violent group, committing violent crimes at only half the rate of white Americans.

These figures must be deeply disheartening to tens of millions of decent African Americans. Yet they do expose as a Big Lie a central tenet of the cultural revolution: the malicious slander that America is a nation where black folks are constantly at risk from the majority. It is in America's minority communities that crime rates are highest; it is out of those communities that interracial crime comes. We solve nothing by self-deception.

The same apparently holds true for England. Analyzing the figures for interracial crime buried in the Home Office's "Statistics on Race and the Criminal Justice System," columnist John Woods found that of "racially motivated" crimes in 1995, "143,000 were committed against minorities, and 238,000 against white people." Woods's conclusion:

> If the ethnic minorities comprise 6% of the population of the UK, and are producing 238,000 assaults per year, and the white population, who comprise 94% of the population, are producing 143,000 racial assaults per year, it would appear that, on a per capita basis, the ethnic minorities are producing about 25 times more racial assaults than the white population.[42]

The New Century Fund is chaired by Jared Taylor, author of *Paved with Good Intentions: The Failure of Race Relations in Contemporary America*, a controversial figure in the debate on crime and race. But the NCF statistics are based on Justice Department numbers and track closely the findings of Wilbanks and Woods. They are also unchallenged and almost ignored.

When the *Washington Times* asked Morgan Reynolds, director of the Criminal Justice Center at the National Center for Policy Analysis in Dallas, to comment on the NCF's study of interracial crime, he shrugged: "It's an issue that most white scholars ignore, because you can only get into trouble. . . . It's no news to anybody who's pursued the differences of race and crime, but it's politically incorrect."[43] Crime scholar James Q. Wilson volunteered that racial aspects of crime are "too sensitive" to be publicly discussed.[44] But if that is true, why have hate crimes statutes at all?

A CRIME IS a crime and should be punished, no matter the creed or color of the perpetrator. Justice should be color-blind. But this campaign to codify certain crimes as "hate crimes" has nothing to do with justice and everything to do with ideology. Our cultural elite wants Americans to see their country as it does—as a racist land in need of redemption, where white males are the most prevalent and dangerous of criminals. And the truth does not matter: if the rape-murder of a thirteen-year-old boy, or the dragging death of a six-year-old boy by a black ex-con, or a racist atrocity in Wichita does not fit, or worse, contradicts the script, bury the story.

In the catechism of the revolution, the thirty murders of young men by the sadist John Wayne Gacy did not qualify as hate crimes, but had Gacy been beaten up outside a gay bar for propositioning a fraternity boy, that would have qualified. The murder of Dr. King would have qualified as a hate crime, as his killer, James Earl Ray, hated King as a black leader; but the murders of John F. Kennedy by a Castroite and Robert Kennedy by a Palestinian extremist would not.

As the Mass, endless reenactments of the Last Supper, is a sacrament of Catholicism, repeated recitations of the lurid details of hate crimes are a virtual sacrament in the new faith. The prototypical hate crime always has the same plot, hero, villain, and victim: progressives standing up to white bigots on behalf of defenseless minorities. And the search for fresh hate crimes by media that have become the propaganda arm of the revolution never ceases. For each newly discovered hate crime reaffirms an infallible doctrine: deep down America is a homophobic, bigoted nation. Per Ms. Sontag, "The white race is the cancer of human history."

But how did this new religion capture a Christian and conservative America of only yesterday? Where did it come from?

# FOUR WHO MADE A REVOLUTION

Who will free us from the yoke of Western Civilization?[1]
—Georg Lukacs
Marxist Theoretician

A really efficient totalitarian state would be one in which the all-powerful executive of political bosses and their army of managers control a population of slaves who do not have to be coerced, because they love their servitude.[2]

—Aldous Huxley
*Brave New World*

The taproot of the revolution that captured the cultural institutions of the American republic goes back far beyond the 1960s to August 1914, the beginning of the Great War that historian Jacques Barzun calls the "blow that hurled the modern world on its course of self-destruction."

On August 4, 1914, the Social Democrats stood in the Reichstag and, to a man, voted the kaiser's war credits, joining the orgy of patriotism as the armies of the Reich smashed into Belgium. Marxists were stunned. The long-anticipated European war was to be their time. "Workers of the world, unite!" Marx had thundered in the closing line of his *Communist Manifesto*. Marxists had confidently predicted that when war came, the workers would rise up and rebel against their rulers rather than fight fellow workers of neighboring nations. But it had not happened. The greatest socialist party in Europe had been converted into a war party, and the workers had thrown down their tools and gone off to fight with songs in their hearts. As historian Barbara Tuchman describes it:

> When the call came, the worker, whom Marx declared to have no Fatherland, identified himself with country, not class. He turned out to be a member of the national family like anyone else. The force of his antagonism which was supposed to topple capitalism found a better target in the foreigner. The working class went to war willingly, even eagerly, like the middle class, like the upper class, like the species.[3]

Marxists had been exposed as fools.

As the horrors of the western front unfolded, they waited. But even Ypres, Passchendaele, and the Somme, where hundreds of thousands of British soldiers went to their deaths over a few yards of mud, did not cause the workers to rise up in the homeland of the Industrial Revolution. Neither the French nor the German working class broke at Verdun. The 1917 mutiny in the French trenches was swiftly put down. New blows came at war's end.

After the Russian Revolution, Communist coups were attempted in Budapest, Munich, and Berlin. The Bavarian Soviet was quickly crushed by German war veterans. Rosa Luxemburg, who had led the Spartacist uprising, and Karl Liebknecht were clubbed and shot to death in Berlin by *Freikorps*. The Budapest regime of Bela Kun lasted a few months. The workers failed to rally to the revolutions launched in their name.

Trotsky sought to make the Red Army the spear point of revolution. Invading Poland, he was hurled back at the Vistula by Polish patriots under Marshal Pilsudski. Nothing the Marxists had predicted had come to pass. Their hour had come and gone. The workers of the West, the mythical proletariat, had refused to play the role history had assigned them. How could Marx have been so wrong?

Two of Marx's disciples now advanced an explanation. Yes, Marx had been wrong. Capitalism was not impoverishing the workers. Indeed, their lot was improving, and they had not risen in revolution because their souls had been saturated in two thousand years of Christianity, which blinded them to their true class interests. Unless and until Christianity and Western culture, the immune system of capitalism, were uprooted from the soul of Western Man, Marxism could not take root, and the revolution would be betrayed by the workers in whose name it was to be fought. In biblical terms, the word of Marx, seed of the revolution, had fallen on rock-hard Christian soil and died. Wagering everything on the working class, the Marxists had bet on the wrong horse.

The first dissenting disciple was the Hungarian Georg Lukacs, an agent of the Comintern, whose *History and Class Consciousness* had brought him recognition as a Marxist theorist to rival Marx himself. "I saw the revolutionary destruction of society as the one and only solution," said Lukacs. "A worldwide overturning of values cannot take place without the annihilation of the old values and the creation of new ones by the revolutionaries."[4] As deputy commissar for culture in Bela Kun's regime, Lukacs put his self-described "demonic" ideas into action in what came to be known as "cultural terrorism."

As part of this terrorism he instituted a radical sex education program in Hungarian schools. Children were instructed in free love, sexual intercourse, the archaic nature of middle-class family codes, the outdatedness of monogamy, and the irrelevance of religion, which deprives man of all pleasures. Women, too, were called to rebel against the sexual mores of the time.[5]

LUKACS'S PURPOSE IN promoting licentiousness among women and children was to destroy the family, the core institution of Christianity and Western culture. Five decades after Lukacs fled Hungary, his ideas would be enthusiastically embraced by baby boomers in the "sexual revolution."

The second disciple was Antonio Gramsci, an Italian Communist who has lately begun to receive deserved recognition as the greatest Marxist strategist of the twentieth century. After Mussolini's march on Rome in 1922, Gramsci fled to Russia. But unlike the "useful idiots" and "infantile left" of Lenin's derision, such as American writer Lincoln Steffens—"I have been over into the future and it works!"—Gramsci was a sharp observer who saw that Bolshevism did not work. Only through terror could the regime compel obedience. Gramsci concluded that Leninism had failed. The Russian people had not been converted to communism; they loathed it. Their land, faith, families, icons, and Mother Russia all meant far more to the Russian people than any international workers' solidarity. The Soviets were deluding themselves, Gramsci concluded. The Russian people had not changed. They were obedient only because resistance meant a knock at the door at midnight and a bullet in the back of the neck in the basement of the Lubianka. Even the czar had evoked more love and loyalty than the hated Bolsheviks.

Gramsci concluded it was their Christian souls that prevented the Russian people from embracing their Communist revolution. "The civilized world had been thoroughly saturated with Christianity for 2000 years," Gramsci wrote; and a regime grounded in Judeo-Christian beliefs and values could not be overthrown until those roots were cut.[6] If Christianity was the heat shield of capitalism, then, to capture the West, Marxists must first de-Christianize the West.

Disillusioned, terrified of Stalin, who had seized power on Lenin's death and who did not relish independent Marxist thinkers, Gramsci went home to lead the Italian Communist party. Mussolini had another idea. He locked Gramsci up and lost the key. Languishing in prison, near death from tuberculosis, Gramsci was finally freed, but died in 1937 at forty-six. But in his *Prison Notebooks* he left behind the blueprints for a successful Marxist revolution in the West. Our own cultural revolution could have come straight from its pages. "In the East," Gramsci wrote of Russia, the state was everything, civil society was primordial . . . in the West there was a proper relation between the state and civil society, and when the state trembled a sturdy structure of civil society was at once revealed. The State [in the West] was only the outer ditch, behind which there stood a powerful system of fortresses and earthworks.[7]

Rather than seize power first and impose a cultural revolution from above, Gramsci argued, Marxists in the West must first change the culture; then power would fall into their laps like ripened fruit. But to change the culture would require a "long march through the institutions"—the arts, cinema, theater, schools, colleges, seminaries, newspapers, magazines, and the new electronic medium, radio. One by one, each had to be captured and converted and politicized into an agency of revolution. Then the people could be slowly educated to understand and even welcome the revolution.

Gramsci urged his fellow Marxists to form popular fronts with Western intellectuals who shared their contempt for Christianity and bourgeois culture and who shaped the minds of the young. Message to the comrades: "It's the culture, stupid!" Since Western culture had given birth to capitalism and sustained it, if that culture could be subverted, the system would fall of its own weight. On the cover of his 1970 runaway bestseller *The Greening of America,* the manifesto of the counterculture, author Charles Reich parroted Gramsci perfectly:

There is a revolution coming. It will not be like revolutions of the past. It will originate with the individual and with culture, and it will change the political structure only as its final act. It will not require violence to succeed, and it cannot be successfully resisted with violence. It is now spreading with amazing rapidity, and already our laws, institutions, and social structure are changing in consequence. . . .

This is the revolution of the new generation.[8]

Gramsci's idea on how to make a revolution in a Western society has been proven correct. Lenin's regime shook the world for seventy years, but ultimately his revolution failed, and his regime collapsed. In the end, the Communist party of Lenin and Stalin remained what it had been from the beginning, a conspiracy of political criminals who used Marxist ideas and rhetoric to disguise what they were really about: absolute power. Lenin's regime died detested and unmourned. But the Gramscian revolution rolls on, and, to this day, it continues to make converts.

## THE FRANKFURT SCHOOL COMES TO AMERICA

In 1923, Lukacs and members of the German Communist party set up, at Frankfurt University, an Institute for Marxism modeled on the Marx-Engels Institute in Moscow. After some reflection, they settled on a less provocative name, the Institute for Social Research. It would soon come to be known simply as the Frankfurt School.

In 1930, a renegade Marxist and admirer of the Marquis de Sade, Max Horkheimer, became its director. Horkheimer, too, had concluded that Marx had gotten it wrong. The working class was not up to its role as the vanguard of the revolution. Already, Western workers were happily moving into the middle class, the detested bourgeoisie. They had failed the Marxists, who would not have been surprised by events on Wall Street in May 1970, when radicals and students protesting Nixon's Cambodian incursion were beaten up by construction workers of the building trades union of Pete Brennan, whom Nixon would then install as his secretary of labor.

At Horkheimer's direction, the Frankfurt School began to retranslate Marxism into cultural terms. The old battlefield manuals were thrown out, and new manuals were written. To old Marxists, the enemy was capitalism; to new Marxists, the enemy was Western culture. To old Marxists, the path to power was the violent overthrow of the regime, as in Paris in 1789 and in St. Petersburg in 1917. To the new Marxist, the path to power was nonviolent and would require decades of patient labor. Victory would come only after Christian beliefs had died in the soul of Western Man. And that would happen only after the institutions of culture and education had been captured and conscripted by allies and agents of the revolution. Occupy the cultural institutions of the West, its "fortresses and earthworks," and the state, the "outer ditch," would fall without a fight.

For old and new Marxists both, however, the definition of morality remained: what advances the revolution is moral, what obstructs it is not. As Hudson Institute scholar John Fonte writes, Gramsci believed in

> "absolute historicism," meaning that morals, values, truth, standards and human nature itself are products of different historical epochs. There are no absolute moral standards that are universally true for all human beings outside of a particular historical context; rather, morality is "socially constructed."[9]

When Ronald Reagan famously blurted that the Soviets "reserve to themselves the right to lie, steal and cheat," he hit on a truth that an honest Marxist would not strenuously contest, though the remark almost caused a collective nervous breakdown at the Department of State.[10]

ABOUT THIS SAME time, music critic Theodor Adorno, psychologist Erich Fromm, and sociologist Wilhelm Reich joined the Frankfurt School. But, in 1933, history rudely intruded. Adolf Hitler ascended to power in Berlin, and as the leading lights of the Frankfurt School were Jewish and Marxist, they were not a good fit for the Third Reich. The Frankfurt School packed its ideology and fled to America.

Also departing was a graduate student by the name of Herbert Marcuse. With the assistance of Columbia University, they set up their new Frankfurt School in New York City and redirected their talents and energies to undermining the culture of the country that had given them refuge.

Among the new weapons of cultural conflict the Frankfurt School developed was Critical Theory. The name sounds benign enough, but it stands for a practice that is anything but benign. One student of Critical Theory defined it as the "essentially destructive criticism of all the main elements of Western culture, including Christianity, capitalism, authority, the family, patriarchy, hierarchy, morality, tradition, sexual restraint, loyalty, patriotism, nationalism, heredity, ethnocentrism, convention and conservatism."[11]

Using Critical Theory, for example, the cultural Marxist repeats and repeats the charge that the West is guilty of genocidal crimes against every civilization and culture it has encountered. Under Critical Theory, one repeats and repeats that Western societies are history's greatest repositories of racism, sexism, nativism, xenophobia, homophobia, anti-Semitism, fascism, and Nazism. Under Critical Theory, the crimes of the West flow from the character of the West, as shaped by Christianity. One modern example is "attack politics," where "surrogates" and "spin doctors" never defend their own candidate, but attack and attack the opposition. Another example of Critical Theory is the relentless assault on Pius XII as complicit in the Holocaust, no matter the volumes of evidence that show that accusation to be a lie.

Critical Theory eventually induces "cultural pessimism," a sense of alienation, of hopelessness, of despair where, even though prosperous and free, a people comes to see its society and country as oppressive, evil, and unworthy of its loyalty and love. The new Marxists considered cultural pessimism a necessary precondition of revolutionary change.

Under the impact of Critical Theory, many of the sixties generation, the most privileged in history, convinced themselves that they were living in an intolerable hell. In *The Greening of America,* which enthralled Senator McGovern, Justice Douglas, and the *Washington Post,* Charles Reich spoke of a "total atmosphere of violence" in America's high schools.[12] This was thirty years before Columbine, and Reich did not mean guns and knives:

> An examination or test is a form of violence. Compulsory gym, to one embarrassed or afraid, is a form of violence. The requirement that a student must get a pass to walk in the hallway is violence. Compulsory attendance in the classroom, compulsory studying in study hall, is violence.[13]

Erich Fromm's *Escape from Freedom* and Wilhelm Reich's *The Mass Psychology of Fascism* and *The Sexual Revolution* reflect Critical Theory. But the most influential book the Frankfurt School ever published was *The Authoritarian Personality*. In this altarpiece of the Frankfurt School, Karl Marx's economic determinism is replaced with cultural determinism. If a family is deeply Christian and capitalist, ruled by an authoritarian father, you may expect the children to grow up racist and fascist. Charles Sykes, senior fellow at the Wisconsin Policy Research Center, describes *The Authoritarian Personality* as "an uncompromising indictment of bourgeois civilization, with the twist that what was considered merely old-fashioned by previous critics was now declared both fascistic and psychologically warped."[14]

Where Marx criminalized the capitalist class, the Frankfurt School criminalized the middle class. That the middle class had given birth to democracy and that middle-class Britain had been fighting Hitler when the comrades of the Frankfurt School in Moscow were cohabiting with him did not matter. Nor did it matter that middle-class America had given Adorno and his colleagues a sanctuary when they had fled the Nazis. The truth did not matter, for these were Marxist ideologues, and they alone defined truth.

Having discovered fascism's nesting ground in patriarchal families, Adorno now identified its natural habitat: traditional culture: "It is a well-known hypothesis that susceptibility to fascism is most characteristically a middle-class phenomenon, that 'it is in the culture' and, hence, that those who conform the most to this culture will be the most prejudiced."[15]

Edmund Burke once wrote, "I would not know how to draw up an indictment against a whole people."[16] Adorno and the Frankfurt School, however, had just done exactly that. They flatly asserted that individuals raised in families dominated by the father, who are flag-waving patriots and follow the old-time religion, are incipient fascists and potential Nazis. As a conservative Christian culture breeds fascism, those deeply immersed in such a culture must be closely watched for fascist tendencies.

These ideas have been internalized by the Left. As early as the mid-1960s, conservatives and authority figures who denounced or opposed the campus revolution were routinely branded "fascists." Baby boomers were unknowingly following a script that ran parallel to the party line laid down by the Moscow Central Committee in 1943:

> Members and front organizations must continually embarrass, discredit and degrade our critics. When obstructionists become too irritating, label them as fascist, or Nazi or anti-Semitic. . . . The association will, after enough repetition, become "fact" in the public mind.[17]

Since the 1960s, branding opponents as haters or mentally sick has been the most effective weapon in the arsenal of the Left. Here is the "secret formula" as described by psychologist and author Thomas Szasz: "If you want to debase what a person is doing . . . call him mentally ill."[18] Behind it all is a political agenda. Our sick society is in need of therapy to heal itself of its innate prejudice. Assessing the Frankfurt School's *Studies in Prejudice,* of which *The Authoritarian Personality* was the best known, Christopher Lasch wrote:

The purpose and design of *Studies in Prejudice* dictated the conclusion that prejudice, a psychological disorder rooted in the "authoritarian" personality structure, could be eradicated only by subjecting the American people to what amounted to collective psychotherapy—by treating them as inmates of an insane asylum.[19]

This is the root of the "therapeutic state"—a regime where sin is redefined as sickness, crime becomes antisocial behavior, and the psychiatrist replaces the priest. If fascism is, as Adorno says, "in the culture," then all of us raised in that old God-and-country culture of the 1940s and 1950s are in need of treatment to help us come face-to-face with the prejudices and bigotries in which we were marinated from birth.

ANOTHER OF THE insights of Horkheimer and Adorno was to realize that the road to cultural hegemony was through psychological conditioning, not philosophical argument. America's children could be conditioned at school to reject their parents' social and moral beliefs as racist, sexist, and homophobic, and conditioned to embrace a new morality. Though the Frankfurt School remains unfamiliar to most Americans, its ideas were well-known at the teachers' colleges back in the 1940s and 1950s.

The school openly stated that whether children learned facts or skills at school was less important than that they graduate conditioned to display the correct attitudes. When Allan Bloom wrote in *The Closing of the American Mind* that "American high school graduates are among the most sensitive illiterates in the world," with some of the lowest test scores on earth in comparative exams, but the highest scores for sensitivity to issues like the environment, Bloom was testifying to the success of the Frankfurt School.[20] Parents may consider today's public schools costly failures where children no longer learn. To the Frankfurt School, they are a success; for the children coming out of them exhibit all the right attitudes. On entering college, these students now go through orientation sessions, where they are instructed in the new values that obtain on college campuses—to get their minds right, as the warden said in *Cool Hand Luke*.

How successful has the cultural revolution been in eradicating the old values and instilling new ones in the souls of the young? In the days after Pearl Harbor, the enlistment lines at navy, army, and marine recruiting stations wound around the block. College boys were as well represented in those lines as farm boys. But in the days after the slaughter at the World Trade Center—before a single U.S. soldier had gone into combat or one cruise missile had been fired at the terrorists' base camps—the antiwar rallies had begun on American campuses.

But the importance of schools in conditioning the minds of the young was soon surpassed by that of the new media: TV and movies. As William Lind, director of the Center for Cultural Conservatism at the Free Congress Foundation, writes:

> The entertainment industry . . . has wholly absorbed the ideology of cultural Marxism and preaches it endlessly not just in sermons but in parables: strong women beating up weak men, children wiser than their parents, corrupt clergymen thwarted by carping drifters, upper-class blacks confronting the violence of lower-class whites, manly homosexuals who lead normal lives. It is all fable, an inversion of reality, but the entertainment media make it seem real, more so than the world that lies beyond the front door.[21]

To appreciate how the cultural revolution has changed the way we think, believe, and act, contrast the values that 1950s films like *On the Waterfront, High Noon,* and *Shane* reflected and undergirded with the values espoused by the leading films of today. At the Academy Awards ceremony in 2000 the two most honored films were *American Beauty* and *Cider House Rules*.

*American Beauty* starred Kevin Spacey and depicted life in an American suburb as a moral wasteland. The villain is an ex-Marine who represses his homosexuality, collects Nazi memorabilia, and becomes a homicidal maniac. In *Cider House Rules,* Michael Caine portrays a soft-spoken abortionist who stands up to the bigotry of Middle America. America's mass media have become siege guns in the culture war and a vast Skinner Box for conditioning America's young.

DURING THE FIFTIES, the Frankfurt School lacked a personality to popularize the ideas buried in the glutinous prose of Horkheimer and Adorno. Enter Herbert Marcuse, ex-OSS officer and Brandeis professor, whose ambition was to be not only a man of words but a revolutionary man of action. Marcuse provided the answer to Horkheimer's question: Who will play the role of the proletariat in the coming cultural revolution?

Marcuse's candidates: radical youth, feminists, black militants, homosexuals, the alienated, the asocial, Third World revolutionaries, all the angry voices of the persecuted "victims" of the West. This was the new proletariat that would overthrow Western culture. Among the "oppressed," the potential recruits for his revolution, Gramsci himself had included all the "marginalized groups of history . . . not only economically oppressed, but also women, racial minorities, and many 'criminals.' "[22] Charles Reich was the echo of Marcuse and Gramsci: "One of the ways the new generation struggles to feel itself as outsiders is to identify with the blacks, with the poor, with Bonnie and Clyde, and with the losers of this world."[23] Coincidentally, in 1968, the year *Bonnie and Clyde,* a film romanticizing two perverted killers, was nominated for an Academy Award, two of Reich's "losers," Sirhan Sirhan and James Earl Ray, achieved immortality with the assassinations of Robert Kennedy and Dr. King.

Past societies had been subverted by words and books, but Marcuse believed that sex and drugs were superior weapons. In *Eros and Civilization,* Marcuse urged a universal embrace of the Pleasure Principle. Reject the cultural order entirely, said Marcuse (this was his "Great Refusal"), and we can create a world of "polymorphous perversity."[24] As millions of baby boomers flooded the campuses, his moment came.

Marcuse's books were consumed. He became a cult figure. When students revolted in Paris in 1968, they carried banners proclaiming "Marx, Mao, and Marcuse."

"Make love, not war" was Marcuse's own inspired slogan. In *One Dimensional Man,* he advocated an educational dictatorship. In "Repressive Tolerance," he called for a new "liberating tolerance" that entails "intolerance against movements from the right, and toleration of movements from the left."[25] Full of Marcusian conviction, sixties students shouted down defenders of the U.S. war effort in Vietnam and welcomed radicals waving Vietcong flags. On some campuses, paroled killers can today find more receptive audiences than can conservatives. The double standard against which the Right rages, and which permits conservatives to be pilloried for sins that are forgiven the Left, is "repressive tolerance" in action. Marcuse did not disguise what he was about. In *Carnivorous Society*, he wrote:

> One can rightfully speak of a cultural revolution, since the protest is directed toward the whole cultural establishment . . . there is one thing we can say with complete assurance. The traditional idea of revolution and the traditional strategy of revolution have ended. These ideas are old-fashioned . . . what we must undertake is a type of diffuse and dispersed disintegration of the system.[26]

The "diffuse and dispersed disintegration of the system" means nothing less than the abolition of America. Like Gramsci, Marcuse had transcended Marx. The old Marxist vision of workers rising up to overthrow their capitalist rulers was yesterday. Today, Herbert Marcuse and his cohorts would put an end to a corrupt Western civilization by occupying its cultural institutions and converting them into agencies of reeducation and of revolution. As Roger Kimball, author and editor at the *New Criterion,* writes:

> In the context of Western societies, the "long march through the institutions" signified—in the words of Herbert Marcuse—

"working against the established institutions while working in them." It was primarily by this means—by insinuation and infiltration rather than confrontation—that the countercultural dreams of radicals like Marcuse have triumphed.[27]

For cultural Marxists, no cause ranked higher than the abolition of the family, which they despised as a dictatorship and the incubator of sexism and social injustice.

Hostility to the traditional family was not new to Marxists. In *The German Ideology,* Marx himself wrote that patriarchal males consider wives and children first as property. In *The Origin of the Family, Private Property, and the State,* Engels popularized the feminist conviction that all discrimination against women proceeds from the patriarchal family. Erich Fromm argued that differences between the sexes were not inherent, but a fiction of Western culture. Fromm became a founding father of feminism. To Wilhelm Reich, "The authoritarian family is the authoritarian state in miniature. . . . Familial imperialism is . . . reproduced in national imperialism." To Adorno, the patriarchal family was the cradle of fascism.

To decapitate the family with the father as its head, the Frankfurt School advocated the alternatives of matriarchy, where the mother rules the roost, and "androgyny theory," where male and female family roles are made interchangeable, and even reversed. Female boxing, women in combat, women rabbis and bishops, God as She, Demi Moore's *G.I. Jane,* Rambo-like Sigourney Weaver comforting a terrified and cringing male soldier in *Aliens,* and all the films and shows that depict women as tough and aggressive and men as sensitive and vulnerable testify to the success of the Frankfurt School and the feminist revolution it helped to midwife.

Like Lukacs, Wilhelm Reich believed the way to destroy the family was through revolutionary sexual politics and early sex education. The appearance of sex education in elementary schools in America owes a debt to Lukacs, Reich, and the Frankfurt School.

IN THE DEATH of the West, the Frankfurt School must be held as a prime suspect and principal accomplice. The propaganda assault on the family it advocated has contributed to the collapse of the family. Nuclear families today represent fewer than one-fourth of U.S. households. And women's liberation from the traditional roles of wife and mother, which the school was among the first to champion, has led to the demeaning and downgrading of those roles in American society.

Millions of Western women now share the feminists' hostility to marriage and motherhood. Millions have adopted the movement's agenda and have no intention of getting married and no desire to have children. Their embrace of Marcuse's Pleasure Principle, their tours of duty in the sexual revolution, mean marriages put off. And, as our divorce and birthrates show, even the marriages entered into are less stable and less fruitful. In the depopulating nations of Europe, even in the old Catholic countries, use of contraceptives is almost universal. Contraception, sterilization, abortion, and euthanasia are the four horsemen of the "culture of death" against which the Holy Father will inveigh to the end of his days. The pill and condom have become the hammer and sickle of the cultural revolution.

In the 1950s, Khrushchev threatened, "We will bury you." But we buried him. Yet, if Western Man does not find a way to halt his collapsing birthrate, cultural Marxism will succeed where Soviet Marxism failed; for in a 1998 report on the depopulation of Europe, the pope's Pontifical Council for the Family tied cultural pessimism directly to infertility.

> A return to a higher fertility rate in those countries whose fertility is declining at the present can be expected only if there is a change in the "mood" in these countries, a shift from present pessimism to a state of mind which could be compared to that of the "baby-boom" era, during the era of post World War Two reconstruction.[28]

No such "mood change" is remotely visible on the Old Continent, where birthrates continue to fall. In helping to undermine the family and induce cultural pessimism, the Frankfurt School can claim a share of the credit for having assisted in the suicide of the West.

Thus did a tiny band of renegade Marxists help subvert American culture and begin the deconstruction of our republic. On the tombstone of architect Christopher Wren is written, "Lector, si monumenta requiris, circumspice."[29] "Reader, if it is monuments you seek, look about you." So it may be said of Lukacs, Gramsci, Adorno, and Marcuse, four who made a revolution.

In a third of a century, what was denounced as the counterculture has become the dominant culture, and what was the dominant culture has become, in Gertrude Himmelfarb's phrase, a "dissident culture."[30] America has become an ideological state, a "soft tyranny," where the new orthodoxy is enforced, not by police agents, but by inquisitors of the popular culture. We see it in the mandatory requirement for "sensitivity training" in the military, in business, and in government. Turn on the TV and observe. The values of the revolution dominate the medium. Political correctness rules. Defiance of our new orthodoxy qualifies as "hate speech," disrespect for its dogmas as a sign of mental sickness. "Get John Rocker to a psychiatrist!" A few years back, a wag described America's universities as "islands of totalitarianism in a sea of freedom." Now even the sea has become inhospitable. Emily Dickinson spoke to our time as well as to her own:

> Assent—and you are sane—
> Demur—you're straightway dangerous
> And handled with a Chain.[31]

Political correctness is cultural Marxism, a regime to punish dissent and to stigmatize social heresy as the Inquisition punished religious heresy. Its trademark is intolerance. By classifying its adversaries as haters, or mentally ill, writes journalist Peter Hitchens in his lament for his country, *The Abolition of Britain,* the new regime imitates the methods of the Soviet Union's Serbsky Institute, which used to classify political dissidents like Natan Sharansky as insane before locking them up in a psychiatric hospital.[32] What Americans describe with the "casual phrase . . . political correctness," says Hitchens, is "the most intolerant system of thought to dominate the British Isles since the Reformation."[33] As it is in the United States.

To oppose affirmative action qualifies one as a racist. To insist there are roles in society unfit for women, such as Navy carrier pilot, is to be branded a sexist. If you believe immigration is far too high for our social cohesion, you are a nativist or a xenophobe. In 1973, the American Psychiatric Association was bullied by gay rights militants into delisting homosexuality as a disorder. Now anyone who considers it a disorder suffers himself from a sickness of the soul called homophobia.

"Homosexual acts are against nature's law," said Pope John Paul II as thousands marched on international gay pride day in Rome.[34] "The church cannot silence the truth, because this . . . would not help discern what is good from evil."[35] This restatement of Catholic moral teaching marks the Holy Father, and all who accept that teaching as true, as homophobic. Scholar and author Paul Gottfried calls it "the dehumanization of dissent."[36]

Words are weapons, said Orwell. Traditionalists have yet to discover effective countermeasures. By calling an enemy a racist or fascist, you no longer need answer his arguments. He must defend his character. In a court of law, the accused is innocent until proven guilty. But if the charge is racism, homophobia, or sexism, there is today the presumption of guilt. Innocence must be proven by the accused beyond a reasonable doubt.

Orwell heard the word "fascist" used so often he assumed that, if Jones called Smith a fascist, Jones meant, "I hate Smith!" But if Jones had said, "I hate Smith," he would be confessing to unchristian hatred. By calling Smith a fascist, he need not explain why he hates Smith or cannot best Smith in debate; he has forced Smith to prove that he is not a closet admirer of Adolf Hitler. Huey Long was right. When fascism comes to America, it will come in the name of anti-fascism.[37]

THAT LUKACS, GRAMSCI, Adorno, Marcuse, and the Frankfurt School had immense influence on America's cultural and intellectual history is undeniable. But, unlike the Bolsheviks, they did not storm a Winter Palace, they did not seize power, and they did not impose their ideas by force and terror; they were not giants, like Marx, to whom men paid homage. Few Americans even know who they were. Not one, not even Marcuse, was a St. Paul, a Luther, or a Wesley. They were intellectual renegades and moral misfits, yes, but they were also men who thought "outside the box" and put into circulation the ideas of how a successful revolution might be launched in the West, against the West. And their ideas have triumphed. America's elites, who may not even know today who the Frankfurt thinkers were, have taken to their ideas like catnip.

Americans who today accept these ideas cannot know that they were hatched in a Marxist nursery in Weimar Germany or thought out in a fascist prison in Mussolini's Italy, or that their purpose was to subvert our culture and overturn our civilization. But that begs the question: Why was the America of the 1960s, if still a country immersed in its Judeo-Christian heritage, history, traditions, and beliefs, receptive to so revolutionary an agenda?

True, a small slice of America's elite, before and during the Great Depression, became complicit in what French author Julien Benda called *The Treason of the Intellectuals*.[38] They despised the Christian capitalist America in which they lived. But why did the ideas of cultural traitors take root in Middle America? Why did they attract a following among children of the Greatest Generation, which had defeated Hitler? Why do so many of the young still buy in? Was America morally adrift in the sixties, searching for something new to believe in, a new way to live? Were the timbers of the old house rotten? Was a revolution inevitable? Were the young, and many of their teachers, simply weary of the demands of the old moral order and looking for a way to say good-bye to all that? Did they all just climb aboard the first train that came through town?

Certainly, the Frankfurt School was not alone in dreaming of and devising a social revolution. In the 1930s, many intellectuals were thinking along the same lines and coming to the same conclusions. Here is a passage from the 1937 *Yearbook of the National Education Association:*

> The present capitalist and nationalist school system has been supplanted in but one place—Russia—and that change was effected by revolution. Hence the verdict of history would seem to indicate that we are likely to have to depend upon revolution for social change of an important and far-reaching character.[39]

Margaret Sanger, the founder of Planned Parenthood, was a more famous radical than any of the Frankfurt School, and she had anticipated their ideas: "Birth control appeals to the advanced radical because it is calculated to undermine the authority of the Christian churches. I look forward to seeing humanity free someday of the tyranny of Christianity no less than capitalism."[40]

Would the 1960s revolution have swept America had Gramsci never written *Prison Notebooks* and had Adorno and Marcuse never gotten out of Germany? Were Lukacs, Gramsci, Adorno, and Marcuse indispensable men? Probably not, but they did devise the strategy and the tactics of a successful Marxist revolution in the West, and the culture they set out to destroy is no longer the dominant culture in America or the West. They began their lives as outcasts and may end on the winning side of history.

WHY DID THEY succeed? Four elements came together in the sixties to create the critical mass that exploded like Dr. Oppenheimer's device in the New Mexico desert at Alamogordo.

First was "the message in a bottle," as the men of the Frankfurt

School called their ideas. And as their ideas were germinating, other Americans, alienated from a Christian and capitalist culture, were working independently on similar strategies and ideas to undermine the culture and abolish the old America they had come to detest. Nurtured for decades, these ideas began to flower in the 1960s.

Second, there arrived on campus, beginning in 1964, a huge cohort of youth who had known neither hardship nor war. The cultural revolution now had a huge, captive, and receptive audience. Spoiled and affluent, carefree, confident, liberated, and bored, these young people were ready for rebellion. And swallowing goldfish was not what they had in mind.

As conservative scholar Robert Nisbet reminds us, bordeom "is one of the most insistent and universal [of the] forces that have shaped human behavior," and the "range of cures or terminations of boredom is a wide one."[41] High among them are sex, narcotics, and revolution. In the 1960s, what Arnold Toynbee called an "internal proletariat" of students, bored with their studies, encountered graduate instructors, bored with their subjects and unexciting lives—a combustible mixture.

Third, 1960s television could convey the tactics and triumphs of campus radicals and urban revolutionaries instantly to their peers. And the medium, now matured, no longer the fifties fiefdom of Howdy Doody and Matt Dillon, could not only transmit the new ideas, it could reinforce them by creating new visual realities.

The fourth indispensable element was Vietnam. If the war meant sacrifice, bloodshed, perhaps death, the Woodstock generation wanted no part of it. What Marcuse offered was intellectual cover for cowardice, a moral argument for malingering, a way to dodge the draft while feeling superior to those who went. The "real heroes" of this war, said Senator Fulbright and New York mayor John Lindsay, are in Canada. The message fell upon receptive ears in the Ivy League and not only there.

Finally, the old American establishment was broken on the wheel of Vietnam—the war that liberalism launched and could not win—

and its moral authority was shattered in the eyes of the young. The path to power was thus opened to the political vessel of the counter-culture, the McGovern campaign of 1972, among whose most enthusiastic workers was young Bill Clinton, the pride and paragon of the Woodstock generation.

BUT ALL THIS raises a greater question: Is the death of a religious-based culture inevitable once a society reaches general affluence? When a nation has overcome the hardships of its infancy and the struggles of its adolescence and manhood, and begins to produce a life of ease and luxury, does it naturally succumb to a disease of the soul that leads to decadence, decline, and death? "America is the only country that has gone from barbarism to decadence without civilization in between," said Oscar Wilde.[42] Did the man have a point?

Jacques Barzun suggests that the sixties generation simply picked up where the twenties generation left off. The era of sex, booze, and jazz led naturally to the era of sex, drugs, and rock and roll. Only the degeneration was briefly interrupted by the intrusive reality of Depression, World War, and Cold War. Once the 1950s were finished, a new generation took up where the Roaring Twenties crowd had left off when the market crashed in 1929.

But if the hedonism of the sixties flowed from the hedonism of the Prohibition Era, there is this difference: that 1920s generation did not hate America. A few "Lost Generation" writers fled the country, but the social rebels of the 1920s were not revolutionaries. After all, they elected Harding, Coolidge, and Hoover in the greatest Republican landslides in history. The sixties intelligentsia was different. As Eric Hoffer wrote, "Nowhere at present is there such a measureless loathing of their country by educated people as in America."[43]

———

AFTER THE COLLAPSE of the Soviet Empire, *Time* magazine asked, "Can the Right Survive Success?"[44] *Time* quoted a conservative scholar as saying, "It is a sign of enormous triumph that there are no galvanizing issues for conservatives today."[45]

"Nothing could be further from the truth," responded James Cooper, the editor of *American Arts Quarterly*. "A major galvanizing issue for conservatives, indeed, for all Americans . . . the great unfinished task that President Reagan alluded to in his farewell speech to the nation . . . is to recapture the culture from the Left. . . ."[46]

While most conservatives had been fighting the Cold War, a small band had been holding down the forgotten front, the culture war. Cooper pleaded with conservatives to take up the culture war as their new cause and spoke of the territory already lost:

> Seventy years ago, the Italian Marxist Antonio Gramsci (1891–1937) wrote the most important mission for Socialism was to "capture the culture." By the end of World War II, the liberal Left had managed to capture not only the arts, theater, literature, music, and ballet, but also motion pictures, photography, education and the media.
>
> Through its control of the culture, the Left dictates not only the answers, but the questions asked. In short, it controls the cosmological apparatus by which most American[s] comprehend the meaning of events.
>
> This cosmology is based on two great axioms: the first is there are no absolute values in the universe, no standards of beauty and ugliness, good and evil. The second axiom is—in a Godless universe—the Left holds moral superiority as the final arbiter of man's activities.[47]

Conservatives ignored Cooper's cry. Instead, they fought against national health insurance and for NAFTA and the WTO. "The Right voted with their feet," said Samuel Lipman, publisher of the *New Criterion*.[48] Added Cooper: "Conservatives returned to money-making and Cold War strategies, straightened out their George Stubbs engravings of English Thoroughbred horses on their office walls, and forgot about the whole matter. After all, they reasoned, how important is culture anyway?"[49]

"Where a man's purse is, there his heart will be also." The hearts of many on the Right are in cutting marginal tax rates and eliminating the capital gains tax. Good causes to be sure. But what doth it profit a man if he gain the whole world and suffer the loss of his country? Is whether the GDP rises at 2 or 3 or 4 percent as important as whether or not Western civilization endures and we remain one nation under God and one people? With the collapsing birthrate, open borders, and the triumph of an anti-Western multiculturalism, that is what is at issue today—the survival of America as a nation, separate and unique, and of Western civilization itself—and too many conservatives have gone AWOL in the last great fight of our lives.

So, let us consider what the death march of the West will mean, not just in future centuries, but in this century, and not just to our children's children, but to the generation growing up today.

# THE COMING GREAT MIGRATIONS

The art of prophecy is very difficult, especially with respect to the future.[1]

—Mark Twain

The Old and New Testaments have many parables of how the first-
born, or first chosen, lose their places in their fathers' houses. A
hungry Esau sells his birthright to his brother Jacob for a mess of
potage. In Matthew 22, Jesus compares heaven to the wedding feast
a king prepares for his son. When the invited guests rudely refuse the
king's invitation, he sends his servants out to the highways and byways
to bring strangers into his house to celebrate the marriage of his son.

As Western peoples have begun to die, the vacant rooms in the
House of the West will not long remain vacant. In America, the places
prepared for the forty million unborn lost since *Roe v. Wade* have
been filled by the grateful poor of Asia, Africa, and Latin America. As
Europeans forgo children, the places prepared for them, too, will be
occupied by strangers.

Let us revisit the UN statistics on the depopulation of Europe. In
2000, there were 494 million Europeans aged fifteen to sixty-five.
That will plunge to 365 million by 2050. But the 107 million Europeans over sixty-five today will soar to 172 million. In fifty years, the
ratio of European young and middle-aged to seniors and elderly will
fall from five to one to two to one.[2] With Europe's welfare states
already buckling under the weight of social programs, who will pay

for the health, welfare, and pensions of the elderly? Who will care for the old people in the retirement centers and nursing homes? With the number of children falling even faster than those of working age, who will mow the lawns, clean the buildings, wash the dishes, prepare and serve the food in the restaurants of Europe? Where will the nannies come from? With a working population 25 percent smaller and an elderly population 90 percent larger, where will the new nurses and doctors come from to care for these seniors?

By 2050, a third of Europe's people will be over sixty. In the U.K., Germany, France, Italy, and Spain, one in ten will be over eighty![3] The median age of a European will be fifty, nine years above the median age of the oldest nation on earth today, Japan. In *Gray Dawn: How the Coming Age Wave Will Transform America and the World,* former commerce secretary Pete Peterson writes:

> Within the next thirty years, the official projections suggest that governments in most developed countries will have to spend at least an extra 9 to 16 percent of GDP annually simply to meet their old age benefit promises. To pay these costs through increased taxation would raise the total tax burden by an unthinkable extra 25 to 40 percent of every worker's taxable wages—in countries where total payroll tax rates often already exceed 40 percent. Or, if we resort to deficit spending, we would have to consume all the savings and more of the entire developed world.[4]

This is the fiscal equivalent of nuclear winter. If Europe wishes to maintain its social safety net, there are three options: trillions of dollars in new tax revenues must be found; European women must begin bearing two and three times as many babies; or Europe must import millions of workers each year. These are the stark choices the Old Continent faces.

Yet, as Joseph Chamie of the UN Population Agency notes, "No demographers believe birth rates will rebound. How much will it take to convince a woman to have four children? People are concerned about their appearances, their education, their careers."[5] Europe's birthrate has been falling for decades. It is no fluke. A birthrate below replacement levels is common to every nation in Europe but Albania, which is Muslim.

This is not a matter of conspiracy but of consensus, of free choice. European women have decided they want one or two children, or none, and they have the means—contraception, sterilization, and abortion—to effect these choices. And European women consider these personal desires to be far more compelling than demographic studies describing what Europe will look like when they are seventy or eighty, or gone.

A "huge decision" confronts Europe, writes Jonathan Steele of the *Guardian*. "If living standards are not to fall, EU countries may have to allow a 60-fold increase in immigration, feeding rightwing protests and causing additional damage to the region's fragile race relations. This is the considered view of demographic experts as they examine the reality of Europe's aging population."[6]

Mass immigration has already begun. In 2000, England took in 185,000 immigrants, a record.[7] In 1999, 500,000 illegal aliens slipped into the European Union, a tenfold increase from 1993.[8] In May 2001, the *Washington Post* reported:

> Just a year ago, discoveries of foundering ships jammed with human cargo of 500 to 1,000 people would have been a novelty that generated headlines and outrage across Europe. But now they have become routine in the waters between Turkey and destinations in Greece, Italy, and as far north as the French Riviera.[9]

*The Camp of the Saints*, Jean Raspail's 1972 novel about an invasion of France by an armada of destitute Third World people, whom Europe, paralyzed by its egalitarianism and liberalism, is powerless to resist, appears to have been prophetic. History has begun to imitate art.

Europe appears unable to stop these millions from coming and taking the jobs opening up as the war generation passes away. Indeed, employers will demand they be brought in. So will the growing millions of seniors and elderly. And as the millions pour into Europe from North Africa and the Middle East, they will bring their Arab and Islamic culture, traditions, loyalties, and faith, and create replicas of their homelands in the heartland of the West. Will they assimilate, or will they endure as indigestible parts of Africa and Arabia in the base camp of what was once Christendom? Consider the numbers.

As the populations of Portugal, Spain, France, Italy, and Greece all shrink, on the other side of the Inland Sea, in Morocco, Algeria, Tunisia, Libya, and Egypt, populations will explode by seventy-three million in twenty-five years. In 1982, when the author was in Cairo, there were forty-four million Egyptians. By 1998, it was sixty-four million. By 2025, Egypt's population is projected to hit ninety-six million. In the nineteenth century, Europe invaded and colonized Africa. In the twenty-first century, Africa invades and colonizes Europe. Writes Nicholas Eberstadt, the AEI population expert, "In 1995 the estimated populations of Europe (including Russia) and Africa were almost exactly equal. In 2050, by these projections, Africans would outnumber Europeans more than 3 to 1."[10] Only the AIDS epidemic stands in the way of a Europe overshadowed and eventually overwhelmed by African peoples.

UNLIKE AMERICA, EUROPE'S nations are homogeneous. They have no history of welcoming strangers or assimilating immigrants. These peoples of different colors, creeds, and cultures will also be arriving in Europe as its nation-states are crumbling. Since 1990, three European nations—the USSR, Czechoslovakia, and Yugoslavia— have subdivided into twenty-one nations. Two more, Kosovo and

Montenegro, may soon be born. Secessionist movements are alive in Russia, Macedonia, Italy, Corsica, the Basque country of Spain, Scotland, Wales, Bavaria, the Skane region of Sweden. In Belgium, the ancient language-and-culture conflict between Flemish and Walloons is flaming up.

"In Europe, with its 40,000-year-old indigenous white population, the rise of a nonwhite majority may not be greeted with . . . equanimity," dryly noted London's *Guardian* in October 2000.[11] The spring race riots in Oldham and Leeds, Bradford and Burnley, between South Asians and whites, underscores the *Guardian*'s point. Anti-immigration parties have sprung up—the National Front of France's Jean-Marie Le Pen, the Freedom party of Austria's Jorge Haider, the Swiss People's party of Christoph Blocher. As waves of immigration from the Islamic nations of North Africa and the Mideast and black nations of the sub-Sahara rise, crest, and crash into Europe, the immigration issue will become even more explosive. Major parties will seize the issue from the minor parties, or minor parties will become the major ones.

The German Christian Democratic party leaders Angela Merkel and Edmund Stoiber already appears to be moving to capitalize on the backlash against Islamic immigration. "The idea of a united Germany as a multicultural society of almost 80 million people with more than 7 million foreign-born appears to trouble [Ms. Merkel]," writes the *New York Times*. "No other nation in Europe has as many foreigners."[12]

Ms. Merkel is irritated at U.S. demands that Turkey be brought into the EU, as membership would confer on Turks the right to move freely across Europe. "About 75 percent of the Turks in the world who live outside Turkey are in Germany," Merkel told the *Times's* Roger Cohen.

> We don't say they should not be Muslims. But we do say that we are a country with a Christian background, and Turks must understand this. . . . Inviting Turkey to become a candidate for

the European Union membership was a mistake. There are differences of values. We do not have the same understanding of human rights. Try opening a Christian Church in Istanbul.[13]

Europe's nations are small, densely populated, and have no experience as "melting pots." Thus, their ruling elites seem more alert, apprehensive, and tough-minded about the social perils of mass immigration than Americans. But those same nations, and their ruling elites, are late, very late, in awakening to the demographic danger presented by a dying population.

## "CATASTROIKA"

No nation will be more adversely affected by its collapsing birthrate than Russia. Her population is projected to fall from 147 million to 114 million by 2050. As Russians are dying, China, even under its one-couple-one-child policy, expects 250 million more people by 2025. They will not be staying home. Chinese men already outnumber the women available to marry by 40 million. If Mother Russia is nervous, she should be. For even after the breakup of the Soviet Union, Russia has twice as much land as China.

Three-forths of the enormous Russian land mass lies east of the Urals, but only 8 million Russians live in the trackless expanses of the Russian Far East, fewer people than there are in the Czech Republic. To their south, however, live 1.25 billion Chinese, with 250 million more on the way. This relative handful of Russians occupies the northern half of the largest continent on earth, a land mass larger than the United States, filled with the world's most vital and desirable resources: timber, oil, gold.

"Russia has been hemmorhaging humanity at a rate unprecedented for a modern, industrialized nation, except during times of famine and war," writes British journalist John O'Mahony.[14] In the winter of 2001, he traveled to the Far East and Kamchatka Peninsula, and returned with a grim tale of despair and death. Since the fall of communism, Kamchatka's capital has already lost a fourth of its population. In nearby regions, the virtual death of civilized society is imminent:

> However, it is at the exposed and vulnerable extremities of the vast Russian territories that the atrophy of the population has been most acute. Perhaps the most startling example is Chukotka, a massive chunk of the far east three times the size of Britain, where the population has withered by a staggering 60% from 180,000 in 1990 to just 65,000 today, a figure that is expected to slump to just 20,000 within the next five years, making the region's infrastructure unsustainable.[15]

China has long looked on slices of Siberia as "lost territories," stolen in the nineteenth century when China was weak and beset by revolution and preyed upon by Western imperial powers. During the Taiping revolt that took twenty-five million lives, the czar's agents swindled the Chi'ing Empire out of 350,000 square miles north of the Amur and between the Ussuri and the sea. This land, now Siberia's Maritime Province, is twice the size of California, and fits around Manchuria like a cupped hand. Vladivostok, Russia's port on the Sea of Japan, naval base of her Pacific Fleet, was founded in 1860 on land that had belonged to the Chinese until that year. And as Russia has had to surrender all the lands taken from Kazakhs, Kirghiz, Uzbeks, Tadziks, and Turkmen, what was taken from China will also be reclaimed.

In Mr. Nixon's first months in office in 1969, Chinese and Russian troops clashed on the long Amur-Ussuri frontier. And, while an entente currently exists between Beijing and Moscow, the Chinese have not forgotten. Before the middle of this century, Beijing will likely try to regain those lands, and Alaska's neighbors across the Bering Strait could be tough young Chinese pioneers, rather than elderly Russians. Already, Chinese settlers are moving into Russian territory, just as Americans once moved into Mexico's northern province of Texas before tearing it away.

"Russians in the Far East worry about China to the point of paranoia," reports the *Financial Times*, "An opinion poll conducted last year [2000] in Primorive, the province around Vladivostok, to the south of Khabarovsk, found 74 percent of the population expected China to annex all or part of their region 'in the long run.' "[16]

RUSSIA'S OTHER THREAT comes from the ex-Soviet republics to its south—Kazakhstan, Uzbekistan, Tajikistan, Kyrgyzstan, Turkmenistan. Let us add Afghanistan, where Islamic rebels delivered the coup de grace to the Soviet Empire. Moscow seeks to reassert its authority in this region it calls its "near abroad," but Russians are historically European and Orthodox Christian, while these people are Asian and Islamic and bitterly resentful at having been colonized and communized. It seems less likely that Russia will be driving south to recapture these lands than that Islamic migrants will be coming north, with, perhaps, Islamic warriors to tear off chunks of Russia, such as Chechnya. Russia's ally in the Caucasus, Armenia, another Christian nation, has joined Russia, Latvia, Bulgaria, and Spain among the nations with the lowest fertility rates on earth. Armenia, too, has begun to die.

By 2025, Iran's population will be approaching that of Russia. Already, Iranians are menacing the former Soviet republic of Azerbaijan. Moscow's retreat from Asia appears as inevitable as Chinese and Islamic encroachment on territories once dominated by czars and commissars. Gazing at these population projections, Russia's Academy of Science has coined a new term, *catastroika*.[17] The scientists understand: demography is destiny. As Russia's population shrinks, consider what will be happening elsewhere in Central Asia.

## CENTRAL ASIA
### (Millions of People)

|                | 2000 | 2025  |
|----------------|------|-------|
| Afghanistan    | 22.7 | 44.9  |
| Kazakhstan     | 16.2 | 17.7  |
| Uzbekistan     | 24.3 | 33.4  |
| Kyrgyzstan     | 4.7  | 6.1   |
| Tajikistan     | 6.2  | 8.9   |
| Turkmenistan   | 4.5  | 6.3   |
|                | 78.6 | 117.3 |

With half of Russia's population today, these six nations in twenty-five years will have almost as many people, and the Russians will be older and grayer and these Islamic peoples younger and more virile.

In the nineteenth century, immense, mighty, and populous Russia pressed down upon what the czars called "the sick man of Europe," the Ottoman Empire. By present projections, the populations of Turkey and Russia will be comparable in 2050. By 2100, there will be only eighty million Russians. Who will be the "sick man of Europe" then; who the predator and who the prey?

Long before then, says Anatoly Antonov, head of the Department of Family Sociology at Moscow State University, a crisis will come: "This is the dilemma of all Western civilizations. Why do we feel happy without having children?"[18] Antonov wants the government to use the media to boost the image of the family. If Russian men and women do not act soon to increase the population, Antonov fears that extremists could seize power in the name of the survival of the Russian people. "If the population decline isn't reversed," warns Antonov, "we will get a fascist state."[19]

If Russia could put its Cold War defeat and resentment at the loss of superpower status behind it, Moscow would see that America is a natural ally in preserving her unity, integrity, and independence. And

Americans should recognize that in any "clash of civilizations," Russians will man the eastern and southeastern fronts of the heartland of the West.

As for Ukraine, the second-most-populous former Soviet republic, the UN projects a population loss of 40 percent, reducing Ukrainians from fifty million today to fewer than thirty million in 2050. And this is optimistic, based on a significant rise in Ukraine's fertility rate from 1.26 children per woman today to 1.70.

## FOR WHOM THE BELL TOLLS

From the the sixteenth to the twentieth century, the great Western nations colonized most of the world. Beginning in 1754, Americans crossed the Alleghenies and drove the French and then the Spanish off their continent, swallowed half of Mexico, corralled the surviving Indians on reservations, pushed over the Rockies to the Pacific, and vaulted to Hawaii, Midway, Guam, and the Philippines. On the other side of the world, Russians under the Romanovs were seizing all the lands from the Arctic to Afghanistan, from Prussia to the Pacific, and down the panhandle of Alaska to Sitka. Led by the British, European nations were invading and colonizing Africa, south and southeast Asia, and establishing enclaves on the coast of a helpless China.

The reels of history are now running in reverse. The great retreat of the West, begun with the collapse of Europe's empires after World War II, reaches climax this century, as the second great Islamic wave rolls into Europe and the peoples of Central Asia and China reclaim what the czars took from them in centuries past. By 2050, Russia will have lost slices of Siberia and will have been pushed out of the Caucusus and back over the Urals into Europe. "If a clod be washed away by the sea," wrote the poet Donne, "Europe is the less, as well as if a promontory were, as well as if a manor of thy friend's or of thine own were . . . therefore never send to know for whom the bell tolls; it tolls for thee."

## IRAN AND THE GULF

In the run-up to Desert Storm, the author argued against the Gulf War thus: an American victory would leave us with imperial duties Americans would not indefinitely sustain. The emirate of Kuwait was not a viable nation; it could not survive without a powerful protector. But Americans would eventually tire and go home, just as the British went home, and Kuwait would be absorbed by Iraq or Iran. All we could do was hold Kuwait temporarily. Moreover, the great adversary in the Gulf, with three times Iraq's population and territory, was Iran.

We lost the debate, and the United States won the war, but the argument seems even more compelling today. With America having adopted a policy of "dual containment" of Iran and Iraq, consider the population projections over the next twenty-five years alone.

### PERSIAN GULF
#### (Millions of People)

|      | 2000 | 2025 |
| --- | --- | --- |
| Iraq | 23.1 | 41.0 |
| Iran | 67.7 | 94.5 |

In 1990, the United States boasted of the six-hundred-ship navy of Ronald Reagan. Since the Gulf War, the U.S. Navy has been cut in half, the army has been cut in half, the air force has been cut in half. By 2010, the United States anticipates a two-hundred-ship navy. The great coalition assembled by the first President Bush to defeat and contain Iraq has collapsed. Arab nations have defected, as have Europeans, save for the British, whose armed forces have also been cut in half since the end of the Cold War.

General Schwartzkopf's army could have marched into Baghdad, hanged Saddam, and imposed a "MacArthur Regency." But, with existing U.S. and allied force levels, and the reluctance of Europeans and Arabs to march again with us, it is not likely there will ever be a Desert Storm II.

By 2025, Iran will have 94.5 million people, a population far greater than that of any European nation but Russia. The technology of the atomic bomb will be eighty years old, and Iran, which already has ballistic missiles, will almost surely have acquired the bomb. And since the atomic age began, no nation with atomic weapons has ever had its homeland invaded or a major war launched upon it. The only nuclear nation ever attacked was Israel, by pin-prick Scud strikes from an Iraq that was being demolished.

As the North Koreans have shown the world, even a rogue nation can get a respectful hearing from the United States if it can build an atom bomb.

## EUROPE – DEAD MAN WALKING

When Bethmann-Hollweg returned from Vienna to brief the kaiser on the condition of their Austro-Hungarian ally on the eve of war, the shaken foreign minister stammered, "Sire, we are allied to a corpse."[20] So are we. Once-great warrior nations that put millions of soldiers onto the battlefields of Europe in the twentieth century today field armies that are little more than national police forces. The Balkan wars of the nineties exposed their impotence without the United States. In Bosnia, Britain and France had to call for the Americans lest their troops be taken hostage by local Serbs.

Alliances are entered into to strengthen nations. How is America strengthened by a treaty to defend forever a continent that refuses to raise the armies to defend itself and whose populations have begun to die? Turkey and Britain excepted, the NATO nations are more dependencies than allies. AWOL in Vietnam, they were only marginally helpful in the Gulf. Outside Europe, their troops are used mainly for UN police duties in sub-Saharan Africa. No longer do they seem able to call up the loyalties and sacrifices of olden times. Today, the fifteen-nation European Union needs several years to muster sixty thousand soldiers for its vaunted Rapid Reaction Force. European threats to "go it alone" are the threats of children to run away from home, who never quite succeed because their mothers told them not to cross the street.

Something vital has gone out of Europe. Once, Western nations were willing to sacrifice for "the ashes of their fathers and the temples of their gods."[21] But Europeans today, though far richer and more numerous than in 1914 or 1939, are not.

The day of Europe is over. The coming mass migrations from the Islamic world will so change the ethnic composition of the Old Continent that Europeans will be too paralyzed by a threat of terrorism to intervene in North Africa, the Middle East, or the Persian Gulf. Europeans already ignore U.S. sanctions on Iran, Iraq, and Libya. As their populations become more Arabic and Islamic, paralysis will set in. We should know. From the 1850s until World War I, U.S. policy toward the British Empire was held hostage by the Irish, whose votes were decisive in states like New York.

With populations declining and children vanishing, Europe has no vital interest to justify sending tens of thousands of their young to war if they are not attacked. At present birthrates, Europe's population in 2100 will be less than a third what it is today. Europe has voted for *la dolce vita*.

But if Europeans are so uninterested in self-preservation that they refuse to have enough children to keep their nations alive, why should Americans defend Europe—and perhaps die for Europe? So they can live the high life until flame-out. Europe has embraced her destiny, perhaps not consciously as a people, but collectively as a people. Europeans do not plan to continue as a great vital race. What then are we defending? Christianity? That is dead in Europe. Western civilization? But, by their decisions not to have children, Europeans have already accepted a twenty-second-century end to their civilization.

## A FINAL SOLUTION
## TO THE AGING QUESTION

In the 1973 *Humanist Manifesto II,* thousands of U.S. intellectuals urged "recognition of an individual's right to die with dignity, euthanasia, and the right to suicide."[22] They were ahead of their time.

On November 28, 2000, the Lower House of the Dutch Parliament voted 104 to 40 to legalize assisted suicide and voluntary euthanasia—"the first nation since Hitler's Germany," wrote Nat Hentoff in *Jewish World Review,* "to legalize . . . the direct killing of patients by physicians."[23] The parliament was rushing to catch up with the Dutch doctors, who have been doing euthanasia for decades. In 1991, a government-backed study found that "the majority of all euthanasia deaths in the Netherlands are involuntary."[24]

Under the new law, children ages twelve to fifteen will need a parent's consent to commit suicide or have a doctor help them kill themselves. But, after sixteen, parental consent will no longer be needed.[25] The Council of Europe accused the Dutch of violating the European Convention of Human Rights, but Dutch doctors are already far down the slippery slope toward the Third Reich. As Rita Marker of the International Anti-Euthanasia Task Force reports:

> A month before the lower house debated the new euthanasia law, a Dutch court ruled that Dr. Philip Sutorius was medically justified when he helped 86-year-old Edward Brongermsa commit suicide. Brongermsa was not physically ill or in pain. He said that he was simply "tired of life" and his aging "hopeless existence."[26]

From his jail cell, Jack Kevorkian saluted the Dutch and predicted America would not be far behind. The U.S. Hemlock Society was equally enthusiastic and hopeful that Holland would show us the way.

Said Hemlock president Faye Grish, "We are very excited. We have admired what the people of Holland have been doing for the last twenty years."[27]

To the Dutch Voluntary Euthanasia Society, however, the new law is gravely deficient, for it does not grant euthanasia rights for those simply weary of life. "We think that if you are old, you have no family near, and you are really suffering from life then it should be possible," said a DVES spokesman.[28] Minister of Health Els Borst agreed. Very old people, who are sick of life, she said, should be allowed to kill themselves: "I'm not against it, as long as it can be carefully enough regulated so that it only concerns very old people who are tired of living."[29] If such a patient wants to die, said the minister, he or she should be given a suicide pill.

In his Christmas message in 2000, John Paul II surely had Holland in mind when he spoke of "alarming signs of the 'culture of death.' "[30]

> We cannot but recall today that shadows of death threaten people's lives at every stage of life and are especially menacing at its earliest beginning and its natural end. The temptation is becoming ever stronger to take possession of death by anticipating its arrival, as though we were masters of our own lives or the lives of others.[31]

Hentoff is on the side of the Holy Father:

> During the Nazi occupation of the Netherlands, that country's physicians rebelled against the culture of death by refusing to cooperate in the killing of patients.
>
> But now, their changed attitude reminds me of an Oct. 17, 1933, *New York Times* report from Berlin that the German Ministry of Justice intended to authorize physicians "to end the suffering of incurable patients, upon request, in the interests of true humanity."[32]

Yet, a hard look at the demographic and moral trends in Europe does not inspire confidence that this is a winning fight for those for whom the Holy Father speaks. For a Christianity that teaches that God is the author of life and that no one has a right to take innocent life is not a growth stock in Europe. By 2050, over 10 percent of the population of the four largest nations in Western Europe—Britain, France, Germany, and Italy—will be over eighty years old. Will Europe's workers, whose taxes must rise and whose retirements must be put off to subsidize the pensions and health care costs of this burgeoning aged population, insist that the sick and senile elderly in their eighties and nineties be kept alive?

A university study in Belgium found that one in ten deaths there is doctor-induced, either by lethal injection without the patient's permission or by withholding treatment.[33] In Zurich, assisted suicide is permissible in homes for the elderly.[34] The baby boomers of Europe may live to see their lives ended, without their consent, by a society that has turned as callous toward their wish to stay alive as they were to the unborn in their own time. What goes around comes around.

AFTER THE NEWARK riot of 1967, its black mayor wittily observed, "I don't know where America is going, but Newark is gonna get there first." Where Europe is at today, America will almost surely arrive tomorrow.

In 1984, Colorado governor Dick Lamm startled seniors when he told a group of doctors, "We've got a duty to die and get out of the way with all of our machines and artificial hearts . . . and let the other society, our kids, build a reasonable life."[35] Princeton now has on faculty an Australian bioethicist, Peter Singer, who argues that if a child is born with disabilities so severe that its parents and doctors think it would be better off dead, it is ethical to kill the newborn and let the couple conceive a healthy child.[36] Singer's argument is not illogical. If we concede parents' rights to abort an unborn infant up to nine months, why do they lose the right to end its life the moment the fetus slips out of the womb?

Singer's ideas have an impressive pedigree. As far back as 1919, Margaret Sanger was admonishing America in her magazine *Birth Control Review:* "More children from the fit, less from the unfit."[37] Americans and Germans were soon competing to advance Sanger's ideas. In 1920, Dr. Alfred Hoche, professor of psychiatry at the University of Freiburg, and Karl Binding, a law professor at Leipzig University, published *The Permission to Destroy Life Unworthy of Life.* The book argued the case for assisted suicide for the terminally ill and euthanasia for those "empty shells of human beings," the mentally retarded, and those with brain damage and psychiatric conditions.[38] A poll found three in four German parents favored letting physicians end the lives of severely retarded children.[39]

In October 1933, the *New York Times* quoted Hitler's Ministry of Justice as saying that ridding society of these poor creatures would make it "possible for physicians to end the tortures of incurable patients, upon requests, in the interests of true humanity."[40] The money saved could be used to benefit "those on the threshold of old age."[41] The language of tenderness is familiar to us all. It calls to mind the words Walker Percy put in the mouth of Father Smith in *The Thanatos Syndrome:* "Do you know where tenderness leads? . . . Tenderness leads to the gas chamber."[42]

In making their case, the Nazis could cite Churchill, who "wanted the curse of madness to die," and George Bernard Shaw, who had said in 1933, "If we desire a certain type of civilization we must exterminate the sort of people who do not fit in."[43] The führer's thoughts exactly, G.B.

Among the first and most famous cases of mercy killing was "Baby Knauer." The little boy's father made a direct plea to Hitler to allow his son, blind, retarded, and missing an arm and leg, to die. Hitler referred the request to his physician Karl Brandt. In 1938, permission was granted.

"Mercy deaths" became common in Germany. In a "Review of *Mein Kampf*," which introduced the 1939 Book of the Month Club selection, journalist Dorothy Thompson excoriated Hitler, except on one issue:

> On the subject of eugenics [Hitler] writes rationally, up to a point. Eugenists all over the world will agree with him that the palpably unfit for reproduction should be sterilized. But the German sterilization laws include habitual drunkards, and it is an amusing thought that had they existed in pre-Hitler Austria, Hitler himself would never have been born! (Neither, incidentally, would Beethoven or Nietzsche.)
>
> There is scientific foundation, though the field needs more exploration, for some of Hitler's eugenic ideas.[44]

Poet W. B. Yeats echoed Ms. Thompson: "Since improvements in agriculture and industry are threatening to remove the last check on the multiplication of the ineducable masses . . . the better stocks have not been replacing their numbers, while the stupider and less healthy have been."[45]

When war came, Hitler's eugenic ideas received "more exploration." He ordered the mercy killing of "life unworthy of life"—"useless eaters"—deformed infants and the severely retarded.[46] Code-named "Aktion 4," the program did away with scores of thousands before Bishop Clemens von Galen, in a fiery sermon in Münster Cathedral in 1940, excoriated Hitler's regime for "plain murder" and called on Catholics to "withdraw ourselves and our faithful from their [Nazi] influence so that we may not be contaminated by their thinking and their ungodly behavior."[47]

Jolted, Berlin publicly put the program on hold, but continued it quietly. One veteran of Aktion 4, Franz Stangl, would do his graduate work at a place called Treblinka. In *Judgment at Nuremburg*, the 1960 film, Montgomery Clift movingly portrayed a victim of the Nazi eugenics program conditionally endorsed by Dorothy Thompson.

But no film ever portrayed Raymond Ludlow, an American hero, who came home from World War II with a Bronze Star, a Purple Heart, and a Prisoner of War Medal. A repeated runaway in his early teens, Raymond Ludlow had been forcibly sterilized under the laws of Virginia, one of thirty-one states to pass compulsory sterilization laws in the halcyon days of Margaret Sanger.[48]

The battle between those who believe in the sanctity of human life, and those who believe some lives are not worth living and ought to be ended, is thus not a new one. And with Europe facing a future where a third of her people will be over sixty-five and one in ten over eighty—and with few Bishop Von Galens and John Paul IIs around—the outcome does not appear to be in much doubt.

## ISRAEL AND THE MIDDLE EAST[49]

Though Israel's population is growing, the neighborhood trend helps one to understand why warrior-statesmen such as Yitzhak Rabin and Ehud Barak concluded that they had no choice but to trade land for peace.

The fertility rate among Palestinians in Israel is 4.5 children per woman; on the West Bank, 5.5 children per woman; in Gaza, 6.6 children per woman. If demography is destiny, Israel is in an existential crisis that can only be exacerbated by continued military occupation and expansion of settlements. Consider the numbers;

(Millions of People)

|  | 2000 | 2025 |
|---|---|---|
| Israel | 6.2 | 8.3 |
| Jordan | 6.7 | 12.1 |
| Egypt | 68.5 | 95.6 |
| Syria | 16.1 | 26.3 |
| Lebanon | 3.3 | 4.4 |
| Saudi Arabia | 21.6 | 40.0 |

In the next twenty-five years, Israel's population (Jewish and Arab) will grow by 2.1 million, while her Arab neighbors will swell by 62.2 million. Now consider Israel's "Palestinian problem."

In twenty-five years, there will be 2 million Palestinians inside Israel, 7 million on the West Bank and in Gaza, and 7 million in Jordan—16 million Palestinians living cheek-by-jowl with 6 million Jewish Israelis. (Sixty percent of the Jordanian population is Palestinian.) In 2050, there will be 3 million Palestinians inside Israel, 12 million on the West Bank and in Gaza, and 10 million in Jordan—25 million Palestinians living alongside 7 million Jewish Israelis at midcentury.

But if Israel must view these numbers with alarm, so should the kings of Jordan and Saudi Arabia. Jordan is among the poorest nations in the Middle East. Saudi Arabia is run by a royal house that has antagonized millions of its people by being seen as America's agent and having invited thousands of infidels onto sacred Islamic soil.

Not one of the twenty-two Arab countries today qualifies as fully democratic. Yet, the more democratic they become, the more responsive their regimes must be to the will of the "Arab street." Those who tell us that democracies never go to war with one another may see that proposition tested, as Arab monarchies fall to more "democratic" regimes, as happened in Teheran with the overthrow of the shah.

## RETURN OF THE PROPHET

At the beginning of the seventh century, the Mediterranean world was Christian. But, within fifty years of Muhammad's hejira to Medina in 622, the armies of Islam had swept over the southern coast of the Inland Sea. Early in the eighth century, Arabs and Berbers brushed aside weak Visigoth resistance, overran Spain, and crossed the Pyrenees into France, where one of the decisive battles of history was fought. At Tours, the "Hammer of the Franks," Charles Martel defeated the Muslims, who withdrew back over the mountains. "Thus was Christendom saved in the tongue between the rivers, a little south of Chatellrault, and a day's march north of Poitiers," wrote Hilaire Belloc.[50] Except for the tiny kingdom of the Asturias, which would be the base camp of the Spanish Reconquista, Islam dominated the Iberian peninsula for centuries. Not until 1492 did Ferdinand and Isabella finally drive the Moors out of Spain.

In the East, the Islamic invasion came later. In the fourteenth century, the Ottoman Empire entered the Balkans and defeated the Serbs at the Battle of Kosovo in 1389. In 1453, Constantinople fell. In 1683, the Turks were at the gates of Vienna when they were stopped by the Polish king John Sobieski. But not until 1913 were they finally driven out of most of the Balkans.

The high tide of Western empire came at the close of World War I. In November 1917, Foreign Minister Arthur Balfour declared it to be His Majesty's policy to create a homeland for the Jews in Palestine, as a British army under Allenby marched into Jerusalem. The Ottoman Empire went into receivership, and, under the Sykes-Picot Agreement, the British and French divided the spoils. Three decades later, a Jewish state was born among the Arabs, under the auspices of the British Empire and a U.S.-dominated UN. But, by 1948, the British Empire was in retreat—out of India, out of Palestine, out of Jordan, out of Egypt, out of Iraq, out of the Gulf, with the French Empire close behind.

Now the signs are everywhere that Islam is rising again. An Islamic secessionist movement is active in the Philippines. Muslim troops battle Christian secessionists in Indonesia. From Palestine to Pakistan, street mobs cheered the slaughter at the Pentagon and World Trade Center. For years, the Taliban gave sanctuary to Osama bin Laden and his terrorist cells and dispatched holy warriors into the old Soviet republics of Central Asia and to assist Chechen rebels fighting in Russia. Before the U.S.-led alliance drove him from power, Taliban ruler Mullah Muhammad Omar ordered all religious statues smashed, including the seventh-century Great Buddhas of Bamiyan, declaring, "These idols have been gods of the infidels."[51]

Israel was driven out of Lebanon by Hezbollah and is being pushed off the West Bank and out of Gaza by *intifadas* in which the suicide bombers of Hamas are assuming the lead role. In Turkey and Algeria, elections in the 1990s brought to power Islamic regimes, which were removed by methods other than democratic. In Egypt, Muslim militants have renewed the persecution of Christian Copts. Islamic law has now been imposed in ten northern states of Nigeria.

In Europe, Christian congregations are dying, churches are emptying out, mosques are filling up. There are five million Muslims in France, and between twelve and fifteen million in the European Union.[52] There are fifteen hundred mosques in Germany.[53] Islam has replaced Judaism as the second religion of Europe. As the Christian tide goes out in Europe, an Islamic tide comes in. In 2000, for the first time there were more Muslims in the world than Catholics.[54]

While the ideology of "Islamism" has failed in Afghanistan, Iran, and Sudan to create a modern state that can command the loyalty of its people and serve as a model for other Islamic nations, the religion of Islam has not failed. In science, technology, economics, industry, agriculture, armaments, and democratic rule, America, Europe, and Japan are generations ahead. But the Islamic world retains something the West has lost: a desire to have children and the will to carry on their civilization, cultures, families, and faith. Today, it is as difficult to find a Western nation where the native population is not dying as it is to find an Islamic nation where the native population is not exploding. The West may have learned what Islam knows not, but Islam remembers what the West has forgot:"There is no vision but by faith."

## ISRAEL AS METAPHOR

As were the American Canal Zone, British Rhodesia, and the Republic of South Africa yesterday, Israel may today be seen as a metaphor and microcosm of the West itself.

In its 1948 war of independence, Israel expanded well beyond the borders set by the UN. Exploiting blunders by Egypt's Nasser and the UN's U Thant in 1967, Israel seized the Syrian Golan Heights, Arab East Jerusalem, the Old City, Gaza, and the West Bank, and occupied all of Sinai to the Suez Canal in six days. In 1982, Israel drove to the suburbs of Beirut and expelled the PLO.

But the retreat of Eretz Israel had already begun. In 1973, the Egyptians recrossed the canal and took back western Sinai. Five years later, the entire peninsula was restored to Egypt. In the 1980s and 1990s, Islamic militants conducted a guerrilla war that forced the Israelis out of Lebanon, and Palestinians launched an *intifada* that forced Israel to offer land for peace. By 2000, Prime Minister Barak offered 99 percent of the Golan Heights for peace with Syria and 95 percent of the West Bank and Gaza, plus East Jerusalem, for peace with an independent Palestine. Assad and Arafat rejected the offers.

Even if accepted by the Arabs, what guarantee has Israel that these are the last territorial demands on the Jewish state? Why should the Arabs, after having digested what Israel gives up, not pursue the goal of expelling the "Zionist entity" from the Middle East? Israelis say they are offering their neighbors a just peace, but Arabs may see Israel as a nation in retreat, trying to cut the best deal it can. Why should the Arabs not believe that as war brought Israel to the table to offer land for peace, more war will produce more land for peace?

From the Arab standpoint, war works. The Yom Kippur War of 1973 led to Israel's surrender of Sinai. Hezbollah's jihad drove Israel out of Lebanon. Two *intifadas* have forced Israel to offer to yield almost all of the West Bank, Gaza, and East Jerusalem. As for Israel's military might, it has no more halted her retreat than military superiority halted the retreat of the West. Did Russia's twenty thousand nuclear weapons prevent the loss of Eastern Europe, the Baltic states, Ukraine, Kazakhstan, and the rest of Moscow's empire in the Caucasus and Central Asia?

Here is the analogy with the West. Is it in the nature of things that nations and civilizations rise, expand, dominate, and rule, only to recede and offer equality to their subject peoples—an offer accepted, until those subject peoples acquire the power to rise, expand, and dominate themselves? Is our era of the equality of nations really the end of history or but a temporary truce, a phony peace, an armistice, a time of transition from a day of Western dominance to a day when the West pays tribute? British historian J. E. Fround once wrote that "if ten men believe in something so deeply they are willing to die for it, and twenty men believe in something so deeply they are willing to vote for it, the ten will give the law to the twenty."[55] As we look at America, Asia, Europe, and the Middle East, which peoples today show a greater disposition to die for their dreams?

Is all our prattle about the equality of peoples willful self-delusion? Is it but the prelude to a renewed struggle to control the destiny of men and nations, a struggle that a rich, depopulating, dying West, with its deep aversion to war, bred of the bloodbaths of the twentieth century, is destined to lose? As Sophocles said, one must wait until evening to see how splendid the day has been. Is it the evening of the West?

MILITANCY, MARTYRDOMS, AND, yes, intolerance are the marks of rising religions and conquering causes. Early Christians who had accepted death rather than burn incense to Roman gods were soon smashing those Roman gods—no equality for them. Baptizing Clovis, the bishop of Reims admonished the king of the Franks, "Bend your neck. Burn what you worship, worship what you burn!"[56] Not very ecumenical, Your Grace. Protestant monarchs and Catholic kings alike did not flinch at burning heretics or drawing and quartering them at the Tyburn tree. The Christianity that conquered the world was not a milquetoast faith, and the custodians of that faith did not believe all religions were equal. One was true; all the rest were false.

From the pulpits of Christian churches today we hear mournful apologias for past sins: "We were wrong to accompany the old conquistadors, wrong to impose our faith on native peoples, wrong to be the handmaidens of empire. We confess, we beg forgiveness from those against whom we and our fathers have sinned."

Now this may be the way to heaven, but it can lead to hell on earth. History teaches it is the whimpering dog that gets kicked. Who will convert to a religion whose priests or preachers go about in sackcloth and ashes doing expiation for the sins of centuries past? Will the people now taught that they were victims of Christian racism be satisfied with apologies? Will they let bygones be bygones? Or will they say, "These Christians, whose ancestors oppressed and robbed us, are now paralyzed with guilt and powerless to resist. Let us take back what they took from us; then let us take what they have"?

Does the remorse of "mainstream" Christian denominations mean they have ascended to a higher moral plane, or is this but a manifestation of their loss of faith in the truth and superiority of Christianity? If the West expects a long life, it had best recapture the fighting faith of its youth. For it is in the nature of things that nations and religions rule or are ruled. Times of equality are temporary truces in an endless struggle. "Homo homini lupus," said the Roman playwright Plautus: "Man is a wolf to man." Added Thomas Hobbes: "I put for a general inclination of all mankind, a perpetual and restless desire of Power after power, that ceaseth only in Death."[57]

AS ISRAEL IS an affluent modern nation surrounded by poor neighbors with historic grievances, so the West is a prosperous modern civilization surrounded by poor neighbors with historic grievances. And as Western intellectuals are harshest about Western history, so Israel's "post-Zionist" "new historians" paint their nation's birth in its blackest hues. And as the West believes all nations will be content with what they have, some Israelis believe the Palestinians will be content in their Bantustans in Gaza and on the West Bank. But why should they? When Chinese outnumber Russians twenty to one instead of ten to one, why should they not seek to reclaim what was taken from them when Russia was strong and China was weak?

Israel confronts an Islam with an ancient history as a fighting faith and peoples willing to die for a cause, while America shares two thousand miles of border with Mexico. So perhaps the analogy is inexact. But then America is not the country she once was. In 1953, an unsentimental old soldier named Ike ordered all illegal aliens out of the United States in "Operation Wetback." Can anyone imagine Mr. Bush ordering five or ten million illegal aliens expelled from the United States?

As Golda Meir once said, Israel never had a better friend than Richard Nixon, who rescued her nation in the 1973 Yom Kippur War. But the Richard Nixon the author recalls was not blind to the forces of history. He used to say, "A statesman must take the long view." In San Clemente once, after he hung up from a courtesy call from Yitzhak Rabin, a friend we had met in Israel days after the Six-Day War, my wife, Shelley, asked the ex-president what the prospects for Israel were.

"The long run?" Nixon responded. He extended his right fist, thumb up, in the manner of a Roman emperor passing sentence on a gladiator, and slowly turned his thumb over and down. I never asked him what he thought about the prospects of the West.

# SIX

# LA RECONQUISTA

The American Southwest seems to be slowly returning
to the jurisdiction of Mexico without firing a shot.[1]
—*Excelsior*
National Newspaper of Mexico

In 1821, a newly independent Mexico invited Americans to settle in
its northern province of Texas—on two conditions: the Americans
must embrace Roman Catholicism, and they must swear allegiance to
Mexico. Thousands took up the offer. But, in 1835, after a tyrannical
general, Santa Anna, seized power, the Texans, fed up with loyalty
oaths and fake conversions, and now outnumbering Mexicans in
Texas ten to one, rebelled and kicked the tiny Mexican garrison back
across the Rio Grande.

Santa Anna led an army north to recapture his lost province. At a
mission called the Alamo, he massacred the first rebels who resisted.
Then he executed the four hundred Texans who surrendered at Go-
liad. But at San Jacinto, Santa Anna blundered into an ambush. His
army was butchered, and he was captured. The Texans demanded his
execution for the Alamo massacre, but Sam Houston had another
idea. He made the dictator an offer: your life for Texas. Santa Anna
signed, and Texas had its independence. On his last day in office,
Andrew Jackson recognized the Lone Star Republic of his old subal-
tern, who had led Old Hickory's Tennesseans in the 1814 slaughter
of the Red Sticks at Horseshoe Bend.

Eight years later, in his final hours in office, Pres. John Tyler decided to write his own page in history by annexing the Texas republic, denying the honor to Jackson's protégé, James K. Polk, who had won the White House on a pledge to bring Texas into the Union. An enraged Mexico now disputed the U.S. claim to all land north of the Rio Grande. To back up that claim, Polk sent Gen. Zachary Taylor to the north bank of the river. When Mexican soldiers crossed and fired on a U.S. patrol, spilling American blood on what Polk claimed was American soil, he demanded and got a swift congressional declaration of war. By 1848, soldiers with names like Grant, Lee, and McClellan were in Montezuma's city. A humiliated Mexico was forced to cede all of Texas, the Southwest, and California. To ease the anguish of amputation, the U.S. gave Mexico fifteen million dollars.

Mexicans seethed with hatred and resentment. In 1910, the troubles began anew. After a revolution that was antichurch and anti-American, U.S. sailors were roughed up and arrested in Tampico. Wilson ordered Veracruz occupied by U.S. Marines until the Mexicans delivered a twenty-one-gun salute to Old Glory. As Wilson explained to the British ambassador, "I am going to teach the South Americans to elect good men."[2] When the bandit Pancho Villa led a murderous raid into New Mexico in 1916, Wilson sent General Pershing and ten thousand troops to do the tutoring.

Despite FDR's Good Neighbor Policy, President Cárdenas, in 1938, nationalized U.S. oil companies on a day still honored in Mexican history. Pemex was born, a state cartel that would collude with OPEC in 1999 to run up oil prices to thirty-five dollars a barrel to gouge the Americans who had led a fifty-billion-dollar bailout of a bankrupt Mexico in 1994. One is reminded of Italian statesman Cavour's response when asked the diplomatic goal of his unified nation in 1859: "To astonish the world with our ingratitude."[3]

The point of this history? Mexico has an historic grievance against the United States that is felt deeply by her people. They believe we robbed their country of half its land when Mexico was young and weak. There are thus deep differences in attitudes toward America between old immigrants from Ireland, Italy, and Eastern Europe, and today's immigrants from Mexico. And with fully one-fifth of all peoples of Mexican ancestry now in the United States, and up to a million more coming every year, we need to understand the differences between the old immigrants and the new, and the America of yesterday and the America of today.

1. The numbers pouring in from Mexico are larger than any wave from any other country in so short a time. In the 1990s alone, folks of Mexican ancestry in the United States grew by 50 percent to twenty-one million, and that does not include the six million Hispanics who refused to tell census takers their country of origin. Mexican Americans are also concentrated in the U.S. Southwest, though the Founding Fathers wanted immigrants spread out among the population to ensure assimilation.

2. Mexicans not only come from another culture, but millions are of another race. History and experience teach us that different races are far more difficult to assimilate. The sixty million Americans who claim German ancestry are fully assimilated, while millions from Africa and Asia are still not full participants in American society.

3. Millions of Mexicans are here illegally. They broke the law to get into the United States, and they break the law by being here. Each year, 1.6 million illegal aliens are apprehended, almost all of them trying to breach our bleeding Southern border.[4]

4. Unlike the immigrants of old, who bade farewell forever to their native lands when they boarded the ship, for Mexicans, the mother country is right next door. Millions have no desire to learn English or to become citizens. America is not their home; Mexico is; and they wish to remain proud Mexicans. They have come here to work. Rather than assimilate, they create Little Tijuanas in U.S. cities, just as Cubans have created a Little Havana in Miami. Only America hosts twenty times as many people of Mexican descent as of Cuban descent. With their own radio and TV stations, newspapers, films, and magazines, the Mexican Americans are creating an Hispanic culture sep-

arate and apart from America's larger culture. They are becoming a nation within a nation.

5. The waves of Mexican immigrants are also coming to a different America than the old immigrants. A belief in racial rights and ethnic entitlements has taken root among our minorities. This belief is encouraged by cultural elites who denigrate the melting pot and preach the glories of multiculturalism. Today, ethnic enclaves are encouraged to maintain their separate identities, and in the barrios ethnic chauvinism is rife. "The integrationist impulse of the 1960s is dead," writes Glenn Garvin in *Reason*, "Liberal chic in the 1990s is segregation, dressed up as identity-group politics."[5] If today Calvin Coolidge declared, "America must remain American," he would be charged with a hate crime.[6]

SAMUEL P. HUNTINGTON, author of *The Clash of Civilizations*, calls migration "the central issue of our time."[7] He divides immigrants into the "converts" who come to assimilate to our way of life, and "sojourners," who come to work a few years and return home. "New immigrants" from south of the border, he writes, "are neither converts nor sojourners. They go back and forth between California and Mexico, maintaining dual identities and encouraging family members to join them."[8] Of the 1.6 million arrested each year crossing the U.S. border, Huntington warns:

> If over one million Mexican soldiers crossed the border Americans would treat it as a major threat to their national security and react accordingly. The invasion of over one million Mexican civilians, as [Mexican president Vicente] Fox seems to recommend, would be a comparable threat to American societal security, and Americans should react against it with vigor.
>
> Mexican immigration is a unique, disturbing and looming challenge to our cultural integrity, our national identity, and potentially to our future as a country.[9]

American leaders are not reacting "with vigor," even though one Zogby poll has found that 72 percent of the people want immigration reduced, and a Rasmussen poll in July 2000 found that 89 percent wanted English to be America's official language.[10] The people want action. The elites disagree and do nothing. Despite our braggadocio about being "the world's last superpower," the U.S. lacks the fortitude to defend its borders and to demand, without apology, that immigrants assimilate into society.

Perhaps our mutual love of the dollar can bridge the cultural chasm, and we shall all live happily together in what one author calls *The First Universal Nation*.[11] But Uncle Sam is taking a hellish risk in importing a huge diaspora of tens of millions from a nation vastly different from our own. And if we are making a fatal blunder, it is not a decision we can ever revisit. Our children will live with the consequences, balkanization, the end of America as we know her. "If assimilation fails," writes Huntington, "the United States will become a cleft country with all the potentials for internal strife and disunion that entails."[12] Is that risk worth taking? Why are we taking it?

Western nations are already breaking up over ethnicity and culture. Secessionist movements have broken apart the Soviet Union, Yugoslavia, and Czechoslovakia and are beavering away in France, Spain, and Italy. In 2001, Germany began a year-long celebration of old Prussia. In England, the Union Jack is being replaced on taxicabs and at World Cup soccer games with the medieval Cross of St. George. People identify less and less with the nation-state, more and more with kith and kin. In Alberta and Saskatchewan, independence parties have been formed, and 14 percent of British Columbia now favors separation from Canada.[13]

A North American Union of Canada, Mexico, and the United States has been proposed by President Fox, with a complete opening of borders to the goods and peoples of the three countries. The idea enraptures the *Wall Street Journal*.[14] But Mexico's per capita GDP of five thousand dollars is only a fraction of America's, and the income gap between us is the largest on earth between two large neighbor countries.[15] Since NAFTA passed in 1993, real wages in Mexico have fallen 15 percent. Half of all Mexicans now live in poverty, and eighteen million subsist on less than two dollars a day, while the U.S. minimum wage is headed for fifty dollars a day. Throw open the border, and millions could flood across into the United States in months. Is our country nothing more than an economy?

OUR OLD IMAGE is of Mexican folks as docile, conservative, friendly, Catholic people of traditional beliefs and values. There are still millions of these hard-working, family-oriented, patriotic Americans of Mexican heritage, who have been among the first to answer America's call to arms. And any man, woman, or child, from any country or continent, can be a good American. We know that from our history.

But the demographic sea change, especially in California, where a fourth of the people are foreign-born and almost a third are Latino, has spawned a new ethnic chauvinism. When the U.S. soccer team played Mexico in the Los Angeles Coliseum a few years back, the "Star-Spangled Banner" was hooted and jeered, an American flag was torn down, and the American team and its few fans were showered with water bombs, beer bottles, and garbage.[16]

Two years ago, the south Texas town of El Cenizo declared Spanish its official language and ordered that all official documents be written in Spanish and all town business conducted in Spanish.[17] Any cooperation with U.S. immigration authorities was made a firing offense. El Cenizo has, de facto, seceded from the United States.

In the New Mexico legislature in 2001, a resolution was introduced to rename the state "Nuevo Mexico," the name it carried before it became a part of the American Union. When the bill was defeated, the sponsor, Rep. Miguel Garcia, suggested to reporters that "covert racism" may have been the cause—the same racism, he said, that was behind naming the state New Mexico in the first place.[18]

A spirit of separatism, nationalism, and irredentism has come alive in the barrio. The Latino student organization MEChA demands return of the Southwest to Mexico.[19] Charles Truxillo, a professor of Chicano Studies at the University of New Mexico, says a new "Aztlan" with its capital in Los Angeles is inevitable, and Mexicans should seek it by any means necessary.[20]

"We're recolonizing America, so they're afraid of us. It's time to take back what is ours," rants Ricky Sierra of the Chicano National Guard.[21] One demonstration leader in Westwood exulted, "We are here . . . to show white Protestant Los Angeles that we're the majority . . . and we claim this land as ours. It's always been ours and we're still here . . . if anybody is going to be deported it's going to be you."[22]

José Angel Gutierrez, a political science professor at the University of Texas at Arlington and director of the UTA Mexican-American Study Center, told a university crowd: "We have an aging white America. They are not making babies. They are dying. The explosion is in our population. They are shitting in their pants in fear! I love it."[23]

Now, this may be Corona talk in the cantina, but more authoritative voices are sounding the same notes, and they resonate in the barrio. The Mexican consul general José Pescador Osuna remarked in 1998, "Even though I am saying this part serious, part joking, I think we are practicing La Reconquista in California."[24] California legislator Art Torres called Proposition 187, to cut off welfare to illegal aliens, "the last gasp of white America."[25]

"California is going to be a Mexican State. We are going to control all the institutions. If people don't like it, they should leave," exults Mario Obledo, president of the League of United Latin American Citizens, and recipient of the Medal of Freedom from President Clinton.[26] Mexican president Ernesto Zedillo told Mexican-Americans in Dallas: "You are Mexicans, Mexicans who live north of the border."[27]

Why should Mexican immigrants not have greater loyalty to their homeland than to a country they broke into simply to find work?

Why should nationalistic and patriotic Mexicans not dream of a *re-conquista*?

Consider the student organization MEChA, whose UCLA chapter, a few years back, was chaired by one Antonio Villaraigosa, who came within forty thousand votes of being mayor of Los Angeles in 2001. MEChA stands for Movimento Estudiantil Chicano de Aztlan, the Chicano Student movement of Aztlan. What is El Plan de Aztlan for which MEChA exists? In its own words, MEChA aims to reclaim the land of their fathers that was stolen in the "brutal 'gringo' invasion of our territories."[28]

> With our heart in our hands and our hands in the soil, we declare the independence of our mestizo nation. We are a bronze people with a bronze culture. Before the world, before all of North America, before all our brothers in the bronze continent, we are a nation, we are a union of free pueblos, we are Aztlan.[29]

In El Plan, "Aztlan belongs to those who plant the seeds, water the fields, and gather the crops and not to foreign Europeans. We do not recognize capricious frontiers on the bronze continent."[30] The MEChA slogan is "Por la Raza todo. Fuera de La Raza nada." Translation: "For our race, everthing. For those outside our race, nothing."[31]

MEChA demands U.S. "restitution" for "past economic slavery, political exploitation, ethnic and cultural psychological destruction and denial of civil and human rights."[32] "Political Liberation," asserts MEChA,

> can only come through independent action on our part, since the two-party system is the same animal with two heads that feed from the same trough. Where we are a majority we will control; where we are a minority we will represent a pressure group; nationally we represent one party: *La Familia de Raza*.[33]

In its constitution, MEChA declares that its official symbol "shall be the eagle with its wings spread, bearing a *macahuittle* in one claw and a dynamite stick in the other with the lighted fuse in its beak."[34]

MEChA is the Chicano version of the white-supremacist Aryan Nation, only it claims four hundred campus chapters across the Southwest and as far away as Cornell and Ann Arbor. With its rhetoric about a "mestizo nation," a "bronze people," a "bronze culture," a "bronze continent," and "race above all," it is unabashedly racist and anti-American. That Villaraigosa could go through a campaign for mayor of America's second-largest city without having to explain his association and repudiate MEChA testifies to the truth that America's major media are morally intimidated by any minority that can make out credentials as a victim of past discrimination.

And nowhere has ethnic intimidation been more successful than in the academy. After years of disruptive MEChA protests, the University of Texas has downgraded Texas Independence Day. In 2000, the university held a "private alumni fund-raising event to milk the holiday for money, while according it virtually no public recognition."[35]

MEANWHILE, THE INVASION rolls on. America's once-sleepy two-thousand-mile Mexican border is now the scene of daily confrontations. Ranches in Arizona have become nightly bivouac areas for thousands of aliens, who cut fences and leave poisoned cattle and trails of debris in the trek north. Even the Mexican army is showing its contempt. The State Department reported fifty-five military incursions in the five years before the incident in 2000, when truckloads of Mexican soldiers barreled through a barbed wire fence, fired shots, and pursued two mounted officers and a U.S. Border Patrol vehicle.[36] Border Patrol agents believe some Mexican army units collaborate with the drug cartels.

America has become a spillway for an exploding population that Mexico is unable to employ. With Mexico's population growing by ten million every decade, there will be no end to the long march north before the American Southwest is fully Hispanicized. Mexican senator Adolfo Zinser conceded that Mexico's "economic policy is dependent on unlimited emigration to the United States."[37] The Yanqui-baiting academic and "onetime Communist supporter" Jorge Castaneda warned in *Atlantic Monthly,* six years ago, that any American effort to cut back immigration "will make social peace in . . . Mexico untenable. . . . Some Americans dislike immigration, but there is very little they can do about it."[38] These opinions take on weight, with Senator Zinser now President Fox's national security adviser and Jorge Castaneda his foreign minister.

Under Fox, Zinser, and Castaneda, Mexican policy has shifted to support of the illegals entering the United States. An Office for Mexicans Abroad has been set up to help Mexicans evade U.S. border guards in the deserts of Arizona and California by providing them with "survival kits" of water, dry meat, granola, Tylenol, antidiarrhea pills, bandages, and condoms. The kits are distributed in Mexico's poorest towns, along with information on where illegals can go for free social services in California, no questions asked. In short, Mexico City is now aiding and abetting an invasion of the United States, and the U.S. political response is one of intimidated silence and moral paralysis.[39]

As the invasion rolls on, with California as the preferred destination, sociologist William Frey has documented an out-migration of African Americans and Anglo-Americans from the Golden State in search of cities and towns like the ones they grew up in.[40] Other Californians are moving into gated communities. A country that cannot control its borders isn't really a country anymore, Ronald Reagan warned us some twenty years ago.

Concerns about a radical change in America's ethnic composition have been called un-American. But they are as American as Benjamin Franklin, who once asked, "Why should Pennsylvania, founded by the English, become a Colony of Aliens, who will shortly be so numerous as to Germanize us instead of our Anglifying them . . . ?"[41] Franklin would never find out if his fears were justified. German immigration was halted during the Seven Years War.

Former president Theodore Roosevelt warned, "The one absolutely certain way of bringing this nation to ruin, of preventing all possibility of its continuing to be a nation at all, would be to permit it to become a tangle of squabbling nationalities."[42]

Immigration is a necessary subject for national debate, for it is about who we are as a people. Like the Mississippi, with its endless flow of life-giving water, immigration has enriched America throughout history. But when the Mississippi floods its banks, the devastation can be enormous. Yet, by the commands of political correctness, immigration as an issue is off the table. Only "nativists" or "xenophobes" could question a policy by which the United States takes in more people of different colors, creeds, cultures, and civilizations than all other nations of the earth combined. The river is rising to levels unseen in our history. What will become of our country if the levees do not hold?

IN LATE 1999, this writer left Tucson and drove southeast to Douglas, the Arizona border town of eighteen thousand that had become the principal invasion corridor into the United States. In March alone, the U.S. Border Patrol had apprehended twenty-seven thousand Mexicans crossing illegally, half again as many illegal aliens crossing in one month as there are people in Douglas.[43]

While there, I visited Theresa Murray, an eighty-two-year-old widow and a great-grandmother who lives in the Arizona desert she grew up in. Her ranch house was surrounded by a seven-foot chain-link fence that was topped with coils of razor wire. Every door and window had bars on it and was wired to an alarm. Mrs. Murray sleeps with a .32-caliber pistol on her bed table, because she has been burglarized thirty times. Her guard dogs are dead; they bled to death when someone tossed meat containing chopped glass over her fence. Theresa Murray is living out her life inside a maximum-security prison, in her own home, in her own country, because her government lacks the moral courage to do its duty and defend the borders of the United States of America.

If America is about anything, it is freedom. But as Theresa Murray says, "I've lost my freedom. I can't ever leave the house unless I have somebody watch it. We used to ride our horses clear across the border. We had Mexicans working on our property. It used to be fun to live here. Now, it's hell. It's plain old hell."[44]

While Theresa Murray lives unfree, in hellish existence, American soldiers defend the borders of Korea, Kuwait, and Kosovo. But nothing is at risk on those borders, half a world away, to compare with what is at risk on our border with Mexico, over which pass the armies of the night as they trudge endlessly northward to the great cities of America. Invading armies go home, immigrant armies do not.

## WHO KILLED THE REAGAN COALITION?

For a quarter of a century, from 1968 until 1992, the Republican party had a virtual lock on the presidency. The "New Majority," created by Richard Nixon and replicated by Ronald Reagan, gave the GOP five victories in six presidential elections. The key to victory was to append to the Republican base two Democratic blocs: Northern Catholic ethnics and Southern white Protestants. Mr. Nixon lured these voters away from the New Deal coalition with appeals to patriotism, populism, and social conservatism. Success gave the GOP decisive margins in the industrial states and a "Solid South" that had been the base camp of the Democratic party since Appomattox. This Nixon-Reagan coalition proved almost unbeatable. McGovern, Mondale, and Dukakis could carry 90 percent of the black vote, but with Republicans taking 60 percent of the white vote, which was over 90 percent of the total, the GOP inevitably came out on top.

This was the Southern Strategy. While the media called it immoral, Democrats had bedded down with segregationists for a century without similar censure. FDR and Adlai Stevenson had put segregationists on their tickets. Outside of Missouri, a border state with Southern sympathies, the only ones Adlai captured in 1956 were Dixiecrat states later carried by George Wallace.

Neither Nixon nor Reagan ever supported segregation. As vice president, Nixon was a stronger backer of civil rights than Senators John F. Kennedy or Lyndon Johnson. His role in winning passage of the Civil Rights Act of 1957 was lauded in a personal letter from Dr. Martin Luther King, who hailed Vice President Nixon's "assiduous labor and dauntless courage in seeking to make Civil Rights a reality."[45]

For a quarter century, Democrats were unable to pick the GOP lock on the presidency, because they could not shake loose the Republican grip on the white vote. With the exception of Lyndon Johnson's landslide of 1964, no Democrat since Truman in 1948 had won the white vote. What broke the GOP lock on the presidency was the Immigration Act of 1965.

During the anti-Soviet riots in East Berlin in 1953, Bertolt Brecht, the Communist playwright, quipped, "Would it not be easier . . . for the government to dissolve the people and elect another?"[46] In the last thirty years, America has begun to import a new electorate, as Republicans cheerfully backed an immigration policy tilted to the Third World that enlarged the Democratic base and loosened the grip that Nixon and Reagan had given them on the presidency of the United States.

In 1996, the GOP was rewarded. Six of the 7 states with the largest numbers of immigrants—California, New York, Illinois, New Jersey, Massachusetts, Florida, and Texas—went for Clinton. In 2000, 5 went for Gore, and Florida was a dead heat. Of the 15 states with the most foreign-born, Bush lost 10. But of the 10 states with the smallest shares of foreign-born—Montana, Mississippi, Wyoming, West Virginia, South Dakota, North Dakota, South Carolina, Alabama, Tennessee, and Arkansas—Bush swept all 10.

Among the states with the most immigrants, only Texas has been reliably Republican, but now it is going the way of California. In the 1990s, Texas took in 3.2 million new residents as the Hispanic share of Texas's population shot from 25 percent to 33 percent.[47] Hispanics are now the major ethnic group in four of Texas's five biggest cities: Houston, Dallas, San Antonio, and El Paso. "Non-Hispanic Whites May Soon Be a Minority in Texas" said a recent headline in the *New York Times*.[48] With the Anglo population down from 60 percent in 1990 to 53 percent, the day when whites are a minority in Texas for the first time since before the Alamo is coming soon. "Projections show that by 2005," says the *Dallas Morning News,* "fewer than half of Texans will be white."[49]

AMERICA IS GOING the way of California and Texas. "In 1960, the U.S. population was 88.6 percent white; in 1990, it was only 75.6 percent—a drop of 13 percentage points in thirty years. . . . [By 2020] the proportion of whites could fall as low as 61 per cent."[50] So writes Peter Brimelow of *Forbes*. By 2050, Euro-Americans, the largest and most loyal share of the electorate the GOP has, will be a minority, due to an immigration policy that is championed by Republicans. John Stuart Mill was not altogether wrong when he branded the Tories "the Stupid Party."[51]

HISPANICS ARE THE fastest-growing segment of America's population. They were 6.4 percent of the U.S. population in 1980, 9 percent by 1990, and in 2000 over 12 percent. "The Hispanic fertility rates are quite a bit higher than the white or black population. They are at the levels of the baby boom era of the 1950s," says Jeffrey Passel, a demographer at the Urban Institute.[52] At 35.4 million, Hispanics now equal African Americans in numbers and are becoming as Democratic in voting preferences. Mr. Bush lost the African-American vote eleven to one, but he also lost Hispanics two to one.

In 1996, when Clinton carried Latino voters seventy to twenty-one, he carried first-time Latino voters ninety-one to six.[53] Aware that immigrants could give Democrats their own lock on the White House, Clinton's men worked relentlessly to naturalize them. In the year up to September 30, 1996, the Immigration and Naturalization Service swore in 1,045,000 immigrants as new citizens so quickly that 80,000 with criminal records—6,300 for serious crimes—slipped by.[54] Here are the numbers of new citizens in the last five years of the Clinton presidency.

| | |
|------|------------|
| 1996 | 1,045,000 |
| 1997 | 598,000 |
| 1998 | 463,000 |
| 1999 | 872,000 |
| 2000 | 898,315[55] |

California took a third of these new citizens. As non-Latino white registration fell by one hundred thousand in California in the 1990s, one million Latinos registered.[56] Now 16 percent of the California electorate, Hispanics gave Gore the state with hundreds of thousands of votes to spare. "Both parties show up at swearing-in ceremonies to try to register voters," says Democratic consultant William Carrick. "There is a Democratic table and a Republican table. Ours has a lot of business. Theirs is like the Maytag repairman."[57] With fifty-five electoral votes, California, home state of Nixon and Reagan, has now become a killing field of the GOP.

VOTING ON REFERENDA in California has also broken down along ethnic lines. In 1994, Hispanics, rallying under Mexican flags, opposed Proposition 187 to end welfare to illegals. In the 1996 California Civil Rights Initiative, Hispanics voted for ethnic preferences. In 1998, Hispanics voted to keep bilingual education. Anglo-Americans voted the other way by landslides.

Ron Unz, father of the "English for the Children" referendum that ended state-funded bilingual education, believes the LA riot of 1992 may have been the Rubicon on the road to the balkanization of California.

> The plumes of smoke from burning buildings and the gruesome television footage almost completely shattered the sense of security of middle-class Southern Californians. Suddenly, the happy "multicultural California" so beloved of local boosters had been unmasked as a harsh, dangerous, Third World dystopia. . . . the large numbers of Latinos arrested (and summarily deported) for looting caused whites to cast a newly wary eye on gardeners and nannies who just weeks earlier had seemed so pleasant and reliable. If multicultural Los Angeles had exploded into sudden chaos, what security could whites expect as a minority in an increasingly nonwhite California?[58]

EXCEPT FOR REFUGEES from Communist countries like Hungary and Cuba, immigrants gravitate to the party of government. The obvious reason: Immigrants get more out of government—in free schooling for their kids, housing subsidies, health care—than they pay in. Arriving poor, most do not soon amass capital gains, estates, or incomes that can be federally taxed. Why should immigrants support a Republican party that cuts taxes they don't pay over a Democratic party that will expand the programs on which they do depend?

After Ellis Island, the Democratic party has always been the first stop for immigrants. Only after they have begun to move into the middle class do the foreign-born start converting to Republicanism. This can take two generations. By naturalizing and registering half a million or a million foreign-born a year, the Democrats are locking up future presidential elections and throwing away the key. If the GOP does not do something about mass immigration, mass immigration will do something about the GOP—turn it into a permanent minority that is home to America's newest minority, Euro-Americans.

As the ethnic character of America changes, politics change. A rising tide of immigration naturally shifts politics and power to the Left, by increasing the demands on government. The rapidly expanding share of the U.S. electorate that is of African and Hispanic ancestry has already caused the GOP to go silent on affirmative action and mute its calls for cuts in social spending. In 1996, Republicans were going to abolish the U.S. Department of Education. Now, they are enlarging it. As Hispanic immigration soars, and Hispanic voters become the swing voters in the pivotal states, their agenda will become America's agenda. It is already happening. In 2000, an AFL-CIO that had opposed mass immigration reversed itself and came out for amnesty for illegal aliens, hoping to sign up millions of illegal workers as dues-paying union members. And the Bush White House—in its policy decisions and appointments—has become acutely attentive to the Hispanic vote, often at the expense of conservative principles.

## AMERICA'S QUEBEC?

Harvard economist George Borjas, who studied the issue, found no net economic benefit from mass migration from the Third World. The added costs of schooling, health care, welfare, social security, and prisons, plus the added pressure on land, water, and power resources, exceeded the taxes that immigrants contribute. The National Bureau of Economic Research puts the cost of immigration at $80.4 billion in 1995.[59] Economist Donald Huddle of Rice University estimates that the net annual cost of immigration will reach $108 billion by 2006.[60] What are the benefits, then, that justify the risks we are taking of the balkanization of America?

Census 2000 revealed what many sensed. For the first time since statehood, whites in California are a minority. White flight has begun. In the 1990s, California grew by three million people, but its Anglo population actually "dropped by nearly half a million . . . surprising many demographers."[61] Los Angeles County lost 480,000 white folks. In the exodus, the Republican bastion of Orange County lost 6 percent of its white population. "We can't pretend we're a white middle class state anymore," said William Fulton, research fellow at USC's Southern California Studies Center.[62] State librarian Kevin Starr views the Hispanization of California as natural and inevitable:

> The Anglo hegemony was only an intermittent phase in California's arc of identity, extending from the arrival of the Spanish . . . the Hispanic nature of California has been there all along, and it was temporarily swamped between the 1880s and the 1960s, but that was an aberration. This is a reassertion of the intrinsic demographic DNA of the longer pattern, which is a part of the California-Mexican continuum.[63]

The future is predictable: With one hundred thousand Anglos leaving California each year, with the Asian population soaring 42 percent in a single decade, with 43 percent of all Californians under eighteen Hispanic, America's largest state is on its way to becoming a predominantly Third World state.[64]

No one knows how this will play out, but California could become another Quebec, with demands for formal recognition of its separate and unique Hispanic culture and identity—or another Ulster. As Sinn Fein demanded and got special ties to Dublin, Mexican Americans may demand a special relationship with their mother country, dual citizenship, open borders, and voting representation in Mexico's legislature. President Fox endorses these ideas. With California holding 20 percent of the electoral votes needed for the U.S. presidency, and Hispanic votes decisive in California, what presidential candidate would close the door to such demands?

"I have proudly proclaimed that the Mexican nation extends beyond the territory enclosed by its borders and that Mexican migrants are an important—a very important—part of this," said President Zedillo.[65] His successor agrees. Candidates for president of Mexico now raise money and campaign actively in the United States. Gov. Gray Davis is exploring plans to have Cinco de Mayo, the fifth of May, the anniversary of Juarez's 1862 victory over a French army at

Puebla, made a California holiday. "In the near future," says Davis, "people will look at California and Mexico as one magnificent region."⁶⁶ Perhaps we can call it Aztlan.

AMERICA IS NO longer the biracial society of 1960 that struggled to erase divisions and close gaps in a nation 90 percent white. Today we juggle the rancorous and rival claims of a multiracial, multiethnic, and multicultural country. Vice President Gore captured the new America in his famous howler, when he translated our national slogan, "E Pluribus Unum," backward, as "Out of one, many."⁶⁷

Today there are thirty-one million foreign-born in the United States. Half are from Latin America and the Caribbean, a fourth from Asia. The rest are from Africa, the Middle East, and Europe. One in every five New Yorkers and Floridians is foreign-born, as is one of every four Californians. With 8.4 million foreign-born, and not one new power plant built in a decade, small wonder California faced power shortages and power outages. With endless immigration, America is going to need an endless expansion of its power sources—hydroelectric power, fossil fuels (oil, coal, gas), and nuclear power. The only alternative is blackouts, brownouts, and endless lines at the pump.

In the 1990s, immigrants and their children were responsible for 100 percent of the population growth of California, New York, New Jersey, Illinois, and Massachusetts, and over half the population growth of Florida, Texas, Michigan, and Maryland.⁶⁸ As the United States allots most of its immigrant visas to relatives of new arrivals, it is difficult for Europeans to come, while entire villages from El Salvador are now here.

The results of the Third World bias in immigration can be seen in our social statistics. The median age of Euro-Americans is 36; for Hispanics, it is 26. The median age of all foreign-born, 33, is far below that of the older American ethnic groups, such as English, 40, and Scots-Irish, 43. These social statistics raise a question: Is the U.S. government, by deporting scarcely 1 percent of an estimated eleven million illegal aliens each year, failing in its constitutional duty to protect the rights of American citizens?[69] Consider:

- A third of the legal immigrants who come to the United States have not finished high school. Some 22 percent do not even have a ninth-grade education, compared to less than 5 percent of our native born.[70]
- Over 36 percent of all immigrants, and 57 percent of those from Central America, do not earn twenty thousand dollars a year. Of the immigrants who have come since 1980, 60 percent still do not earn twenty thousand dollars a year.[71]
- Of immigrant households in the United States, 29 percent are below the poverty line, twice the 14 percent of native born.[72]
- Immigrant use of food stamps, Supplemental Social Security, and school lunch programs runs from 50 percent to 100 percent higher than use by native born.[73]
- Mr. Clinton's Department of Labor estimated that 50 percent of the real-wage losses sustained by low-income Americans is due to immigration.[74]
- By 1991, foreign nationals accounted for 24 percent of all arrests in Los Angeles and 36 percent of all arrests in Miami.[75]
- In 1980, federal and state prisons housed nine thousand criminal aliens. By 1995, this had soared to fifty-nine thousand criminal aliens, a figure that does not include aliens who became citizens or the criminals sent over by Castro in the Mariel boat lift.[76]
- Between 1988 and 1994, the number of illegal aliens in California's prisons more than tripled from fifty-five hundred to eighteen thousand.[77]

None of the above statistics, however, holds for emigrants from Europe. And some of the statistics, on low education, for example, do not apply to emigrants from Asia.

Nevertheless, mass emigration from poor Third World countries is "good for business," especially businesses that employ large numbers at low wages. In the spring of 2001, the Business Industry Political Action Committee, BIPAC, issued "marching orders for grass-roots mobilization."[78] The *Wall Street Journal* said that the 400 blue-chip companies and 150 trade associations "will call for continued normalization of trade with China . . . and easing immigration restrictions to meet labor needs. . . ."[79] But what is good for corporate America is not necessarily good for Middle America. When it comes to open borders, the corporate interest and the national interest do not coincide, they collide. Should America suffer a sustained recession, we will find out if the melting pot is still working.

But mass immigration raises more critical issues than jobs or wages, for immigration is ultimately about America herself.

## WHAT IS A NATION?

Most of the people who leave their homelands to come to America, whether from Mexico or Mauritania, are good people, decent people. They seek the same better life our ancestors sought when they came. They come to work; they obey our laws; they cherish our freedoms; they relish the opportunities the greatest nation on earth has to offer; most love America; many wish to become part of the American family. One may encounter these newcomers everywhere. But the record number of foreign-born coming from cultures with little in common with Americans raises a different question: What is a nation?

Some define a nation as one people of common ancestry, language, literature, history, heritage, heroes, traditions, customs, mores, and faith who have lived together over time on the same land under the same rulers. This is the blood-and-soil idea of a nation. Among those who pressed this definition were Secretary of State John Quincy Adams, who laid down these conditions on immigrants: "They must cast off the European skin, never to resume it. They must look forward to their posterity rather than backward to their ancestors."[80] Theodore Roosevelt, who thundered against "hyphenated-Americanism," seemed to share Adams's view. Woodrow Wilson, speaking to newly naturalized Americans in 1915 in Philadelphia, echoed T.R.: "A man who thinks of himself as belonging to a particular national group in America has yet to become an American."[81] This idea, of Americans as a separate and unique people, was first given expression by John Jay in *Federalist 2:*

> Providence has been pleased to give this one connected country to one united people—a people descended from the same ancestors, speaking the same language, professing the same religion, attached to the same principles of government, very similar in their manners and customs, and who, by their joint counsels, arms, and efforts, fighting side by side throughout a long and bloody war, have nobly established their general liberty and independence.[82]

But can anyone say today that we Americans are "one united people"?

We are not descended from the same ancestors. We no longer speak the same language. We do not profess the same religion. We are no longer simply Protestant, Catholic, and Jewish, as sociologist Will Herberg described us in his *Essay in American Religious Sociology* in 1955.[83] We are now Protestant, Catholic, Jewish, Mormon, Muslim, Hindu, Buddhist, Taoist, Shintoist, Santeria, New Age, voodoo, agnostic, atheist, humanist, Rastafarian, and Wiccan. Even the mention of Jesus' name at the Inauguration by the preachers Mr. Bush selected to give the invocations evoked fury and cries of "insensitive," "divisive," and "exclusionary."[84] A *New Republic* editorial lashed out at these "crushing Christological thuds" from the Inaugural stand.[85] We no longer agree on whether God exists, when life begins, and what is moral and immoral. We are not "similar in our manners and customs." We never fought "side by side throughout a long and bloody war." The Greatest Generation did, but it is passing away. If the rest of us recall a "long and bloody war," it was Vietnam, and, no, we were not side by side.

We remain "attached to the same principles of government." But common principles of government are not enough to hold us together. The South was "attached to the same principles of government" as the North. But that did not stop Southerners from fighting four years of bloody war to be free of their Northern brethren.

In his Inaugural, President Bush rejected Jay's vision: "America has never been united by blood or birth or soil. We are bound by ideals that move us beyond our background, lift us above our interests, and teach us what it means to be a citizen."[86] In his *The Disuniting of America,* Arthur Schlesinger subscribes to the Bush idea of a nation, united by shared belief in an American Creed to be found in our history and greatest documents: the Declaration of Independence, the Constitution, and the Gettysburg Address. Writes Schlesinger:

> The American Creed envisages a nation composed of individuals making their own choices and accountable to themselves, not a nation based on inviolable ethnic communities. For our values are not matters or whim and happenstance. History has given them to us. They are anchored in our national experience, in our great national documents, in our national heroes, in our folkways, our traditions, and standards. [Our values] work for us; and, for that reason, we live and die by them.[87]

But Americans no longer agree on values, history, or heroes. What one-half of America sees as a glorious past the other views as shameful and wicked. Columbus, Washington, Jefferson, Jackson, Lincoln, and Lee—all of them heroes of the old America—are all under attack. Those most American of words, equality and freedom, today hold different meanings for different Americans. As for our "great national documents," the Supreme Court decisions that interpret our Constitution have not united us; for forty years they have divided us, bitterly, over prayer in school, integration, busing, flag burning, abortion, pornography, and the Ten Commandments.

Nor is a belief in democracy sufficient to hold us together. Half of the nation did not even bother to vote in the presidential election of 2000; three out of five do not vote in off-year elections. Millions cannot name their congressman, senators, or the Supreme Court justices. They do not care.

Whether one holds to the blood-and-soil idea of a nation, or to the creedal idea, or both, neither nation is what it was in the 1940s, 1950s, or 1960s. We live in the same country, we are governed by the same leaders, but can we truly say we are still one nation and one people?

It is hard to say yes, harder to believe that over a million immigrants every year, from every country on earth, a third of them breaking in, will reforge the bonds of our disuniting nation. John Stuart Mill warned that "free institutions are next to impossible in a country made up of different nationalities. Among a people without fellow-feeling, especially if they read and speak different languages, the united public opinion necessary to the working of representative government cannot exist."[88]

We are about to find out if Mill was right.

# SEVEN

# THE WAR AGAINST THE PAST

"To destroy a people, you must first sever their roots."[1]
—Alexander Solzhenitzyn

How does one sever a people's roots? Answer: Destroy its memory. Deny a people the knowledge of who they are and where they came from.

"If we forget what we did, we won't know who we are," said Ronald Reagan in his farewell address to the American people. "I am warning of the eradication of . . . the American memory, that could result, ultimately, in an erosion of the American spirit."[2]

In the Middle Ages, Ottoman Turks imposed on Balkan Christians a blood tax—one boy out of every five. Taken from their parents, the boys were raised as strict Muslims to become the fanatic elite soldiers of the sultan, the Janissaries, who were then sent back to occupy and oppress the peoples who had borne them. For a modern state the formula for erasing memory was given to us by Orwell in the party slogan of Big Brother, "Who controls the past controls the future. Who controls the present controls the past."[3]

Destroy the record of a people's past, leave it in ignorance of who its ancestors were and what they did, and one can fill the empty vessels of their souls with a new history, as in *1984*. Dishonor or disgrace a nation's heroes, and you can demoralize its people. The cause of Irish independence was crippled by the revelation that the great Charles Stewart Parnell was living in adultery with the wife of

Captain O'Shea. Baseball almost did not survive the Black Sox scandal of 1919, when popular hero "Shoeless Joe" Jackson was found to have taken money from gamblers and his team had thrown the World Series. The loss of faith was caught in the kid's lament, "Say it ain't so, Joe!"

Richard Nixon's New Majority was shattered by Watergate and the resignation of a president and vice president who had carried forty-nine states. The success of Nixon's enemies in ousting from office a hated adversary became the archetype for the "politics of personal destruction," the defeat of causes by disgracing their flawed champions. It has become standard operating procedure in American politics.

CULTURAL MARXISTS UNDERSTOOD this. Their Critical Theory was a prototype of the politics of personal destruction. What the latter does to popular leaders, Critical Theory does to an entire nation through repeated assaults on its past. It is the moral equivalent of vandalizing the graves and desecrating the corpses of its ancestors.

Many of the institutions that now have custody of America's past operate on the principles of Big Brother's Ministry of Truth: drop down the "memory hole" the patriotic stories of America's greatness and glory, and produce new "warts-and-all" histories that play up her crimes and sins, revealing what we have loved to be loathsome and those we have revered to be disreputable, even despicable. Many old heroes have not survived the killing fields of the New History. Ultimate goal: Destroy patriotism, kill the love of country, demoralize the people, deconstruct America. History then will no longer unite and inspire us, but depress and divide us into the children of victims and the children of the villains of America's past.

A CHILD'S LOVE of its mother grows naturally, but love of country must be taught. Only by learning can a child know of the people and nation to which he or she belongs. For those born before World War

II, love of country came easily. Radio, movies, newspapers, comic books, and conversations conveyed the same message: We were a good and trusting people, attacked without warning at Pearl Harbor. Many brave Americans had died there, others were bayoneted on a Death March in a place called Bataan. Now we were paying Japan back.

There was a spirit of solidarity and unity then unlike any we have known since. We were truly one nation indivisible and one people. But the war was not unquestioned. Nightly, one heard arguments over the "blackout," whether the Germans could bomb Washington, the wisdom of aiding Stalin, the merits of Eisenhower versus those of MacArthur, the "sellout" of Poland, and who was responsible for our being caught unprepared at Pearl Harbor. Today "the Good War" is among the few events in history that retains its luster, still a bright shining moment. Whatever the wisdom of the decisions, our enemies were the incarnation of evil, and we were on God's side.

Korea was different, a divisive war in a divided nation, Truman's America. But, unlike Vietnam, no patriot suggested that the North Koreans or Chinese Communists were right and America was wrong. The dissent was General Bradley's dissent: Korea was "the wrong war, in the wrong place, at the wrong time, with the wrong enemy."[4]

With Eisenhower came an end to Korea and the savage arguments over the "sellout at Yalta" and "Who lost China?" and the beginning of a new Era of Good Feelings, which lasted until November 22, 1963. But after the assassination of President Kennedy, an adversary culture arose that set about dynamiting America's legends, demythologizing her history, and demolishing her heroes. With its media collaborators, this counterculture has left scarcely an institution unscarred or a hero unsullied. We grew up in an era of belief. We grow old in an era of disbelief, feebly fending off the relentless pounding of the artillery of an adversary culture that accepts no armistice.

## THE OLD HISTORY

Not long ago, every American child knew the names of all the great explorers—Magellan, da Gama, de Soto, Cortes, Henry Hudson—but the greatest of all was Columbus, for he had discovered America in one of the greatest events of world history. Our history books began here. In the Catholic schools, stories of the French and Spanish explorers and of the North American martyrs like Fr. Isaac Joques, the Apostle to the Iroquois tomahawked to death near Albany, were accented. But we, too, got around to John Smith and Jamestown and the Pilgrims and Plymouth Rock.

From there, our histories leapt 150 years to the French and Indian War, the Stamp Act, the Boston Massacre, the Boston Tea Party, "Give me liberty or give me death," Bunker Hill, the Declaration of Independence, Valley Forge, "I regret that I have but one life to give for my country," Benedict Arnold, Saratoga, and Cornwallis's surrender at Yorktown.

From triumph to triumph, American history marched. The British burned the White House, but Dolley Madison saved the paintings. Our men held "through the night" of the bombardment of Fort McHenry, and Andy Jackson paid the British back at New Orleans. The Alamo came quickly, where Crockett and the Texas heroes refused to surrender and died to a man on Mexican bayonets. No one suggested America stole anything. After the Alamo the Mexicans had it coming. In the 1950s, a Davy Crockett craze swept America, with a movie, a TV show, and even a bestselling record about the "King of the Wild Frontier." Davy made actor Fess Parker famous. There were so many kids walking around in coonskin caps that the raccoon population took a serious hit. Rock star Johnny Horton recorded Jimmy Driftwood's "Battle of New Orleans": "In 1814 we took a little trip / Along with Colonel Jackson / Down the mighty Mississip / And we took a little bacon / And we took a little beans / And we caught the bloody British / In a town called New Orleans."[5]

In our Civil War histories, Lee and Jackson were great soldiers and men of nobility. Sherman's March to the Sea was a black page in history. Reconstruction was cruel. Southerners were, after all, fellow Americans who had fought bravely and should have been treated with honor. "Dixie" was more popular than "The Battle Hymn of the Republic." But Lincoln was the great hero, with a holiday in his honor. He had saved the Union and freed the slaves, only to be assassinated by John Wilkes Booth in one of the great tragedies of American history, for Honest Abe would never have allowed Reconstruction. So we were taught.

After the Civil War came the Winning of the West. Pioneers—men, women, and children alike—crossed the Great Plains, braving the terrible weather and constant threat of Indian massacres. General Custer and the Seventh Cavalry were heroic in our history books. *They Died with Their Boots On,* starring Errol Flynn and Ronald Reagan, told us so. This was also the time of the Robber Barons, who had grabbed the railroads and banks until they met their match in the great "trust-buster" Teddy Roosevelt. The hero of San Juan Hill also built the Panama Canal, a marvel of American engineering genius. Those were the days of Edison, the Wright Brothers, and Alexander Graham Bell, when we Americans had invented pretty much everything worth inventing.

Then came World World I, when President Wilson sent our soldiers off to "make the world safe for democracy." Led by General Pershing, with Sergeant York as the hero of the war, we defeated Germany, which had started the war by torpedoing our ships. Soon after, Japan treacherously attacked us at Pearl Harbor. So we had to go back again and finish the job, destroying Mussolini and Hitler, although in Catholic schools Stalin was every bit as monstrous. There was no Popular Front at the Blessed Sacrament school the author attended. Now we had to save the world from "atheistic Communism." At the end of the daily mass, we recited a Prayer for the Conversion of Russia—later dropped for the more détentist "Prayer for Peace."

NOW THE ABOVE is not a nuanced rendering of American history. Yet at its core is this truth: We Americans have a glorious history, the richest and greatest of any modern people or nation, or of any republic that went before us. Were wrongs committed and crimes covered up? Surely. That is true of every nation. But none had triumphed in as many endeavors as America had, and there is no need for eight-year-olds to debate Fort Pillow or the trysts of Warren Harding or John F. Kennedy.

We established public schools in America to create good citizens and patriots who will protect and preserve their country. These schools should lead children through courses that will teach them to love America. As a child reads the biographies, histories, stories, and poems, and hears the songs and sees the paintings that tell of a glorious national past, patriotism takes root. With a growing love of country comes a growing desire to be forever a part of this people, and a willingness to sacrifice, even to die, to defend this people, as one would defend one's family.

In the New Testament, Christ holds out a hellish punishment for any who would destroy the belief of "these little ones": "It were better for him that a millstone were hanged about his neck and that he were drowned in the depth of the sea."[6] Yet, American children are today being robbed of their heritage, cheated of their right to know the magnificent history of their country. In *The Disuniting of America*, Arthur Schlesinger cites a character out of Milan Kundera's *The Book of Laughter and Forgetting:*

> The first step in liquidating a people is to erase its memory. Destroy its books, its culture, its history. Then have someone write new books, manufacture a new culture, invent a new history. Before long the nation will begin to forget what it is and what it was.[7]

Another character adds, "The struggle of man against power is the struggle of memory against forgetting."[8] This is the struggle of the old America against the cultural revolution. Yet, look at what our Ministry of Truth has already done to our heroes and our history.

## GOOD-BYE, COLUMBUS

On the three-hundredth anniversary of Columbus's voyage, 1792, New York's King's College was renamed Columbia, and the U.S. capital was named the District of Columbia. In 1882, to honor "a prophet . . . an instrument of Divine Providence," Irish Catholics organized the Knights of Columbus.[9] The *Admiral of the Ocean Sea* was the Columbus we grew up with; but, as columnist Garry Wills chortled in the *New York Review of Books*:

> A funny thing happened on the way to the quincentennial observation of America's Discovery. . . . Columbus got mugged. This time the Indians were waiting for him. He comes now with an apologetic air—but not, for some, sufficiently apologetic. . . . He comes to be dishonored.[10]

Kirkpatrick Sale's *Conquest of Paradise* and Jan Carew's *Columbus: The Rape of Paradise* accused the explorer of having "introduced slavery to the West and set off a legacy of shame and racism that continues to this day."[11] The UN canceled its Columbus celebration, and the National Council of Churches urged that the five-hundredth anniversary of his voyage be set aside as a time for penitence for the "genocide, slavery, ecocide and exploitation" the Italian explorer introduced to the Americas.[12] Writes columnist George Szamuely of the *New York Press*:

In 1992, the quincentenary of Christopher Columbus' transatlantic journey came and went with scarcely any national celebration; only rote condemnation of the cruelty, greed and
savagery of the continent's European conquerors punctured the
embarrassed national silence.[13]

When Italian Americans sought to carry a banner of Columbus in
their October 2000 parade in Denver, radicals of the American Indian
Movement threatened violence. AIM's veteran troublemaker Russell
Means said that Columbus "makes Hitler look like a juvenile delin-
quent."[14] Marching in step with the forces of progress, the University
of California at Berkeley hastily changed Columbus Day into Indigenous Peoples Day.[15]

The diabolization of the great Spanish explorers and conquistadors
as irredeemable racist murderers is almost complete. America, it is
said, was not "discovered," but invaded by disease-ridden Europeans
who burned out native cultures as they razed native villages. Cortes's
burning of his ships and march inland with a handful of soldiers to
conquer and convert the Aztecs is now cultural genocide against a
peace-loving people. That the Aztecs were themselves conquerors who
made slaves of defeated enemies and offered human blood sacrifices
to Huitzilopochtli, their god of sun and war, is ignored. And what is
meant by "cultural genocide"? When the Europeans arrived in the
Americas, some indigenous tribes were still practicing cannibalism—
and not one had invented the wheel.

## THE FOUNDING FATHERS

Now comes the turn of the Founding Fathers. Five of our first seven
presidents, excepting only the Adamses, owned slaves. Jefferson was
a hypocrite whose "all men are created equal" clause in the Declaration of Independence is contradicted by his lifelong ownership of

slaves. His sexual exploitation of Sally Hemings, whose mulatto children he cowardly refused to recognize, was disgraceful. Washington, too, was a slave owner and a participant in the greatest evil in U.S. history. Madison was yet another. The abolitionist William Lloyd Garrison was right to call the Constitution Madison wrote "an agreement with death and a covenant with hell."[16] By the corrupt bargain that sealed the success of that constitutional convention, slaves counted as only three-fifths of a person. As for Andrew Jackson, Old Hickory was, in the judgment of commentator-author Robert Novak, "a murderer, a demagogue, a brute, a racist, and corrupt to boot"—and guilty of genocidal massacres in his Indian wars.[17]

HOW SUCCESSFUL HAS our Ministry of Truth been in shaping the view of Americans toward their country's past? When our parents were young, 89 percent of American men and 94 percent of American women thought this was the greatest country on earth.[18] Today, only 58 percent of American men identify the United States as "the best country in the world," and only 51 percent of American women agree.[19]

Dr. David Yeagley, a columnist with *FrontPage* Magazine, tells a story of how the new antihistory is killing love of country in the souls of the young. Himself a descendant of Comanches, Yeagley was leading his class in social psychology at Oklahoma State in a spirited discussion of patriotism and what it means to be an American when a beautiful young white girl jolted the class with these remarks:

> Look, Dr. Yeagley, I don't see anything about my culture to be proud of. It's all nothing. My race is just nothing. . . . Look at your culture. Look at American Indian tradition. Now I think that's really great. You have something to be proud of. My culture is nothing. . . . I'm not proud of how America came about.[20]

"On one level I wasn't surprised," said Dr. Yeagley. "I knew the head of our American History department at Oklahoma State . . . and I recognized his hackneyed liberal jargon. . . . She had taken one of his courses with predictable results."[21] Still, Yeagley was stunned by the timidity and silence of the rest of the class, as this woman denounced her own people and nation as well as theirs. No Indian woman would have dared say such a thing in the presence of Indian men.

The rewrite men of America's past have done their work well.

CONSIDER THE REACTION to one of the most popular movies of 2000, *The Patriot.*

The film stars Mel Gibson as Benjamin Martin, an American hero of the French and Indian War and a father of seven who wants to stay out of the Revolution. Martin is drawn into the fighting when his teenage son is murdered before his eyes by a brutal British officer and his eldest boy, a rebel, is taken away to be executed. The story is set in South Carolina, and Martin is based on Francis Marion, the "Swamp Fox," and Daniel Morgan, the famed guerrilla. The British antagonist is based upon the legendarily ruthless Col. Banastre Tarlton.

Two powerful and memorable scenes enraged critics. The first is when Martin, having witnessed his son's cold-blooded killing, instructs his two younger boys, aged thirteen and ten, to grab muskets and follow him. They ambush the British patrol, which is shot to pieces, with Martin finishing the last British soldier off with his hatchet. Father and sons have avenged an atrocity and rescued a son and brother about to be lynched. The second scene has the British officer taking his revenge. Corralling dozens of civilians from Martin's village in a church, he orders the doors locked and the church burned.

On seeing *Patriot,* some movie reviewers went more berserk than Martin had on seeing his son executed. "Don't mistake 'The Patriot' for history," wrote James Verniere in the *Boston Herald*. "It's a sales pitch for America."[22] And what would be wrong with that?

"Overblown sanctimony and sentimentalism," wrote Ann Hornaday in the *Baltimore Sun*, "as corny as the Fourth of July"; indeed, "much more dishonest and damaging than anything that's sprung from Oliver Stone's imagination."[23] But damaging to whom? Stone had implied that the CIA, the U.S. military, and Lyndon Johnson conspired in the murder of John F. Kennedy.

Film director Spike Lee emerged from the movie apoplectic, choking with rage. His letter to the *Hollywood Reporter* deserves quotation at length. For it mirrors the mind-set of our new cultural elite.

> I along with millions of other Americans went to see "The Patriot." We both came out of the theater fuming . . . "The Patriot" is pure, blatant . . . propaganda. A complete whitewashing of history, revisionist history. . . .
>
> For almost three hours, "The Patriot" dodged around, skirted about or completely ignored slavery. . . .
>
> America was built upon the genocide of Native Americans and the enslavement of African people. To say otherwise is criminal. . . . [24]

In his enraged epistle, Lee confessed that he had to hold himself back from shouting at the screen. He attacked screenwriter Robert Rodat for not making the Gibson character a slave owner and not putting at least some Indians into the Revolutionary War film: "Where were they? Did the two Johns—Ford and Wayne—wipe them out already?" Incensed by the final scene in which Benjamin Martin holds aloft a thirteen-star American flag and heroically charges the British lines, Lee castigated it as "laughable."

What comes out of Lee's letter is virulent anti-Americanism—i.e., our country was built on "genocide" and "enslavement"—and his settled conviction that anyone who rejects this view of U.S. history is "criminal." Only a sick or criminal mind, Lee is saying, could paint the American Revolution as heroic, honorable, and moral, and not deal with slaughtered Indians. And to portray any blacks in America as free, happy, or loyal is "propaganda," an outrage; it cannot be true.

In *Salon.com,* Jonathan Foreman explores for the roots of this evil film and finds them where you might expect: "The savage soldiers in 'The Patriot' act more like the Waffen SS than actual English troops. Does 'The Patriot' have an ulterior motive?"[25]

> You could actually argue . . . that "The Patriot" is as fascist a film (and I use the term in its literal sense, not as a synonym for "bad") as anything made in decades. . . . "The Patriot" presents a deeply sentimental cult of the family, as it casts unusually Aryan-looking heroes. . . .
>
> In one scene tow-headed preteens are armed by their father and turned into the equivalent of the Werewolf boy-soldiers that the Third Reich was thought to have recruited for the Hitler Youth to carry out guerrilla attacks against the invading allies.
>
> In the film's most exciting sequence, Gibson is provoked by the foreigner into becoming one of those bloodiest, ax-wielding forest supermen so beloved in Nazi folk-iconography. . . .
>
> The black population of South Carolina—where the film is set—is basically depicted as happy loyal slaves, or equally happy (and unlikely) freemen.[26]

The church burning, writes Foreman, replicates the Nazi atrocity in the French village of Oradour sur Glane in June 1944. "*German* director Roland Emmerich" may just have "a subconscious agenda."[27] By shifting Oradour to South Carolina, he and screenwriter Robert Rodat "have done something unpleasantly akin to Holocaust revisionism. They have made a film that will have the effect of inoculating audiences against the unique historical horror of Oradour . . . implicitly rehabilitating the Nazis. . . ."[28] This is the type of film, wrote

Foreman, that Nazi propaganda minister Joseph Goebbels used in "efforts at inflaming isolationist Anglophobia."[29]

"Lighten up, man!" one is tempted to say. Unfortunately, at work here is a mind deeply conditioned and steeped in antihistory. An affecting portrayal of a father and seven loving and dutiful children represents the "cult of the family." Their heroic fight together to overthrow British rule and win America's freedom is "fascist." Martin's thirteen- and ten-year-old sons are like "Werewolf boy soldiers" of the Reich, because they are "tow-headed" and "Aryan-looking."[30] To Foreman, the fascists are everywhere.

No more than Spike Lee can Foreman tolerate a depiction of slaves or freedmen as proud American soldiers and patriots. Yet, this is but a cinematic portrayal of a forgotten slice of our history. Free Negroes did soldier and fight in the Revolution, under Jackson at New Orleans, and for the Union, and for the Confederacy under Bedford Forrest. The over-the-top reaction to Gibson's *Patriot* testifies to how our cultural elites have indoctrinated our newest tribe of scribblers in an almost reflexive hatred of America's past and of the men we once revered as patriot-fathers.

TO OUR NEW cultural elite, America's Civil War was a revolt of slave owners and traitors to destroy the Union to preserve their odious institution, and the Lost Cause was ignoble and dishonorable. Hence, the Confederate flag should be as repulsive as a Nazi swastika, and only white racists and the morally obtuse would defend that bloody banner. As for Lee and Jackson, they led hundreds of thousands to their deaths in an evil cause, and if the NAACP demands we rid the public square of all plaques, statues, or flags of the Confederacy, they are not only within their rights, they are morally right.

Not long ago, stories of the pioneers, soldiers, settlers, and cowboys who "won the West" and tamed a continent in an historic struggle against an unforgiving nature, outlaws, and Indians were the stuff of books, films, and TV shows that enthralled not only Americans, but the rest of the world as well. But the revisionists have done their work. No film today would dare paint Indians as backward, capricious, or cruel. Rather, as in *Little Big Man* and *Dances with Wolves,* Indians are seen as early environmentalists who cherished, nurtured, and protected the land and wildlife they depended on. These peaceful, trusting people were cheated, murdered, and massacred by amoral white men who butchered their way across the plains, slaughtering the buffalo and corrupting the Indians they did not wantonly kill. Custer and the Seventh Cavalry are now the role models for the Einsatzgruppen.

## ONLY YESTERDAY

To see how America's heroes of old have been cast out of the Pantheon by the Taliban of Modernity, consider:

• Washington's Birthday, once a national holiday for the Father of Our Country, a soldier and statesman without equal in American history, greatest man of the eighteenth century, has been replaced by "Presidents' Day," when we can all recall the greatness of Millard Fillmore, Chester Arthur, and William Jefferson Clinton.

• The New Orleans School Board has taken Washington's name off an elementary school. Its new policy prohibits honoring "former slave owners or others who did not respect opportunity for all."[31] That rules out Presidents Jefferson, Madison, Monroe, Jackson, Tyler, Taylor, and Grant, as well as Clay, Calhoun, and Robert E. Lee.

Should African Americans, tens of thousands of whom carry these great names, go to court to get them changed? Is it Andrew Jackson, the Indian killer, or Stonewall Jackson, the Confederate legend, whose name Jesse Jackson proudly carries?

• Thomas Jefferson, author of the Declaration of Independence, was last year declared persona non grata in New Jersey. The legislature twice defeated a bill that would have required public school students to recite in class each day a brief passage from the Declaration. Every Democrat in the statehouse voted "no" on the Declaration, which was denounced as "anti-women, anti-black and too pro-God."[32] State senator Wayne Bryant, an African American, led the fight to spare students from the indignity of having to recite Jefferson's "all men are created equal." Bryant berated the bill's sponsor: "You have nerve to ask my grandchildren to recite the Declaration. How dare you? You are now on notice that this is offensive to my community."[33]

• Andrew Jackson, who seized Florida from Spain for the United States, is the target of an American Indian Movement campaign. Calling Jackson a "genocidal maniac" who served as a "Hitler prototype," AIM wants to prevent America's seventh president from being honored in the annual Springtime Tallahassee parade.[34]

"Old Hickory" has trouble in North Carolina, too. There, a self-described "vice chief" of the Tuscaroras, Robert Chavis, wants U.S. 74, now Andrew Jackson Highway, to be renamed American Indian Highway. "Andrew Jackson is no hero to us. He's like Hitler. He's a killer," says Chavis, who claims to have four thousand signatures on a petition to effect the name change.[35]

As the face of the U.S. twenty-dollar bill is now graced by a portrait of "King Andrew," who was a slave owner, an Indian fighter, and the president who signed the law that moved the Cherokees out of Georgia and the Carolinas to Oklahoma, this could get interesting.

• Custer National Battlefield has lately been renamed Little Big Horn National Battlefield, as the Indians consider the massacre of Custer's entire command a great victory. Alongside the small obelisk that now honors the American dead of the Seventh Cavalry will rise a monument to the Indians who killed and scalped them and mutilated their bodies.[36]

• Militant Indians have demanded that all sports teams drop Indian names. In 2001, the U.S. Civil Rights Commission agreed, arguing that the collegiate use of Indian team names and mascots is "disrespectful and offensive" and creates a "racially hostile educational environment."[37] We were not told when exactly it became so. But with political correctness now the prevailing orthodoxy on campuses, the campaign is succeeding. The Dartmouth Indians are now Big Green, the Stanford Indians are now Cardinals, and St. John's University's Redmen are now the Red Storm. North Dakota, however, decided to retain "Fighting Sioux" after an alumnus threatened to withdraw his 100-million-dollar pledge if the name was changed.

The Washington Redskins and Atlanta Braves have also balked, as Braves's fans continue to use their famed "tomahawk chop," though it is said to be insulting to the inventors of the tomahawk. The Portland *Oregonian* has adopted a policy of refusing to mention team names that include the words *indians, braves, redmen, redskins,* or *chiefs.*[38]

• In San Jose, California, Indian and Hispanic rage prevented a statue of Thomas Fallon, the American adventurer who captured the town in the Mexican War and became its mayor, from being placed in a public park. "The statue is an insult to our ancestors, people who were lynched here," said Pascual Mendevil of Pueblo Unido, "It's like a red flag to racists out there that it's open season on Mexicans."[39] San Jose, however, does boast a new statue of Quetzalcoatl, a feathered serpent god of the Aztecs, whose empire never came close to reaching San Jose.

Perhaps Mexicans and Indians should reconsider Quetzalcoatl. The Aztec emperor Montezuma II was a deeply superstitious fellow, terrified that Quetzalcoatl would return from the east to claim his throne. When his emissaries reported that Cortes and his bearded white men were ashore at Veracruz, the fearless Montezuma and his court went into a panic.

• In St. Augustine, Florida, oldest city in the United States, founded by Columbus's lieutenant Ponce de Leon, removal of Ponce's bayfront statue is being demanded by American Indians. The Spanish explorer, mortally wounded by an arrow in his search for the Fountain of Youth, is said by the Indians to have been a "genocidal maniac."[40]

• In Southampton, Long Island, the local Anti-Bias Task Force is demanding the scrapping of the town's seventy-year-old official seal, a medallion featuring a white man in Pilgrim dress and an Indian in a loincloth. The seal reads, "First English Settlement in the State of New York," and has in its background a square-rigger and the rock called Conscience Point, where the first colonists, from Lynn, Massachusetts, landed in 1640. The seal is on road signs and all town documents.

"The seal represents one race, one gender and one part of history," protests task force ex-chair Susana Powell. "History did not start in 1640. Native Americans were here long before that."[41] Adds the Anti-Bias Task Force chairman Robert Zeller, the seal is inaccurate. "They didn't wear loincloths here the year round, it was too cold."[42] Perhaps the seal can be altered to put the Shinnecock Indian into something nice from L. L. Bean.

BUT IT IS the South and anything associated with the Lost Cause that is today's inflamed front of the culture war. In 1898, President McKinley, a veteran of Antietam, could go to Atlanta, stand for the playing of "Dixie," wave his hat to his old enemies, and recommend the preservation of Confederate graves—a splendid gesture that helped heal a country about to go to war with Spain. Today, McKinley would be charged with giving moral sanction to a racist cause. One hundred years after McKinley's beau geste, America's cultural elite is almost slavishly on the side of those who wish to dishonor every banner and disgrace every leader associated with the Confederate States of America.

• In Richmond, which was defended for four years by his Army of Northern Virginia, Robert E. Lee's portrait was ordered removed from a display of famous Virginians, and the painting was then desecrated by vandals.[43] On Monument Avenue, where statues of the four great sons of the Confederacy stand—Lee, Jackson, Stuart, and Davis—a statue of black tennis star Arthur Ashe stands in their midst, put there to disrupt and contradict the symbolism. Lee-Jackson Day has been severed from Martin Luther King Day, and many believe it will soon be terminated in Virginia, where both Confederate heroes lie buried.

• After a decade-long boycott led by the NAACP, the Confederate battle flag was ordered down from the South Carolina capitol, which still bears the scars of the shelling by Sherman's army, which burned Columbia to the ground. South Carolinians wanted to keep the flag where it had flown since 1962, after President Eisenhower urged Americans to memorialize the centennial of the war. But what South Carolina wanted did not matter. Conventions were canceled. Entertainers and athletes threatened not to appear in the state. The legislature capitulated, and the flag came down, moved to a battle monument on the capitol grounds. But that did not satisfy the NAACP. The boycott continues until the flag disappears.

• Georgia, threatened with a boycott, abolished its state flag, which had a replica of the Confederate battle flag, prompting ex-Atlanta mayor Maynard Jackson to thank the governor, "who fought to get rid of the swastika."[44]

• In Texas, on the orders of Gov. George W. Bush, two plaques to Confederate war dead, paid for from a Confederate widows' fund, were removed from the state Supreme Court building.[45]

• In Florida, on February 2, 2001, Gov. Jeb Bush removed the Confederate battle flag from atop the state capitol in Tallahassee, where it had flown since 1978.[46]

• In Mississippi, students at Ole Miss have been forbidden by court order from waving tiny battle flags in the stadium. Boycotts of the state were threatened if Mississippi's flag was not altered to remove the replica of the battle flag. But when the issue was put to a statewide vote, in April 2001, the old flag won by two to one.[47] It seems that Southern politicians of both parties, to pacify minorities and placate a national cultural elite, are ignoring the will of the people they are elected to represent.

• In Harpers Ferry, West Virginia, there is a stone memorial to the freedman Hayward Shepherd, the baggagemaster who was the first man killed in John Brown's terrorist raid on the federal arsenal, which was crushed by marines led by Bvt. Col. Robert E. Lee and Lt. J. E. B. Stuart.[48] The memorial, near the corner of Potomac and Shenandoah, was put there in 1931 by the United Daughters of the Confederacy. An inscription states that Hayward Shepherd exemplified "the character and faithfulness of thousands of Negroes who, under so many temptations throughout subsequent years of war, so conducted themselves that no stain was left upon a record which is the peculiar heritage of the American people and an everlasting tribute to the best of both races." While the stone has been covered for years, repeated efforts to have it removed have thus far failed.

• At Point Lookout Cemetery in southern Maryland, a Memorial Day tradition of putting tiny Confederate flags on the graves of the four thousand Southern soldiers who died in the Union prison there was ended by the Department of Veterans Affairs.[49] In 1997, Maryland ordered a recall of the license plates issued to the Sons of Confederate Veterans, which carried a tiny image of the battle flag. The SCV was the only one of 215 nonprofit organizations to have its plates rejected.[50]

• At Antietam, a campaign is underway to prevent the erection, even on private property, of any statues to the Confederate commanders at that bloodiest of battles on American soil. Of 104 statues there now, only 4 honor Southerners.[51]

• In Selma, the Alabama town defended by Gen. Nathan Bedford Forrest, a statue to the Civil War legend has been repeatedly trashed. The city council wants it down. Memphis's City Council has proposed turning the city's Confederate Memorial Park, which also features a statue of Forrest, into a memorial park for cancer victims.[52]

Forrest was the greatest cavalry commander America has ever produced, and though a slave trader before the war who "embraced the Klan as a weapon in a savage fight for individual and sectional survival," Forrest "thrust [the Klan] away soon after he saw that it injured, instead of aided, the best interests of the South and the nation."[53] Following a lynching in 1874 in Trenton, Tennessee, General Forrest threatened to "exterminate the killers."[54] By 1875, he was urging that blacks be "allowed entry into the practice of law and anywhere else they were capable of going. Even the Great Emancipator, another Southerner born in a log cabin, never said that. . . ."[55] As columnist Walter Williams writes, Forrest always praised the bravery of the black soldiers who served in his command: "[T]hese boys stayed with me and better Confederates did not live."[56] But America is not as big a country today as the America that paid homage to Bedford Forrest as a peerless fighting man.

• "Gilmore Surrenders Virginia's Heritage" ran the headline over the front page story in the *Washington Times*.[57] Gov. James S. Gilmore III, President Bush's choice as national chairman of the Republican party, had just abolished Confederate History Month after the NAACP threatened a boycott of Virginia if the governor did not terminate the tradition.

"Va. Scraps Tribute to Confederacy" was the *Washington Post* page one headline.[58] "Striking at a core belief of the Confederate remembrance groups," wrote the *Post* reporter, "Gilmore expanded the resolution to say for the first time, 'that had there been no slavery there would have been no war.' "[59] Heritage groups argue that Lincoln's refusal to let South Carolina, Georgia, and the Gulf states depart in peace brought on the war.

The *Post* story quoted only one critic of Gilmore and was heavily weighted with comments supporting an end to Confederate History Month. With this decision, the *Post* suggested, Gilmore's national career was now on an upward trajectory:

> Black leaders generally hailed Gilmore's revised proclamation as a positive step that could be a political boost to the white conservative Republican who . . . may have his eye on a Senate seat. . . .
>
> Tony-Michelle Travis, an African American who teaches

government at George Mason University, said any aspirations for federal office that Gilmore may have could be bolstered by what she called "his [the governor's] effort to reach out."[60]

• "Carry Me Back to Old Virginny" is no longer Virginia's state song. It was removed because it contains the phrases "darkey's heart" and "old massa," though it was written in 1875 by the black composer James Bland, a New Yorker, who also wrote "Oh Dem Golden Slippers."[61]

• Book-banning has begun. *The Adventures of Huckleberry Finn*, from which "all modern American literature" proceeds, as Hemingway said, has been removed from school reading lists across America. Twain's great satirical attack on slavery, hypocrisy, and prejudice in antebellum America has as its central black character the slave Jim, a man of great dignity and moral courage. But to black educator John Wallace, who has made a career attacking it, *Huckleberry Finn* is the "most grotesque example of racist trash ever given our children to read. . . . Any teacher caught trying to use that piece of trash with our children should be fired on the spot, for he or she is either racist, insensitive, naive, incompetent, or all of the above."[62]

Hemingway, T. S. Eliot, and Lionel Trilling thought *Huckleberry Finn* an American classic, but who are they to contradict John Wallace?

Not far down the target list is Harper Lee's Pulitzer Prize–winning *To Kill a Mockingbird*, set in the segregated South before World War II, which inspired the film of the same name that gave Gregory Peck his finest role as the lawyer Atticus Finch. To those who detest the book, *To Kill a Mockingbird* represents "institutionalized racism."[63]

Opelousas Catholic High in Louisiana has the distinction of being the first U.S. high school to ban the work of Flannery O'Connor, perhaps the finest Catholic fiction writer of twentieth-

THE DEATH OF THE WEST

century America. Black parents and a black priest at Opelousas Catholic demanded that O'Connor's collection *A Good Man Is Hard to Find,* containing the short story "The Artificial Nigger," be removed from school reading lists.[64]

But, as Catholic film critic and *New York Post* columnist Ron Dreher writes, O'Connor, by featuring "white bigots as protagonists," "exposes and condemns the hellish pride that leads these characters to dismiss black people as 'niggers' and 'pickaninnies.' "[65] He writes that "The Artificial Nigger," which O'Connor considered her best work, "offers a psychologically penetrating portrait of cracker racism."[66]

Bhp. Edward O'Donnell initially fended off demands for O'Connor's purge from the curriculum by pointing out that her books were taught at Xavier, Grambling, Southern, and other black colleges. But His Eminence quickly capitulated and ordered that all O'Connor books be removed from diocesan Catholic schools and that "no similar books" replace them.[67] Any book containing racial epithets is forbidden, no matter the context, which would seem to rule out not only Twain, O'Connor, and Harper Lee, but William Faulkner and black authors Ralph Ellison and James Baldwin. Writes Dreher:

> "Essentially, O'Connor is not about race at all, which is why it is so refreshing, coming, as it does, out of such a racial culture," the black novelist Alice Walker once wrote about O'Connor. "If it can be said to be 'about' anything, then it is 'about' prophets and prophecy, 'about' revelation and 'about' the impact of supernatural grace on human beings who don't have a chance of spiritual growth without it."[68]

"Prime stuff, you would think for study in a Catholic high school in the deep South," Dreher adds.[69] Yes, you would think so.

• In 1999, Chief Justice William H. Rehnquist was admonished in a formal resolution by the National Bar Association for singing

"Dixie" at the judicial conference of the Fourth Circuit Court of Appeals.[70] Rehnquist annually attends and leads the sing-along.

Yet "Dixie" was ordered played by Lincoln himself when he visited the Confederate capital after Richmond had fallen to Grant's army. For generations after the Civil War, "Dixie" was as popular at Democratic party conventions as "Happy Days Are Here Again" after FDR. Yet the National Bar Association insists that the song is a "symbol of slavery and oppression."[71] Here are the words; let the reader be the judge:

First Verse:

> I wish I was in the land of cotton,
> Old times there are not forgotten,
> Look away, look away, look away, Dixie land.
> In Dixie land where I was born in, early on a frosty mornin',
> Look away, look away, look away, Dixie land.

Chorus:

> Then I wish I was in Dixie, hooray! Hooray!
> In Dixie land I'll take my stand, to live and die in Dixie,
> Away, away, away down south in Dixie,
> Away, away, away down south in Dixie.[72]

Not as weighty as the *Cantos* of Ezra Pound, but what does this little ditty have to do with slavery and oppression? In Gaslight Square in the St. Louis of the early 1960s, the black Dixieland jazz band closed each nightly performance with a rendition of "Dixie," followed by "The Battle Hymn of the Republic." All mellowed patrons stood, sang, and cheered both. How insensitive we all were.

By 1999, however, Justice Rehnquist was already a citizen under suspicion by the thought police for refusing to redesignate the Supreme Court's Christmas party as a "Holiday Party."[73] The singing chief justice apparently also insists on taking the lead in warbling the Christmas carols his colleagues have outlawed from America's public schools.

• Though the Cross of St. Andrew only flew over the Civil War battlefields for four years, the American flag flew for more than four generations over a country whose constitution countenanced slavery. It was thus inevitable that the turn of Old Glory would also come. And so it has. In the spring of 2001, Democratic representative Henri Brooks of Memphis, former membership chairman of the NAACP's Political Action Committee, refused to stand in the Tennessee legislature during the Pledge of Allegiance. Said Brooks: "This flag represents the former colonies that enslaved our ancestors."[74] While the NAACP "did not respond to requests" for comment on Brooks's defiance, columnist Julianne Malveaux did. It is "ridiculous," said Malveaux, for African Americans to recite the Pledge of Allegiance to the flag, for the words "are nothing but a lie, just a lie."[75] For some Americans, racial consciousness now conflicts with, and supersedes, national consciousness.

But the war on the past is not unique to America.

The new mayor of London, "Red Ken" Livingstone, wants to knock off their pedestals British generals whose names are associated with empire and rule of peoples of color. Among the statues the iconoclastic mayor wanted down are those of Adm. Sir Charles Napier, who conquered Sindh in 1843, and Sir Henry Havelock, who suppressed the Sepoy Mutiny in 1857.[76] Napier is remembered for having sent back to his commanders the coded message "*Peccavi*"—Latin for "I have sinned."

But the most famous of those whom Red Ken no longer wants in his London is Maj. Gen. Charles "Chinese" Gordon, who suppressed the Taiping Rebellion in China, helped end the slave trade, and died in Sudan when his small force suffered the fate of Custer's, fighting the dervishes of the Mahdi.[77] Gordon's head was put on a pole and brought to the Mahdi's tent, to the immense consternation of Queen

Victoria. Two decades after that battle of Khartoum, the British took their revenge at Omdurman, where eleven thousand wildly charging dervishes were cut down by the rifles and Maxim guns of General Kitchener. Among those making history's final great cavalry charge was young Winston Churchill. The Anglo-Egyptian army lost forty-eight men, and Hilaire Belloc tipped his cap to British technology:

> Whatever happens, we have got
> The Maxim gun, and they have not.[78]

Kitchener proceeded to desecrate the Mahdi's tomb and thought of using his skull as an inkstand, so perhaps his statue should come down as well. In the 1966 film *Khartoum,* the Mahdi was played by Lawrence Olivier and General Gordon by Charlton Heston, currently of the National Rifle Association. Meanwhile, plans advance to erect in Trafalgar Square, where Adm. Horatio Nelson's column stands, a nine-foot statue of Nelson Mandela.

France also hosts the new iconoclasts. When the government tried to organize a 1996 celebration to mark the fifteen-hundredth anniversary of the baptism of Clovis, king of the Franks, Socialists, Communists, and all the parties of the Left—half of France—protested any commemoration of the year that France became Christian.[79]

WHAT DO THESE incidents tell us? That those who loudly preach diversity often do not practice it, that those who decry intolerance may be found among the most intolerant. Like the Taliban and the Great Buddhas of Bamiyan, our cultural revolution intends to tear down all the flags and statues of the old America that it abhors. And it will hear no appeal.

Whether a state chooses to honor Dr. King or Robert E. Lee should be a decision for its own people. No stigma should attach to any state that chooses to honor one, both, or neither. But that is unacceptable.

Not to honor Dr. King today is intolerable. When Arizona voted not to have a holiday for King, the state was threatened with loss of the Super Bowl and convention boycotts, and berated by the national press.[80] The pressure and abuse were so unbearable that the state overturned a popular vote and ratified the holiday. Only then was Arizona permitted to rejoin the Union.

THE CITADEL IN South Carolina, one of two U.S. colleges with an all-male cadet corps, a 150-year-old tradition, was the target of repeated and bankrupting court challenges to force the school to admit women. The Citadel wanted to keep its tradition. The women of the Citadel—wives, sisters, mothers, daughters of graduates—wanted to keep the tradition. So did South Carolina. But what people want no longer matters in America. A federal court ordered the Citadel to bring women into the cadet corps.

In our Orwellian world of Newspeak, diversity means conformity. In the name of diversity, every military school must look alike. None may be all-male, even if that is what those to whom the school belongs desire. Is this freedom? Is this democracy? No. Orwell got it right: "One makes the revolution . . . to establish the dictatorship."[81] The French and Russian and Maoist and Khmer Rouge and Taliban revolutions all dethroned the old gods and desecrated their temples. So it is with our cultural revolution. It cannot abide dissent. Only after Senator McCain apologized for not having denounced the Confederate battle flag over the South Carolina capitol, and confessed to opportunism and weakness, was he restored to the good graces of the revolution.

## THE NEW HISTORY

"Every child in America should be acquainted with his own country. As soon as he opens his lips, he should rehearse the history of his

own country; he should lisp the praise of liberty, and of those illustrious heroes and statesmen, who have wrought a revolution in her
favor."[82] So said Noah Webster. So we once believed. But the cultural
revolution is purging the history "of those illustrious heroes and
statesmen" from public schools to prepare a new curriculum, to separate children from parents in their beliefs, and to cut children off
from their heritage. Said Solzhenitzyn: "To destroy a people you must
first sever their roots."[83] To create a "new people," the agents of our
cultural revolution must first create a new history; and that project is
well advanced.

In 1992, UCLA was awarded two million dollars by the National
Endowment for the Humanities and the U.S. Department of Education to develop new National History Standards for the textbooks
for children from the fifth through twelfth grades.[84] In 1997, UCLA
completed its assignment. In the history texts to be studied by American children in the public schools of the future:

- No mention was made of Samuel Adams, Paul Revere, Thomas
  Edison, Alexander Graham Bell, or the Wright Brothers.
- There were seventeen references to the Ku Klux Klan and nine
  references to Sen. Joseph R. McCarthy.
- Harriet Tubman was referenced six times, while Robert E. Lee
  was ignored.
- The founding dates of the Sierra Club and the National Organization for Women were recommended for special notice.
- Instructions for teaching students about the traitor Alger Hiss
  and executed Soviet spies Julius and Ethel Rosenberg, who gave
  the atom bomb secrets to Stalin, urged "leeway for teachers to
  teach it either way."
- The Constitutional Convention was never mentioned.
- The presidency of George Washington was unmentioned, as was
  his Farewell Address. Instead, students were "invited to construct
  a dialogue between an Indian Leader and George Washington at
  the end of the Revolutionary War."

- America's 1969 moon landing did not appear, but the Soviet Union was commended for its great "advances" in space exploration.
- The only congressional figure included was House Speaker "Tip" O'Neill, cited for calling President Reagan a "cheerleader for selfishness."
- Teachers were urged to have their pupils conduct a mock trial of John D. Rockefeller of Standard Oil.
- Students were instructed to "analyze the achievements of and grandeur of Mansa Musa's court, and the social customs and wealth of the kingdom of Mali," and to study Aztec "skills, labor system, and architecture." No mention of the quaint old Aztec custom of human sacrifice.

Were the National History Standards "flushed down the toilet," as Rush Limbaugh recommended? It would not appear so. In December 2000, the *Washington Times* reported on the new Virginia State Standards for Learning History.[85] First graders will find Pocahontas gets equal time with Capt. John Smith. In introducing younger children to the Civil War, teachers have dropped Lee and "Stonewall" Jackson. Third graders will study the "highly developed West African kingdom of Mali" of our old friend Mansa Musa. A new emphasis is to be placed on Confucianism and Indus Valley civilization. Who and what were dropped to make room for Confucius? Paul Revere, Davy Crockett, Booker T. Washington, John Paul Jones, Thanksgiving, the Pilgrims, Independence Day, and Virginia statesman Harry F. Byrd, Sr.

THE WAR ON America's past and the dumbing down of American children—to make their minds empty vessels into which the New History may be poured—is succeeding. In a recent student survey, 556 seniors, from fifty-five of the nation's top-rated colleges and universities, were asked thirty-four questions from a high school course on U.S. history. Four out of five flunked.[86] Only one-third of the college seniors could name the American general at Yorktown. Only 23 percent named Madison as the principal author of the Constitution. Only 22 percent linked the words "government of the people, by the people, and for the people" to Lincoln's Gettysburg Address. The good news—98 percent knew rapper Snoop Doggy Dog, and 99 percent identified Beavis and Butthead.[87]

"We cannot escape history," said Lincoln. But thanks to our cultural revolution, the Gen-Xers may have just done it.

Ten years ago, Jesse Jackson led a Philistine parade across the Palo Alto campus of Stanford chanting, "Hey, hey, ho, ho, Western culture's got to go."[88] Faced with so convincing an argument, Stanford replaced its required course in Western civilization with a new one, "Culture, Ideas and Values."[89] Today, not one of the fifty-five elite colleges and universities, as rated by *U.S. News and World Report,* requires a course in American history to graduate.[90]

"The debate about curriculum," writes Dr. Schlesinger, "is a debate about what it means to be an American. What is ultimately at stake is the American future."[91] But what will America's future be when it is decided by a generation oblivious to American history and suffering from cultural Alzheimer's?

About the time the UCLA standards became public, the Smithsonian Institution held its fiftieth anniversary exhibit of V-J Day. That exhibit, which featured the cockpit of the B-29 that dropped the bomb on Hiroshima, the *Enola Gay,* had ignited an explosion of veterans' and public wrath for its portrayal of America's war in the Pacific as racist. Columnist John Leo of *U.S. News* took the occasion to visit other museums on the Mall that teach tourists and schoolchildren about America's past.

At the Museum of American History, Leo found the "Science in American Life" exhibit to be a "disparaging, politically loaded look at American science, concentrating single-mindedly only on failures and dangers: DDT, Three Mile Island, the ozone hole, acid rain, the explosion of the *Challenger*, Love Canal."[92] At the Air and Space Museum, he found the airplane indicted as an invention whose primary use has been for mass slaughter. In future scripts, however, Leo found that Japanese kamikaze pilots, whose suicide crashes took a terrible toll on U.S. Navy ships and American sailors, would be painted as heroes of the air. The children of Gramsci had captured the museums of America.

Almost alone, novelist Tom Wolfe noted the astonishing absence of any celebration of the "First American Century" at its close on December 31, 1999, the eve of the millennium.

> Where was I. On the wrong page? The wrong channel? Outside the bandwidth? . . . [D]id a single solitary savant note that the First American Century had just come to an end and the Second American Century had begun?
>
> Was a single bard bestirred to write a mighty anthem—along the lines of James Thomson's "Rule, Britannia! Britannia rule the waves! Britons never shall be slaves!" for America, the nation that in the century just concluded had vanquished two barbaric nationalist brotherhoods, the German Nazis and the Russian Communists, two hordes of methodical slave-hunting predators who made the Huns and Magyars look whimsical by comparison. . . .
>
> Did any of the America-at-century's-end network TV specials strike the exuberant note that Queen Victoria's Diamond Jubilee struck in 1897?
>
> My impression was that one American Century rolled into another with all the pomp and circumstance of a mouse pad. America's great triumph inspired all the patriotism and pride . . . all of the yearning for glory and empire . . . all of the martial jubilee music of a mouse click.[93]

Who looked back in pride at all America had accomplished in the century just ended? In all the celebrations from London to New York to Tokyo to Beijing, who looked back to the Man whose two-thousandth birthday it was? Almost none, for, by the coming of the new millennium, Americans were living in a civilization, culture, and country that, in its public life, was well along the way to de-Christianization.

# EIGHT

# DE-CHRISTIANIZING AMERICA

Religion blushing veils her sacred fires,
And unawares Morality expires.[1]
— Alexander Pope

A people without religion will in the end find that it
has nothing to live for.[2]
— T. S. Eliot, 1939

In the Great War of 1914–18, Catholic France fought Catholic Austria, and Protestant Germany fought Protestant England. Nine million Christian soldiers marched to their deaths. Yet only Orthodox Russia succumbed to a Communist revolution, and that was more coup d'état than mass conversion. Gramsci concluded that two thousand years of Christianity had made the soul of Western Man impenetrable to Marxism. Before the West could be conquered, its faith must be uprooted. But how?

Gramsci's answer—a "long march" through the institutions. The Marxists must cooperate with progressives to capture the institutions that shaped the souls of the young: schools, colleges, movies, music, arts, and the new mass media that came uncensored into every home, radio, and, after Gramsci's death, television. Once the cultural institutions were captured, a united Left could begin the de-Christianization of the West. When, after several generations, this was accomplished, the West would no longer be the West, but another civilization altogether, and control of the state would inevitably follow control of the culture.

But, as Christianity began to die in the West, something else occurred: Western peoples began to stop having children. For the correlation between religious faith and large families is absolute. The more devout a people, whether Christian, Muslim, or Jewish, the higher its birthrate. In New Square, New York, in the first wholly Orthodox Jewish community in the United States, the average family has ten children.[3] In Kostroma, Russia, Vladimir Alexeyev, father of a poster family of sixteen children, and his pregnant wife have a home full of icons. "Even before we were believers," Alexeyev told the AP, "we found meaning in this."[4] In the Baptist state of Texas, the birthrate among whites is higher than among white folks in sybaritic California. Wherever secularism triumphs, populations begin to shrink and die.

In 1999, Pope John Paul II convoked a continental Episcopal Synod to take the pulse of the faith in the Old Continent. The news was not good. Secularism, reported the bishops, "poisons a large section of Christians in Europe. There is a great risk of de-Christianization and paganization of the Continent."[5] Fewer than 10 percent of the young people in Belgium, Germany, and France attend church regularly. There is not a major city in northwest Europe where half the newborns are baptized.

A 1999 *Newsweek* survey found that 39 percent of the French profess no religion and only 56 percent of the English believe in a personal God.[6] In Italy, only 15 percent attended Sunday mass, while in the Czech Republic, Sunday attendance at church barely reaches 3 percent.[7] What we are creating, said Czech president Vaclav Havel, is "the first atheistic civilization in the history of mankind."[8] Havel went on to ask:

> Could not the whole nature of our current civilization with its shortsightedness, with its proud emphasis on the human individual . . . and with its boundless trust in humanity's ability

to embrace the universal by rational cognition, could it not all be but the natural manifestation of a simple phenomenon which, in simple terms, amounts to the loss of God.[9]

But as this new "atheistic civilization" rises in Europe, the peoples needed to sustain it have begun to die. It appears an iron law: Kill a nation's faith, and its people will cease to reproduce. Foreign armies or immigrants then enter and fill the empty spaces. By de-Christianizing America, the cultural revolution has found a contraceptive as effective as the little pill of Dr. Rock. But how did a nation as "churched" as America and as steeped in traditional Christianity as the United States in the 1950s permit itself to be publicly de-Christianized, almost without a fight?

"AMERICA IS A Christian nation," Gov. Kirk Fordice famously said back in 1992.[10] Before the Mississippi governor sat down, he was being denounced as an intolerant bigot for not using "Judeo-Christian." Yet, as Gary DeMar writes in *America's Christian History: The Untold Story,* the governor was right about America's origins and first 250 years.

The earliest settlements in America were Protestant enterprises. Jews and Catholics were only tiny minorities. When the author was in parochial school in the 1940s, nuns spoke proudly of how *one* of fifty-seven signers of the Declaration of Independence was a Catholic: Charles Carroll of Carrollton, Maryland.

In the First Charter of Virginia, the colonists' declared goal is to "spread the Christian religion to such people as yet live in darkness and miserable ignorance of the true knowledge and worship of God." "In the name of God, Amen" are the first six words of the Mayflower Compact, which proceeds, "by the grace of God . . . having undertaken for the glory of God and advancement of the Christian faith . . ." In the Fundamental Orders of Connecticut in 1639, the assembled declared, "The word of God requires that to maintain the peace and union of such a people there should be orderly and decent government established according to God . . . to preserve the liberty and purity of the Gospel of our Lord Jesus Christ."[11]

Reflecting on this history at a prayer breakfast of the International Council of Christian Leadership in 1954, Chief Justice Earl Warren said:

> I believe no one can read the history of our country without realizing that the Good Book and the spirit of the Savior have from the beginning been our guiding geniuses. . . . Whether we look to the first Charter of Virginia . . . or to the Charter of New England . . . or to the Charter of Massachusetts Bay . . . or to the Fundamental Orders of Connecticut . . . the same objective is present: a Christian land governed by Christian principles.[12]

DeMar establishes the truth beyond refutation. A century before Governor Fordice, the U.S. Supreme Court declared in 1892, "This is a Christian nation."[13] "America was born a Christian nation," said New Jersey governor Woodrow Wilson in 1911, "born to exemplify that devotion to the elements of righteousness which are derived from the revelations of the Holy Scripture."[14] In 1931, Justice George Sutherland reaffirmed the court's 1892 decision, calling Americans "a Christian people."[15]

At Placentia Bay, where he crafted the Atlantic Charter with Winston Churchill, FDR declared that America was "founded on the principles of Christianity" and led the American and British sailors in singing "Onward Christian Soldiers."[16] In a 1947 letter to Pius XII, Harry Truman affirmed, "This is a Christian nation."[17] In a 1951 Supreme Court decision, Justice William Douglas wrote, "We are a religious people and our institutions presuppose the existence of a Supreme Being."[18] Added Jimmy Carter, "We have a responsibility to try to shape government so that it does exemplify the will of God."[19]

The reaction to Fordice—visceral, bristling, hostile—tells us more about our cultural elite than about the beliefs of the Great Silent Majority. But the cultural revolution has been rewriting history and replacing true history with bogus history—that America never was a Christian country and only bigots like Governor Fordice insist on saying so. As for President Carter's assertion that we have a "responsibility to try to shape government so that it does exemplify the will of God," that, according to the Supreme Court, is forbidden by the First Amendment. If you wish to reshape American society through law, says the court, you may use as guides the books written by Karl Marx, Rachel Carson, Betty Friedan, or Al Gore, but not the books written by Matthew, Mark, Luke, or John.

HOW WAS AMERICA de-Christianized? Answer: Tyrannically, and with surprisingly small resistance from a people whose forebears rank among history's fiercest enemies of undemocratic rule.

Half a century ago, the Supreme Court was captured by judicial ideologues who understood its latent power to reshape society. Using the incorporation clause of the Fourteenth Amendment, the Court asserted a right to impose on the states all the restrictions the Constitution had imposed on Congress. At that point, the Tenth Amendment was dead, and the states of the Union became subject provinces of the Supreme Court.

Where the First Amendment prohibited Congress from making any law "respecting an establishment of religion," and required Congress to respect the "free exercise" of faith, the Supreme Court reinterpreted the words to justify a preemptive strike on Christianity. All Christian Bibles, books, crosses, symbols, ceremonies, and holidays were ordered out of the public square and public schools. Out went Adam and Eve; in came *Heather Has Two Mommies*. Out went paintings of Christ ascending into heaven; in came pictures of apes ascending into *Homo erectus*. Out went Easter; in came Earth Day. Out went Bible teachings about the immorality of homosexuality; in came the homosexuals to teach about the immorality of homophobia. Out went the Commandments; in came the condoms.

Going back fifty years, the Supreme Court has inflicted an almost uninterrupted string of defeats upon the faith of our fathers. In 1948, voluntary religious instruction was outlawed in public schools. In 1962, school prayer went. In 1963, voluntary daily reading from the Bible was declared unconstitutional. In 1980, a Kentucky law that called for posting the Ten Commandments on classroom walls was overturned because the Commandments serve "no secular purpose." In 1985, Alabama's "moment of silence" at the start of the school day was declared unconstitutional. In 1989, the Supreme Court ordered a Nativity scene removed from the grounds of the Allegheny County Courthouse outside Pittsburgh. In 1992, all prayers at high school graduations were prohibited. In 2000, students were forbidden to pray over the loudspeakers at high school games.

Having sat for three decades on the bench, Chief Justice Rehnquist had heard enough and issued a stinging dissent. This Court's decision, said Rehnquist,

> bristles with hostility to all things religious in public life. . . . Neither the holding nor the tone of the opinion is faithful to the meaning of the Establishment Clause, when it is recalled that George Washington himself, at the request of the very Congress which passed the Bill of Rights, proclaimed a day of "public thanksgiving and prayer to be observed acknowledging with grateful hearts the many and signal favors of Almighty God."[20]

Imitation is the sincerest form of flattery. Sensing Christianity was on the run, lower courts began to outdo the Supreme Court. In 1996, the Ninth Circuit ruled that a large cross erected as a war memorial in a public park in Eugene, Oregon, violated the Constitution. In 1999, the Sixth Circuit ordered the Cleveland Board of Education to cease opening its meetings with a prayer, though Congress does every day. The Eleventh Circuit outlawed any invocations, prayers, or benedictions at high school graduations.

Since 1959, Ohio has had as its state motto, "With God, All Things Are Possible." It is used on state documents and tax forms, and is on a bronze plate in the sidewalk at the entrance to the statehouse. In 2000, a three-judge panel of the Sixth Circuit ordered the motto removed. Why? Because the words come from the New Testament. Even worse, they are Christ's own words. Had Ohio adopted as a motto Nietszche's "God is dead" or the line from Dostoyevsky's *Brothers Karamazov* that states that if God is dead, all things are permissible, that would be fine.

Shock rocker Marilyn Manson once said, "Each age has to have at least one brave individual that tries to bring an end to Christianity, which no one has managed to succeed [sic] yet."[21] Cheer up, Marilyn, the Supreme Court is in your corner. In May 2001, it upheld a U.S. appellate court decision ordering Elkhart, Indiana, to remove a six-foot granite pillar engraved with the Ten Commandments from the lawn of City Hall. The pillar had stood for over forty years. By six to three, the Court refused to hear the town's appeal. However, a dissenting chief justice pointed out to his colleagues that a portrait of Moses carrying those same Ten Commandments adorns a wall in the Supreme Court's own courtroom.[22]

RELIGIOUS RIVALRY IS a zero-sum game. Every gain for one faith is a loss for another. The rise of Christianity was recognized as a mortal threat in Jerusalem by Saul of Tarsus, who held the coats of the men who stoned St. Stephen the Martyr. Islam's conquest of Arabia and North Africa alarmed Christian Europe. The Reformation and the rise of Protestantism were a crisis for Rome. Where communism triumphed, Christians went to the wall. And when secularism was awarded custody of America's schools, it was a crushing defeat for Christianity.

From kindergarten through twelfth grade, the public schools shape the hearts and minds of America's children and the future of the nation. This is where children are taught what to believe, what to value, how to think, how to live. Now, Christianity, like some vagrant, has been ordered off the school grounds, another bloodless coup of the revolution. How great a defeat was it? Spend an hour with the *Humanist Manifesto* of 1973.

You will find there the dogmas that govern what is now taught, and what is no longer taught, in public schools. "Faith in a prayer-hearing God . . . is an unproved and outmoded faith."[23] "Traditional moral codes . . . fail to meet the pressing needs of today."[24] "Promises of immortal salvation or fear of eternal damnation are both illusory and harmful."[25] "Science affirms that the human species is an emergence from natural evolutionary forces."[26] Children emerge from schools receptive to these ideas, because they have been imparted by their teachers in what was included and what was excluded from classroom discussions where Christianity was an unwelcome intruder.

Secular humanists have not concealed their agenda. Their manifesto asserts a "right to birth control, abortion and divorce," and adds, "The many varieties of sexual behavior should not in themselves be considered 'evil.' "[27] Freedom "includes a recognition of an individual's right to die in dignity, euthanasia and the right to suicide."[28] Now that the exorcists of the ACLU have purged Christianity from the public schools, these secularist dogmas are taught as truth to children. Thus, while America remains a predominantly Christian society and country, her public institutions and popular culture have been thoroughly de-Christianized.

REMARKABLY, THIS MANIFESTO was published within months of Richard Nixon and Spiro Agnew rolling up a forty-nine-state landslide over the choice of Consciousness III, George McGovern, in the "acid, amnesty, and abortion" campaign of 1972. But despite liberal defeats in 1972, 1980, 1984, 1988, and 1994, the *Humanist Manifesto*—miles outside America's mainstream when first published—is being gradually implemented by the Democratic party as Republican resistance fades. On one point, however, the manifesto is deceptive. It asserts that "the separation of church and state and the separation of ideology and state are imperatives."[29] But secular humanism *is* a faith, the faith of America's elite, and it is being imposed by the Supreme Court. Perhaps the greatest success of Christianity's great rival is to have convinced Christians it is not a rival, just ideas reached by reason alone.

Christians have been dispossessed by a militant minority, whose beliefs were alien to Middle America, but which managed to have its allies capture the Supreme Court and impose its agenda by diktat. Whatever may be said against the ACLU, it does not lack for patience and perseverance. As Cervantes said, give the devil his due.

Christians who still believe the Court only created a level playing field for all faiths are whistling past the graveyard. The Court just took their stadium into receivership and turned it over to their rivals. What Christians have lost, they will not get back without a struggle. In *When Nations Die,* Jim Nelson Black is particularly hard on Evangelicals:

> But one of the greatest reasons for the decline of American society over the past century has been the tendency of Christians who have practical solutions to abandon the forum at the first sign of resistance. Evangelicals in particular have been quick to run and slow to stand by their beliefs. In reality, most Christians had already vacated "the public square" of moral and political debate by their own free will, long before civil libertarians and others came forth to drive us back to our churches.[30]

This may be too harsh, but Christians need a wake-up call if they are not to lose their country, and they need leaders prepared to fight to save it. C. S. Lewis warned against a spirit of compromise that was but a cloak to cover up the nakedness of irresolution and timidity:

> As Christians we are tempted to make unnecessary concessions to those outside the Faith. We give in too much . . . there comes a time when we must show that we disagree. We must show our Christian colours, if we are to be true to Jesus Christ. We cannot remain silent or concede everything away.[31]

By the twenty-first century, the de-Christianization of our public life was complete. Easter celebrations, Nativity scenes, Christmas carols, and Christian books, stories, pageants, and holidays had all but vanished from public schools and the public square. The schools were no longer run according to the wishes of the parents of the children who attend them, or the taxpayers who sustain them, but according to the dictates of courts imposing the agendas of the ACLU and *Humanist Manifesto*.

In Republic, Missouri, the ACLU, suing on behalf of a Wiccan witch, managed to get the image of a fish cut out of the city seal because the "symbol is often found in Christian establishments, not non-Christian ones, and . . . most of the people who wrote letters supporting the fish identified it as a Christian symbol."[32]

In May 2001, the ACLU sued the Virginia Military Institute on behalf of two students who wanted to put an end to the saying of grace before evening meals.

The dethronement of God from American public life was not done democratically, it was done dictatorially, and our forefathers would never have tolerated it. Why did people of a once-fighting faith permit it, when prayer, Christmas carols, Bible reading, and posting the Ten Commandments were backed by huge majorities? Because we live under a rule of judges, Congress is unwilling to confront. If America has ceased to be a Christian country, it is because she has ceased to be a democratic country. This is the real coup d'état.

"Here, sir, the people rule!" Americans once proudly boasted. It is no longer true. We do not live by majority rule in America. We live under the rule of minorities whose vision of what America ought to be is shared by five justices on the Supreme Court, most of whom not one in ten Americans could name.

WITH THE DE-CHRISTIANIZATION of America has come the overthrow of the old moral order based on Judeo-Christian teachings and the establishment of the new moral order of the *Humanist Manifesto*. Again, this was not done by popular vote, but by court order. Abortion had been a crime; now it is a right. So sayeth the Court. Voluntary school prayer now violates the First Amendment, but nude nightclub dancing no longer does. When Colorado voted in a referendum to stop the legalization of homosexuality, the Supreme Court decided that the motives of the voters were suspect and threw it out.

"Our law and our institutions must necessarily be based upon and embody the teachings of the Redeemer of mankind," said the Supreme Court in the 1892 decision *Church of the Holy Trinity v. United States*. "Our civilization and our institutions are emphatically Christian."[33] That America has been abolished, by order of a different Court. The old moral consensus has collapsed, and the moral community built upon it no longer exists.

Seeing Americans bow to its will, the Supreme Court became supremely confident in its coup. In the *Richmond Newspapers* decision (1980), Justice William J. Brennan described the new order. Judges, he wrote, "are not mere umpires, but, in their own sphere, lawmakers."[34] In 1985, he told Georgetown Law School, "Majoritarian process has appeal under some circumstances, but I think ultimately it will not do." It is the Court's role "to declare certain values transcendent, beyond the reach of temporary political majorities."[35] What Justice Brennan meant was that his personal values were transcendent, the will of the American majority notwithstanding.

"The Court, not the people, is now the agent of change in American society," writes Prof. William Quirk, coauthor of *Judicial Dicta-*

*torship*. This contradicts what Jefferson called the "mother principle, that 'governments are republican only in proportion as they embody the will of the people, and execute it.' "[36]

Warren, Douglas, Brennan, and Blackmun have triumphed. We no longer have a republic. And Christianity, driven out of the public square, is slowly losing its hold. In a 1999 Gallup Poll, 62 percent of young adults said religion was losing influence in American life.[37] Another study revealed, "America has more atheists and agnostics than Mormons, Jews or Muslims."[38] Of fourteen million nonbelievers, half are Gen-Xers and 31 percent baby boomers. Only 42 percent of Americans still believe Christianity is the one true faith.[39] In a 1996 Princeton survey, 62 percent of Protestants and 74 percent of Catholics said all religious faiths were equally good.[40] America remains the most "Christianized" nation of the West, but for millions it is not the demanding and fighting faith of old. What Catholic evangelist Bhp. Fulton J. Sheen predicted in 1931 has come to pass. We are producing, said Sheen,

a group of sophomoric latitudinarians who think there is no difference between God as Cause and God as a "mental projection"; who equate Christ and Buddha, Saint Paul and John Dewey; and then enlarge their broad-mindedness into a sweeping synthesis that says not only that one Christian sect is just as good as another, but even that one world-religion is just as good as another.[41]

Yet, no court ordered any church to rewrite its prayers, hymns, or Bibles to conform to the new secular catechism. This the churches have done, voluntarily and even eagerly. Why? For the most human of reasons.

As many young priests and pastors themselves no longer believed in the inerrancy of the truths they had been taught, and they did not want to be left behind as the young departed, they attempted the impossible: to reconcile Christianity to the counterculture. But in their desperation to make themselves relevant, they only made themselves ridiculous.

"Amazing grace how sweet the sound that saved a wretch like me" is the opening line of perhaps the most famous of all hymns, written by repentant slave ship captain John Newton in 1779. In some hymnals that has been changed to "that saved and strengthened me," or "that saved and set me free."[42] Why? To get away from the uncomfortable idea of man's sinfulness and his need to accept Jesus Christ as his Savior.

The stanza of "America the Beautiful" that contains the lines, "O beautiful for pilgrim feet / Whose stern impassioned stress / A thoroughfare for freedom beat . . ." has been dropped in some hymnals and song books.[43] Why? Because, says Rev. Harold Jacobs of the Lumbee Indian tribe, "white men have trampled over the Indian to beat that freedom path."[44]

"Whiter than snow, dear Lord, / Wash me now . . ." from "Have Thine Own Way, Lord" is now rendered in some hymnals as "Wash me just now, Lord / Wash me just now."[45] It seems that "Whiter than snow" has racist connotations. "Father, Son and Holy Ghost" is being replaced with "Creator, Redeemer, and Sustainer" to make the phrase more gender-neutral.[46] New York's Riverside Church prefers "Father, Son and Holy Spirit, One God, Mother of us all."[47]

Mother of God, pray for us.

"Onward, Christian Soldiers" and "Am I a Soldier of the Cross" have been denounced as excessively militaristic. "He Leadeth Me" and "Dear Lord and Father of Mankind" are chauvinistic. "God Rest Ye Merry Gentlemen" is exclusionary. "Faith of Our Fathers" is naturally under fire. Those who love the hymn, but like not the lyrics, may use "mothers" or "ancestors." "God of Our Fathers" has become "God of the Ages." Instead of "Son of Man," some congregations prefer "the Human One."

In 1980, the National Council of Churches established a committee of feminist academics to write a nonsexist lectionary. "Lord" was replaced with "Sovereign One," "Son of God" with "Child of God."

God's decision to create Eve for Adam was rewritten to read: "It is not good that the human being should be alone; I will make a companion corresponding to the creature."[48]

When Volume I of the *Inclusive Language Lectionary* appeared in 1983, writes Michael Nelson, a political science professor at Rhodes College, "after a week or so of alternative outrage and hilarity, the larger church abandoned it to gather dust."[49]

On his deathbed, the atheist Voltaire said, "I have never made but one prayer to God. Oh Lord! Make my enemies look ridiculous. And God has answered it."[50] No court forced these churches to make fools of themselves. They wanted to be relevant and made themselves irrelevant. And before berating fifteen-year-olds for caving in to peer pressures on sex and drugs, consider the performance of their moral superiors.

## NOW, THE PROVOCATIONS

In the Communist lexicon, peaceful coexistence did not mean peace. It meant continuing the struggle by means other than war. So, too, the struggle for moral hegemony will end only when one side is defeated and the other triumphs. If traditionalists believe that they can peacefully coexist with the cultural revolution, they might revisit the recent controversies at the National Endowment for the Arts, for most involved desecrations of Christian images and deliberate affronts to Christianity's moral code.

Andreas Serrano's *Piss Christ* was a photograph of a large crucifix immersed in his urine. Robert Mapplethorpe twisted an altarlike image of the Virgin Mary into a bloody tie rack and featured a photograph of himself with a bullwhip protruding from his rectum. In *Queer City,* a "poet" depicted Jesus in an act of perversion with a six-year-old boy. In an art catalog funded by the NEA, an AIDS activist called the late Card. John O'Connor a "fat cannibal from that house of walking swastikas up on Fifth Avenue."[51] That house was St. Patrick's Cathedral, desecrated by homosexuals who spat out consecrated hosts at Sunday mass. The altarpiece of the 1999 "Sensations" exhibit at the Brooklyn Museum of Art was *The Holy Virgin Mary,* a painting with the visage of the Mother of God splattered with elephant dung, with a halo of female genitalia. In an adjacent room were half a dozen life-size mannequins of naked little girls with penises sprouting from their bodies.

"Art is what you can get away with," said Andy Warhol, but Picasso saw it as having a more serious purpose. "Art" he said, "is not to decorate apartments. Art is a weapon of revolution. . . ."[52] Wheeler Williams, one of America's great sculptors, "acknowledged that the purpose of modern art 'was to destroy man's faith in his cultural heritage.' "[53] In other words, art is but another front of the cultural revolution's relentless war on Christianity.

In 2001, Brooklyn Museum hosted Renee Cox's *Yo Mama's Last Supper,* featuring a photo of a stark-naked Ms. Cox as Jesus, with eleven black friends as apostles and a white man as Judas.[54] When Mayor Giuliani denounced the "pattern of anti-Catholicism at Brooklyn Museum" and announced a commission to set "decency standards," Bronx borough president Fernando Ferrer said the proposal "sounds like Berlin in 1939."[55]

In truth, the obscene and vile abuse that the arts colony heaps upon Catholics and their holiest symbols does recall Berlin in 1939, specifically Julius Streicher's *Der Stürmer,* which treated Jews and their beliefs the way Mapplethorpe, Serrano, and Cox treat Catholics and their beliefs. The difference? Anti-Catholicism, the anti-Semitism of the intellectuals, is the bigotry du jour of the cultural establishment. And that prejudice is not confined to our cultural capitals.

Early in 2001, Santa Fe's Museum of International Folk Art featured a computerized photo collage of Our Lady of Guadalupe, naked except for a bikini of roses, and held up by a bare-breasted angel.[56] When Arch. Michael J. Sheehan protested and angry demonstrators showed up, State Museum director Thomas Wilson said, "We never expected anything like this."[57] Exhibit curator Tey Marianna Nunn was puzzled, telling the *New York Times* that "reimaging" Our Lady

of Guadalupe, the holiest icon of Mexican Americans, is quite common, and the Virgin Mother has been portrayed as a Barbie doll, a
karate kicker, and a tattooed lesbian.[58]

Art, it is said, is the mirror of the soul. T. S. Eliot called art the
incarnation of a people's religion. If that is true, who or what inhabits
the souls of these "artists"? What would happen if they mocked the
Holocaust by presenting a computerized photo collage of a naked
Anne Frank frolicking with SS troops at Auschwitz? Or put on a
satirical minstrel show that mocked Dr. King?

We know the answer. When the French company Alcatel, with
permission of the King family, used film of King's speech at the Lincoln Memorial in a TV ad, Julian Bond of the NAACP said, "Some
things ought to be sacred."[59] In the new paganism a pornographic
image of the Blessed Virgin Mary is permissible, but Dr. King's words
are sacrosanct.

Years ago, when the film *The Prophet* came out, in which the face
of Muhammad was shown, an act of blasphemy to Islam, theaters
refused to run it for fear of violent retaliation. When Salman Rushdie
published *Satanic Verses,* a novel judged an obscene insult by Islam,
he spent years hiding from the fatwa, a death sentence imposed by
the Ayatollah Khomeini. Now, fatwas and firebombings are not the
American way of protest, but economic boycotts and political retribution are. When Christians were told to "turn the other cheek," it
was for offenses against them, not against God. Christ himself used
a whip to drive the money changers out of the temple.

IN 1990, EDITOR James F. Cooper of *American Arts Quarterly* ran
a want ad. As Horace Greeley had admonished Civil War veterans to
"Go West, young man!" Cooper exhorted Cold War veterans, "Recapture the culture!"[60] Conservatives, he said,

> seemingly never read Mao Tse-tung on waging cultural war
> against the West. [Mao's] essays were prescribed reading for

the Herbert Marcuse-generation of the 1960s, who now run
our cultural institutions. . . . Conservatives were oblivious to
the fact that . . . modern art—long separated from the idealism
of Manet, Degas, Cezanne and Rodin—had become the pur-
veyor of a destructive, degenerate, ugly, pornographic, Marxist,
anti-American ideology.[61]

To these assaults upon their God, their beliefs, their sacred sym-
bols, and their sainted heros and heroines by Serrano, Mapplethorpe,
Cox & Co., the response of Christians has been feeble, even pathetic.
As Regis Philbin likes to say, "Is that your final answer?"

## GAY RIGHTS AND CIVIL RIGHTS?

The struggle for the soul of America is not going to fade away. In the
spring of 2000, a lesbian student at Tufts University filed a charge of
discrimination against the campus chapter of the Inter-Varsity Christian Fellowship for refusing to permit her to serve on its leadership
council. In its defense, a chapter leader responded, "When you ask
us to give up the Bible, you're asking us to give up the heart of our
religion."[62]

Result: A student court ordered Tufts Christian Fellowship de-
recognized, defunded, and denied the right to meet on campus. The
chapter was told to drop Tufts from its name. A majority of students
applauded the tribunal. Not to treat homosexuals equally, they said,
is bigotry. After taking its case public, TCF won a reversal. But this
is a harbinger of what is coming.

What happened at Tufts was a collision of faiths. The catechism
of the revolution teaches that homosexuality is a preference, not a
sin, and that those who treat gays and lesbians differently are bigots
who must be exposed and reeducated. In biblical Christianity, homosexuality is unnatural and immoral. And this is the heart of the
culture war: Whose beliefs shall be the basis of law? At Tufts, the
new faith briefly replaced the old, and Christians were ordered to

conform or leave. The revolution will coexist until it attains hegemony. Then it will dictate.


BUT WHICH STATEMENT is true? Is homosexuality a moral disorder or a moral and legitimate lifestyle? Dr. Charles Socarides, author
of numerous books and winner of the Distinguished Professor Award
of the Association of Psychoanalytic Psychologists of the British
Health Service, has treated homosexuals for forty years. He has helped
a third of his patients to lead normal lives by marrying and having
children. Dr. Socarides describes how the cultural revolution changed
what was a "pathology" into a "lifestyle." The "reinventers," he writes,

> didn't go after the nation's clergy. They targeted the members
> of a worldly priesthood, the psychiatric community, and neu-
> tralized them with a radical redefinition of homosexuality itself.
> In 1972 and 1973, they coopted the leaders of the American
> Psychiatric Association and through a series of maneuvers, lies
> and outright flim-flams, they "cured" homosexuality over-
> night—by fiat. They got the A.P.A. to say that same-sex was
> "not a disorder." It was merely a "condition"—as neutral as
> left-handedness.[63]

"Those of us who didn't go along with the political redefinition,"
said Dr. Socarides, "were soon silenced at our own professional meetings. Our lectures were canceled inside academe and our research
papers turned down in the learned journals. Worse things were to
follow in the culture at large."[64] What were they?

> Television and movie producers began to do stories promoting
> homosexuality as a legitimate lifestyle. A gay review board told
> Hollywood how it should deal or not deal with homosexuality.
> Mainstream publishers turned down books that objected to the
> gay revolution. Gays and lesbians influenced sex education in
> our nation's schools and gay and lesbian libbers seized wide

control of faculty committees in our nation's college[s]. State legislatures nullified laws against sodomy.[65]

In *Philadelphia,* Tom Hanks portrayed a lawyer with AIDS who is victimized by bigoted colleagues. Hollywood gave Hanks an Oscar for his politically correct performance. But Socarides, who claims a cure rate for homosexuals as good as the Betty Ford Clinic, never gave up. Nor should traditionalists. For homosexuality is not liberation, it is slavery. It is not a lifestyle; it is a death style. With the onset of AIDS, Dr. Socarides's own patients would tell him, "Doctor, if I weren't in therapy, I'd be dead."[66]

Those who believe the gay rights movement is the twenty-first century's civil rights movement miss a basic difference. The civil rights cause could successfully invoke the Bible, natural law, and Thomas Jefferson on behalf of equal justice under law. Gay rights cannot. Jefferson considered homosexuality worse than bestiality. As governor of Virginia in 1779, he urged the same punishment for sodomy as for rape.[67] The Bible, Catholic doctrine, and natural law hold the practice to be abhorrent and a society that embraces it to be decadent. Christians are to reform such societies or separate from them.

In *Letter from a Birmingham Jail,* Martin Luther King wrote, "A just law is a man-made code that squares with the moral law or the law of God. An unjust law is a code that is out of Harmony with the moral law. To put it in the terms of St. Thomas Aquinas: An unjust law is a law that is not rooted in eternal law and natural law."[68] But gay rights laws do not square with the "law of God." They are not "rooted in eternal law or natural law." By Dr. King's conditions, gay rights laws are unjust laws "out of Harmony" with the moral law. When imposed, they will be resisted by Christians. Hardly a formula for national unity.

The only way the gay rights movement can succeed in making society accept homosexuality as natural, normal, moral, and healthy is to first de-Christianize that society. And, admittedly, they are making headway.

## THE GREAT EXPERIMENT

What we are attempting is truly audacious. Like Lucifer and Adam, Western Man has decided he can disobey God without consequence and become his own God. In casting off Christianity, Western Man is saying: "Through medical and biological science, we have learned how to prevent life, how to prolong life, how to create life, how to clone life. Through our military technology, we know how to win wars now without losing a single soldier. Through our understanding of monetary and fiscal policy, we know how to prevent depressions. Soon we will know how to prevent recessions. Our global economy promises prosperity for all through free markets and free trade. Global democracy will bring us world peace, and we have in place the institutions of a world government. Time and goodwill will take us there. God was a good flight instructor, but now we no longer need Him. We will take over from here."

The de-Christianization of America is a great gamble, a roll of the dice, with our civilization as the stakes. America has thrown overboard the moral compass by which the republic steered for two hundred years, and now it sails by dead reckoning. Reason alone, without Revelation, sets our course. The Founding Fathers warned that this was a bridge too far. No country could remain free unless virtuous, they said, and virtue could not exist in the absence of faith. Do not "indulge the supposition that morality can be maintained without religion," said Washington in his Farewell Address. "Of all the dispositions and habits which lead to prosperity, religion and morality are indispensable supports."[69] John Adams agreed: "Our constitution was made only for a moral and religious people. It is wholly inadequate to the government of any other."[70] Consider what has happened to our society with the overthrow of the old moral order.

- One in four children born to white women are out of wedlock. In 1960, it was 2 percent.[71] Three in four unmarried white women have had affairs by age nineteen. In 1900, the figure was 6 percent.[72] Teenage suicides are triple what they were in the early 1960s.[73] The test scores of high school students are now among the lowest of the industrialized nations.

- Abortions in the United States now run at 1.2–1.4 million per year, the highest rate in the West, with 40 million performed since *Roe v. Wade*. Births to married women in the United States, 4 million in 1960, fell to 2.7 million in 1996.[74]
- The U.S. divorce rate is up 350 percent since 1962, and one-third of all American children now live in single-parent homes.[75]
- Nearly 2 million Americans are in jails or prison, 4.5 million on probation or parole. In 1980, the prison and jail population was 500,000.[76]
- There are six million narcotics addicts in the United States.[77]
- In the African-American community, 69 percent of all births are out of wedlock, two-thirds of the children live in single-parent homes, and 28.5 percent of the boys can expect to serve a jail or prison sentence.[78] In major cities four in ten black males aged sixteen to thirty-five are in jail or prison, or are on probation or parole. Drugs are pandemic. Children do not learn in schools. Conscientious kids are intimidated and beaten up. Girls are molested and assaulted by gang members high on dope and rap.

These are the statistics of a decadent society and dying civilization, the first fruits of the cultural revolution that is de-Christianizing America. Reading these statistics, one is reminded of Whittaker Chambers in *Witness:* "History is cluttered with the wreckage of nations that have become indifferent to God, and died."[79] Again, Jim Nelson Black:

> No matter how far back you look, you will find that religion was always foundational to the great societies. Whether in India, China, Palestine, Greece, Carthage, Africa, or the civili-

zations of South and Central America, the story is always the same: Civilization arises from religion, and when the traditional religious beliefs of a nation are eroded, the nation dies.[80]

Europe has begun to resemble the United States. Between 1960 and 2000, out-of-wedlock births soared in Canada from 4 percent to 31 percent, in the U.K from 5 percent to 38 percent, in France from 6 percent to 36 percent.

As a guide to people's moral lives in Britain, Chistianity has been "vanquished," Card. Cormac Murphy-O'Connor, the archbishop of Westminster, told a gathering of priests in September 2001. People now seek happiness in alcohol, drugs, pornography, and recreational sex, said the cardinal in echo of the archbishop of Canterbury, Dr. George Carey, who had observed, a year earlier, "A tacit atheism prevails. Death is assumed to be the end of life. Our concentration on the here and now renders a thought of eternity irrelevant."[81]

But what is one man's septic tank is another's hot tub. To a devout Marxist, Castro's Cuba is paradise compared to the Cuba of the 1950s and a more just and decent society than what the exiles have created in Miami. To our cultural elite, divorces, abortions, and the junking of obsolete Christian concepts like sacramental marriage may be seen as milestones of freedom.

But how do we create a moral nation and good society if we no longer even agree on what is moral and good?

## WHEN BOY SCOUTS BECAME BIGOTS

"Culture is religion externalized and made explicit," said theologian Henry Van Til. Echoing historian Christopher Dawson, Russell Kirk wrote that all culture is rooted in the "cult," i.e., in religion. "This is no mere wordplay," argues Bruce Frohnen, senior fellow at the Russell Kirk Center for Cultural Renewal.

Culture and cult share a common root in the Latin *colere*, which means to cultivate, as in cultivating one's garden or one's character. . . . Dawson's point was that a people grow together from its common worship. As a people develop common liturgical habits—be they a formal liturgy or the simple singing of hymns—they also develop social habits concerning things like cuisine, art, and daily ritual. These common habits bind them together as a people into a common culture. They also tie, forever, the culture of people with its common religion.[82]

The goal of the secularists is to cut the ties between our culture and "common religion." If that happens, the culture dies. Again, Dr. Kirk:

All culture arises out of religion. When religious faith decays, culture must decline, though often seeming to flourish for a space after the religion which has nourished it has sunk into disbelief. But neither can religion subsist if severed from a healthy culture; no cultured person should remain indifferent to erosion of apprehension of the transcendent.[83]

That this culture war is thus a religious war may be seen in the latest skirmish—the Battle of the Boy Scouts. By the 1911 Scout handbook, "No boy can grow into the best kind of citizen without recognizing an obligation to God."[84] "On my honor I will do my duty to God and my country," reads the Boy Scout Promise.[85] "Homosexual conduct is inconsistent with the requirements in the Scout Oath that a Scout be 'morally straight,' " reads the Scouts's official position.[86]

Since its founding, the Boy Scouts of America has held faithfully to these principles. But while the Scouts have remained true to their beliefs, fashionable opinion has done a somersault. What was morally upright in 1980 is intolerable bigotry in 2001. To the *New York Times*, the Boy Scouts of today are "something akin to a hate group."[87] And either the Scouts will conform to the altered moral code of the cultural revolution, or they will be ostracized, defunded, and destroyed.

The revolution simply cannot coexist with a Boy Scout organization that is huge, respected, and beloved, but shapes the souls of boys in ways it finds abhorrent. Thus a nonnegotiable demand is on the table: the Boy Scouts may retain their respected position in society only if they cut out certain core beliefs and substitute the opposite beliefs. Specifically, atheists and homosexuals must be allowed to become Scouts and Scoutmasters.

"Make him an offer he can't refuse," said Don Corleone. The revolution is making the Boy Scouts an offer it can't refuse: yield, change your beliefs, or we destroy you.

Given what has happened to the Catholic Church, where a screening process failed to weed out potential pedophile priests, resulting in tragedies for altar boys and the worst scandal in the history of the Catholic Church in America, the policy of not permitting homosexuals to take Boy Scouts and Cub Scouts camping would seem simple common sense. But ideology has crippled common sense. The ACLU today defends both the right of homosexuals to lead Scout troops *and* the right of the North American Man-Boy Love Association to publish manuals on how to pick up kids and evade the cops—i.e., a how-to manual to help pedophiles get away with statutory rape. The plaintiffs in the case against NAMBLA are the parents of a ten-year-old boy who was raped and murdered by a NAMBLA member.[88]

WHERE DOES THE Battle of the Boy Scouts stand?

Dismissing the Scouts's claim that they are a private organization and thus exempt from state antidiscrimination laws, New Jersey's Supreme Court ordered the Scouts to admit homosexuals in the name of a higher goal: "eradicating the 'cancer of discrimination.' "[89] Thus, the court equated the Scout creed and Christian doctrine that homosexuality is "not morally straight" with a "cancer" on American society.

In a five-to-four decision, the U.S. Supreme Court spared the Scouts from having to decide whether to be true to their God-centered beliefs or to be broken by state power. But the Scouts's courage cost them one million dollars in funding. In New York, California, Massachusetts, and Minnesota, school boards have cut ties and denied the Scouts access to school facilities. Local governments in Miami Beach and Fort Lauderdale have denounced them. Thirty-two United Way chapters have severed connections. Levi Strauss, Wells Fargo, and Textron have ended support. The Union of American Hebrew Congregations sent a memo to its affiliates urging a cutting of ties. Film director Steven Spielberg resigned from the BSA advisory board with a statement reading: "The last few years in scouting have deeply saddened me to see the Boy Scouts of America actively and publicly participating in discrimination. It's a real shame."[90] When Eagle Scouts participated in opening ceremonies at the Democratic Convention in Los Angeles, delegates booed them. Wrote reporter Valerie Richardson:

> Under normal circumstances, jeering at children is the sort of behavior that might get a delegate sanctioned, if not booted from the convention altogether. But anyone who expected the Democratic leadership to scold the Boy Scouts of America bashers is attending the wrong convention.
>
> Support for homosexual rights has become an integral part of the Democratic orthodoxy, as unassailable as the party's pro-choice or civil rights planks.[91]

In April 2001, the cultural revolution rolled out its siege gun, CBS's *Sixty Minutes*, and, in what columnist Nat Hentoff called an "attack" and "prejudicial reporting," blasted the Scouts for bigotry.[92] Hentoff, for the defense, quoted Alexis de Tocqueville's *Democracy in America*: "The right of association is as inalienable as individual liberty."[93]

But such rights are early casualties in a cultural war in which there will be no truce. Traditionalists can run, but they can't hide. With our public schools and public square de-Christianized, our private schools and private institutions are next. Through the hook of public money, all will be made godless, all forced to conform to the catechism of a revolution that declares infallibly, "All lifestyles are equal." Who says otherwise—let him be anathema. What, then, is the future of the West? Again, Eliot:

> If Christianity goes, the whole of our culture goes. Then you must start painfully again, and you cannot put on a new culture ready-made. You must first wait for the grass to grow to feed the sheep to give the wool out of which your new coat will be made. You must pass through many centuries of barbarism. We should not live to see the new culture, nor would our great-great-great-grandchildren; and if we did not one of us would be happy in it.[94]

# INTIMIDATED MAJORITY

Civil rights laws were not passed to protect the rights
of white men and do not apply to them.[1]
—Mary Berry, Chairman
U.S. Civil Rights Commission

**W**hy did Christians permit their God and faith to be driven out of
the temples of their civilization? Why was their resistance so feeble?
Napoleon said that God is on the side of the big battalions. But in
America the Christians *were* the big battalions, and they were supposed to be on God's side. Yet they were beaten—horse, foot, and
dragoons. In his book *Long March,* Roger Kimball, an editor at *New
Criterion,* attributes the rout on the cultural front to a failed conservative movement.

> The long march of America's cultural revolution has succeeded
> beyond the wildest dreams of all but the most starry-eyed uto-
> pians. The great irony is that this victory took place in the
> midst of a significant drift to the center-Right in electoral pol-
> itics. The startling and depressing fact is that supposed con-
> servative victories at the polls have done almost nothing to
> challenge the dominance of left-wing, emancipationist attitudes
> and ideas in our culture. On the contrary, in the so-called
> "culture wars," conservatives have been conspicuous losers.[2]

Despite the hollow boasts of some conservatives that "we won" the
culture war, candor compels one to concede Kimball is right. But why

are traditionalists in retreat? Christians and conservatives did not lack
for pulpits or microphones, from talk radio to cable TV, from the
Internet to the magazines. After 1968, Republicans won more battles
than they lost and did not lack political power. Polls showed the
country was on their side of the barricades in the culture wars: Americans opposed women in combat, abortion on demand, and racial
preferences. They favored prayer in the public schools and posting the
Ten Commandments. They wanted immigration reduced and English
made America's language. Yet, on the moral, social, and cultural
fronts, Republicans, conservatives, and Christians have been in almost
continuous retreat and are today, by and large, an intimidated lot.

The White House refused to step in while John Ashcroft was
beaten bloody by Teddy Kennedy and the Democrats of the Judiciary
Committee. Neither Mr. Bush nor his running mate attended the
2000 convention of the Christian Coalition. Mr. Bush sent a tape.
But he did make time in his campaign schedule to meet with the gay
Republicans from the Log Cabin Club. When the Confederate battle
flag became a blazing controversy, Governor Bush said it was for
South Carolinians to decide. But, as soon as the primary was over,
he ordered memorial plaques to Confederate war dead taken down
from the Texas Supreme Court.

Not one speaker at the Republican convention in Philadelphia was
allowed to defend the party's position on the defining moral issue of
life. Yet Colin Powell was given prime time to lecture the party on
its supposed hypocrisy in opposing affirmative action, and the chas-
tened Republicans dutifully smiled through their public caning. On
the social and moral issues that once defined Reaganism, the party
has fled the field.

"It's a different Republican party" was the convention spin. Yes, it
is, with pandering the fashion in Philadelphia. Malevolent wit Bill
Maher mocked that "the last time the Republicans had this many
blacks up on the stage, they were selling them."[3] When Mr. Bush
sought to "reach out" to the NAACP by addressing its convention,
the NAACP reciprocated with an attack ad featuring the daughter of

James Byrd, implying that Mr. Bush's opposition to a hate crimes law meant he did not care about her father's lynching. Whenever critics demand that Republicans reach out to those who have again and again bitten their hand, the party obediently reaches out, and is bitten again—to the undying amusement of its tormentors. *National Review* summarized the success of the politics of appeasement.

> Bush tried, more than any previous Republican candidate had, not to offend liberal sensitivities on race. He embraced immigration, supported bilingual education, obscured his position on race preferences, appeared before the NAACP, split the difference on hate crimes, and had Colin Powell guilt-trip the Republican convention. His reward: 35 percent of the Hispanic vote and a smaller share of the black vote than Bob Dole got in 1996.[4]

Conservatives have lost the moral certitude they had when they were young and theirs was a fighting faith. Now, they seem desperately anxious to reassure the public that they are really not bigots, but every bit as warmhearted and well-intentioned as their accusers. After Mr. Bush chose his cabinet, NAACP chair Julian Bond said he had "selected nominees from the Taliban wing of American politics, appeased the wretched appetite of the extreme right wing and chose[n] Cabinet officials whose devotion to the Confederacy is nearly canine in its uncritical affection."[5]

House Majority Leader Richard Armey wrote NAACP president Kwasi Mfume that such language was "racial McCarthyism" and "reverse race-baiting."[6] "Deliberate or not," said Armey, "if left unchallenged, this practice will continue to divide our nation."[7] Armey asked for a meeting, but Bond dismissed his letter as "a typical complaint of those who oppose justice and fairness."[8]

The episode is instructive. One of the highest-ranking Republicans in the nation had requested a meeting with an NAACP whose leaders had smeared his party and vilified the president-elect, and Bond had treated him with contempt. A morally self-confident Republican party would have lacerated Bond, demanded that the IRS look into the NAACP to ensure it was not violating its tax exemption by engaging in partisan attacks, cut off discretionary federal funds to the NAACP until Bond was fired, written the major donor corporations of the NAACP to ask if they support demagogic attacks on the president, and amended the tax laws to punish foundations like Ford, which finance, with tax-free dollars, the trashing of the president and the Republican party. How should conservatives deal with the NAACP? The same way liberal Democrats deal with the Religious Right.

Instead, Mr. Armey asked for dialogue. Fighting back in the culture war has become incompatible with the new Republican image. Since Ronald Reagan departed, the media have whispered in Republican ears, "Moral and social issues are losers. Drop them, or go down to defeat." Republicans have gotten the message and become conscientious objectors in the culture war.

AMERICA, TOO, SEEMS to have lost her moral certitude. In the 1950s, President Eisenhower sent illegal aliens packing in Operation Wetback and apologized to no one for defending U.S. borders and ordering intruders to go home. Republicans today will not even demand that we seal a border that 1.5 million aliens attempt to breach every year. No one wants to be called a nativist. When the conservative weekly *Human Events* interviewed seventeen members of the House and Senate, asking if they supported the deportation of illegal aliens who broke our laws and broke into the country, only two flatly said yes.[9] Because Hispanic Americans might retaliate against members of Congress who demand that our immigration laws be enforced, Congress will not insist that the president enforce them. Such cowardice could cost us our country. There has been a terrible attrition of will to do what is necessary to preserve the unique nation that America once was.

At that Portland State commencement where Mr. Clinton said that in fifty years there would be "no majority race left in America," students broke out in spontaneous applause.[10] Surely, it is a rarity in history that a people would cheer news that they and their children would soon be dispossessed of their inheritance as the majority in the nation their ancestors built.

The moral rot is even more widespread in Europe. Nations that in the twentieth century fielded million-man armies today lack the will to raise sufficient troops to provide for their own defense. They prefer to let the Americans do it. Europe's populations are shrinking, and its nations are breaking apart, but few seem to care. Full of guilt, the Germans seem to want to lose themselves inside the warm cocoon of a united Europe. Other nations, too, seem weary of striving to be independent and free, as they prepare to accept the dictates of a European superstate. "Nations are the wealth of mankind, they are its generalized personalities: the smallest of them has its own particular colors, and embodies a particular facet of God's design," said Solzhenitzyn. "The disappearance of nations would impoverish us no less than if all the peoples were made alike, with one character, one face."[11] Yet the nations of Europe seem reconciled to the reality that their time on this earth may be coming to an end.

LEADERS WHO WISH to preserve their unique national identity and character are branded as racists and xenophobes. In Denmark, interior minister Karen Jespersen, a 1960s radical, ignited a storm of indignation by suggesting that refugees with criminal records be put on a "deserted island." She did "not wish to live," said Jespersen, in a multicultural nation "where the cultures were considered equal."[12]

Denmark has become a haven for political refugees, but Danish hospitality is being exploited by criminal gangs from Azerbaijan, Armenia, and Ukraine. Jespersen's comment about preferring her own culture followed a series of gang rapes by Middle Eastern immigrants of Danish women and demands that Danish law be made to conform to Islamic law, with new restrictions on women, return of the death penalty, and mutilations as punishments for theft.

Europe was aghast—at Ms. Jespersen. Reactions "were fast and furious," wrote Henrik Bering in *Policy Review*.[13] The European Monitoring Center on Racism and Xenophobia was instantly on her case. But, as 33 percent of Denmark's social budget goes for that 4 percent of the nation's population that consists of non-Western immigrants, Danes are starting to tune out Europe and tune in Karen.

Something vital has gone out of Europe. In *The Suicide of the West*, written in 1964, Cold War strategist James Burnham detected a mind-set that reconciles Western peoples to the death of their empires and the eclipse of their civilization. Burnham called it an "ideology of Western suicide."[14] The disease now appears to have become an epidemic.

Why have conservatives not acted more decisively to roll back a revolution that threatens their civilization and culture? There are several reasons.

FIRST, THE FOLLOWERS of Barry Goldwater and Ronald Reagan were drawn into politics by the conviction that America was losing the Cold War. Their movement was unprepared, unequipped, untrained for a culture war. And with the election of Ronald Reagan, the fall of the Berlin Wall, and the collapse of the Soviet Empire, the great cause that had united them was gone.

Moreover, many conservatives in politics, journalism, and broadcasting are far better versed in economics and foreign policy than in history, philosophy, or theology. As one wit has observed, "Republicans were put on this earth to cut taxes." At times, it seems that is the only reason they were put on this earth. Unschooled in matters of morality and culture, many are uncomfortable with such issues, have no interest in them, and don't believe they belong in politics. The late Richard Weaver had these conservatives in mind when he wrote that "many traditional positions in our world have suffered not so much because of inherent defect as because of the stupidity, ineptness and intellectual sloth of those who . . . are presumed to have their defense in charge."[15]

Confronted with moral, social, or cultural issues, these conservatives move swiftly off them and onto taxes and defense, where they feel on terra firma. But despite an ardent Republican wish that this culture war would just pass away, it will not pass away. For, as Trotsky said, "You may not be interested in war, but war is interested in you."[16]

Second, by capturing the institutions where the young spend most of their waking hours—MTV and prime-time, movies and magazines, schools and colleges—the revolution is able to shape the values, beliefs, and attitudes of the young. Artists, actors, playwrights, songwriters, and popular singers are almost all on the other side. Op-ed page commentators and radio and TV talk show hosts cannot match this cultural firepower. The arsenals are unequal. Moreover, the entertainment that the cultural revolution has on offer is far more attractive and alluring; thus, many of the children of traditionalists defect. Though, as they grow older, many prodigal sons and daughters do ruefully return to their father's house.

Half a century ago, literary critic Lionel Trilling could write, "In the United States at this time liberalism is not only the dominant but even the sole intellectual tradition. For it is the plain fact that nowadays there are no conservative or reactionary ideas in general circulation."[17] Though an exaggeration even then, Trilling's line yet contains a core of truth. And since the sixties, there has been a population explosion among the creators of culture and shapers of thought—intellectuals, social critics, teachers, journalists, writers, bureaucrats, and artists. Suddenly, conservatives were not just outnumbered, they were overwhelmed.

Crane Brinton, in his *Anatomy of Revolution,* writes that one sign of a "markedly unstable society" is the sudden appearance of a great host of intellectuals:

bitterly attacking existing institutions, and desirous of a con-
siderable alteration in society, business and government. Purely
metaphorically, we may compare intellectuals of this sort to the
white corpuscles, guardians of the bloodstream; but there can
be an excess of white corpuscles, and when this happens you
have a diseased condition.[18]

By Brinton's definition, America would appear to be close to that
"diseased condition."

Third, unlike normal politics, where a middle ground can usually
be found and a compromise reached, culture war is a zero-sum game.
One side's gain is the other's loss. Abortion, assisted suicide, and gay
marriage are moral questions that call for a yes or no from politicians
who prefer to split the difference and meet in the moderate middle.
Republicans, most of whom do not consider politics a blood sport,
are unprepared for the no-quarter combat that Critical Theory entails,
with its savage rhetoric and attack politics.

In the old politics, incumbents "pointed with pride" and challeng-
ers "viewed with alarm." In a culture war, the revolution is always on
the attack, and traditionalists are always on the defensive. "Strength
lies not in defense but in attack," wrote a budding cultural revolutionary by the name of Adolf Hitler.[19]

Consider the thirty-years war for control of the command post of
the culture war, the Supreme Court. Two of Mr. Nixon's nominees,
federal judges Clement Haynesworth and G. Harrold Carswell, were
scourged and rejected. Two of Ronald Reagan's nominees, federal
judges Robert Bork and Douglas Ginsburg, were savaged and rejected,
the latter for marijuana indiscretions as a law professor. Bork's name
became a verb, to Bork, meaning to shred a nominee's reputation
before casting him aside. George Bush's nominee, Clarence Thomas,
had to run an Iroquois gauntlet.

Contrast this back-alley butchery of conservative jurists to the high
tea treatment accorded Clinton nominees Stephen Breyer and Ruth
Bader Ginsberg. Each was introduced with respect and easily confirmed. The core constituencies of the Democratic party understand

culture war, while many Republicans seem blissfully unaware there even is a war.

"Politics stops at the water's edge" and "partisanship ends when the sun goes down" are the clichés of yesterday. A culture war is what Mao called "a permanent revolution." If the Confederate battle flag comes down in South Carolina, Georgia, and Florida, the front moves to Mississippi. When all the flags are down, the statues and portraits go next, then the school names, until all public homage paid to Dixie's heroes is forever abolished.

Fourth, thirty years of pounding have pulverized Christian morale. Unlike the era of *The Bells of St. Mary's* and *The Song of Bernadette,* priests and preachers are now, as often as not, portrayed in movies and on TV as hypocritical and lecherous or intolerant and backward. Who wants to stand up for family values when the price is public ridicule? Like every institution, the churches have been under constant fire and exhibit signs of battle fatigue. Beset by schisms over abortion and homosexuality, plagued by scandals from womanizing televangelists to pedophile priests, to enabling bishops they are not the churches of yesterday. Like muscle tissue, moral authority unexercised atrophies and dies. To watch Catholic senators, without sanction by their bishops, sustain Bill Clinton's veto of a ban on partial-birth abortion—"infanticide," to Senator Moynihan—is to see how far downhill the old church has slipped and stumbled since the confident years of Pius XII.

Constant charges of racism, sexism, homophobia, and bigotry have taken a toll on traditionalist morale. The cost of continuing to fight seems intolerably high. Many have given in to defeatism and despair and whine like Hollywood stars and starlets who threaten to leave the country rather than live in George Bush's America. So, Christians save their protest for the privacy of the voting booth, but those they elect often have no more stomach for this battle than they do.

Justice Clarence Thomas spoke of the price of resistance at the American Enterprise Institute dinner in 2001. "Active citizens are often subjected to truly vile attacks, they are branded as mean-spirited, racist, Uncle Tom, homophobic, sexist," said the justice.[20] Under such assaults, he added, "We censor ourselves. This is not civility. It is cowardice."[21] As a federal official, Thomas had questioned the wisdom of affirmative action and busing for racial balance. Black leaders charged him with "treason" to his people. The purpose, said Thomas, was "intimidation."[22]

The intimidators failed with Clarence Thomas but succeeded with some conservatives who, like defeated peoples, no longer make demands. They just want to get along. But, in a culture war, where the other side is always making demands, and the other side is always ready to fight, this translates into endless retreats and eventual defeat.

Fifth, God-and-country people are raised to respect and obey their rulers. Judicial revolutionaries like Warren, Douglas, and Brennan relied on the innate conservatism of the silent majority when they imposed their radical agenda. Many Americans were enraged, but felt they must obey. After all, this was the Supreme Court. As long as Americans believe that their government is acting constitutionally, they will obey. By definition, conservatives are not rebels. But neither were the Founding Fathers until pushed to the wall.

Finally, a new generation has now grown up for whom the cultural revolution is not a revolution at all, but the culture they were born into and have known all their lives. Public homosexuality, pornography, abortion, trash talk on TV and in movies, and filthy lyrics in popular music have all been around since before they can remember. No big deal. Many have come to accept the axioms of modernity about how wicked the old America was. It is the traditional culture they find odd. They have passed through schools and universities, consumed the fare, and come to believe what they were taught about the country's old heroes and history. "We will steal your children!" the sixties radicals howled at Middle America. They did.

And with an intolerant new cultural elite now ascendant, a failing of conservatives is that they are conservatives. In the 1770s, there came a time when conservative men like Washington and John Hancock realized they, too, must become rebels like Patrick Henry and Sam Adams. When the French Revolution was on the march in the persons of Robespierre and Bonaparte, it was good to have Edmund Burke, but one also needed Nelson and the Iron Duke. "The first thing we have to learn about fighting and winning a culture war," said Dr. Sam Francis, the syndicated columnist and author of *Revolution from the Middle*, "is that we are not fighting to 'conserve' something, we are fighting to overthrow something."[23]

> We must understand clearly and firmly that the dominant authorities in . . . the major foundations, the media, the schools, the universities, and most of the system of organized culture, including the arts and entertainment—not only do nothing to conserve what most of us regard as our traditional way of life, but actually seek its destruction or are indifferent to its survival. If our culture is going to be conserved, then we need to dethrone the dominant authorities that threaten it.[24]

We traditionalists who love the culture and country we grew up in are going to have to deal with this question: Do we simply conserve the remnant, or do we try to take the culture back? Are we conservatives, or must we also become counterrevolutionaries and overthrow the dominant culture?

Americans who look on this cultural revolution as politics-as-usual do not understand it. It means to make an end of the country we love. It cannot be appeased. Its relentless, reckless use of terms like *extremist, sexist, racist, homophobe, nativist, xenophobe, fascist,* and *Nazi* testifies to how seriously it takes the struggle and how it views those who resist. To true believers in the revolution, the Right is not just wrong; the Right is evil.

Here is Jesse Jackson, premier voice of black America, after the 1994 GOP victory: "Hate and hurt are on a roll in America. If what was happening here was happening in South Africa, it'd be called racist apartheid. If it was happening in Germany, we'd call it Nazism.

And in Italy, we'd call it fascism. Here we call it conservatism."[25] As Mr. Bush's team was winning the Florida recount battle, Jackson reverted: "If George Bush wins, it'll be by Nazi tactics. . . . We'll take to the streets right now. We'll delegitimize Bush, discredit him, do whatever it takes but never accept him."[26]

To Julian Bond, critics of affirmative action are "neo-fascists."[27] To Atlanta's ex-mayor Maynard Jackson, the Confederate battle flag is a "swastika."[28] To Cong. Maxine Waters, John Ashcroft is a "racist."[29] Missouri congressman William Clay said of Mr. Bush's decision to name Ashcroft, this is the "way the Ku Klux Klan members worked to improve race relations—they too reached out to blacks with nooses and burning crosses."[30]

Equating conservatives with Nazis and Klansmen dates at least as far back as Dr. King, who professed to see in the Goldwater campaign the "danger signs of Hitlerism."[31] The slander is now common, because the cost is free. Few journalists will call black leaders to account, for some share their animus against conservatives, while others agree with Marcuse, who advocated intolerance toward conservatives to delegitimize the Right as beyond the pale of acceptable politics.

Calling opponents Nazis, fascists, and Klansmen, when it carries no penalty, can be rewarding. It places an opponent outside the company of decent men, discredits in advance what he says, and forces him to defend his character rather than his positions. And there are psychic rewards. After all, if one is standing up to Nazis or night riders, that is surely more heroic than standing up to Denny Hastert or Dick Armey. The more one demonizes an enemy, the more one "heroizes" oneself.

In the demonization of the Right there is also fantasizing by the Left. Mr. Clinton spoke grimly of black churches being burned by racists in the Arkansas of his boyhood, but it never happened. Mr. Gore can break into tears relating how he vowed to fight Big Tobacco to the last ditch as he watched his beloved sister die of lung cancer. Only later did we learn that Mr. Gore was still bundling with Big Tobacco long after his sister's death. This Walter Mitty fantasizing explains how Al Gore invented the Internet, discovered Love Canal, and saw his steamy romance with Tipper inspire the writing of *Love Story*. In Gore's mind, it may just have happened that way. And when Jesse Jackson compares a Florida legal battle to Selma, he not only casts Republican lawyers as the club-wielding troopers of "Bull" Connor with their attack dogs—but himself as the Hero of Selma Bridge.

"I have measured out my life with coffee spoons," laments T. S. Eliot's J. Alfred Prufrock.[32] So, too, have our cultural elites. But in their minds they daily heave a cutlass against Nazis, fascists, and Klansmen who would otherwise fall upon defenseless and persecuted minorities. Why shouldn't one feel good about oneself? For today's progressive, *The West Wing* of Pres. Josiah Bartlett is the real world.

The politics of posture entails no pain. Consider again Ms. Sontag's "the white race is the cancer of human history . . . the white race and it alone . . . eradicates autonomous civilizations wherever it spreads."[33]

Rewrite that sentence with "Jewish race" in place of "white race" and the passage would fit nicely into *Mein Kampf*. Had Sontag so savaged the Jewish people, her career would have ended there. But her diatribe against the "white race" no more diminished her standing than her 1968 visit to Hanoi, when the North Vietnamese were torturing American POWs. Sontag subsequently won a MacArthur Foundation genius grant, and one recent survey found her the most respected intellectual of our time. Yet, as Tom Wolfe, of *Radical Chic* and *Bonfire of the Vanities* fame, asked about Sontag:

> Who was this woman? Who and what? . . . a Max Weber . . .
> an Arnold Toynbee. Actually, she was just another scribbler
> who spent her life signing up for protest meetings and lum-
> bering to the podium, encumbered by her prose style, which
> had a handicapped parking sticker valid at *Partisan Review*.[34]

Sontag, said Wolfe, seemed "hellbent on illustrating" the truth of McLuhan's observation that "moral indignation is a technique used to endow the idiot with dignity."[35]

ULTIMATELY IT IS the dream of every victim to exchange places with his oppressor," wrote Franz Fanon, the revolutionary.[36] Fanon's insight helps to explain the transformation of the civil rights movement from a social movement in the American tradition of women's suffrage and the labor movement into an arm of the revolution.

In the 1950s, African Americans could still be described as socially conservative, patriotic, proudly Christian. What they wanted, demanded, was to be full and equal members of our national family, to which they and their people had contributed all their lives. America said yes. Black and white together, America went out and buried Jim Crow. We seemed on the way to a more united country. But when the valid grievances had been redressed and the legitimate demands for equal rights under law had been met, America's attention moved elsewhere. Civil rights became yesterday's story.

To recapture the nation's attention, new demands had to be invented, and when they were met, still newer demands. Desegregation was now no longer enough. Affirmative action, quotas, set-asides, equality of result in jobs, pay, and income, and legislative and congressional districts redrawn to guarantee a "fair" share of the seats of power were demanded. Racial balance had to be achieved in classrooms, even if it meant forced busing of white children into dangerous inner-city schools. The old battle cry of freedom gave way to the new "nonnegotiable demands" for Black Power.

In 1971, the Supreme Court heard a case in which a white law student was protesting his failure to be admitted to the Arizona bar though he had a higher score on the bar exam than black students who had been admitted. During court discussion, Justice Thurgood Marshall turned to his colleague William Douglas and said, "You guys have been discriminating for years. Now it is our turn."[37]

The civil rights movement melded with the cultural revolution, and militant leaders had even newer demands. Songs like "Dixie" must never again be publicly sung. Robert E. Lee must no longer be honored. As Washington was a slave owner, his name and the names of all former slave owners should be removed from schools that black children attend. Mark Twain's books contain racial slurs; get them out. The Confederate battle flag is a symbol of racism. Replicas must be removed from all state flags, or boycotts will be imposed. Immigration laws must put Third World peoples first in line to increase "diversity." We also need new hate crimes laws that single out for special punishment and reeducation whites who attack blacks. And now we would like to sit down and discuss reparations for slavery.

"Every successful revolution puts on in time the robe of the tyrant it has deposed," said Barbara Tuchman.[38] Every political cause, added Eric Hoffer, eventually becomes a business and then degenerates into a racket. Civil rights has become a racket. All Americans of goodwill would offer a hand to alleviate the social catastrophe in black America. For, after all, African Americans are children of the same God and citizens of the same republic. But the Jacksons, Sharptons, and Bonds do not want our help. They want to bait us, provoke us, and demonize us, for that is how they keep the pot boiling, the TV producers calling, and the federal and foundation grants rolling in. If Theodore Bilbo and Bull Connor are dead and gone, new white racists must be found, even if they have to be invented, like John Ashcroft and George W. Bush. Booker T. Washington warned America to be wary of these race racketeers:

> There is a class of colored people who make a business of keeping the troubles, the wrongs and the hardships of the Negro race before the public. Having learned that they are able to make a living out of their troubles, they have grown into the settled habit of advertising their wrongs—partly because they want sympathy and partly because it pays. Some of these people do not want the Negro to lose his grievances, because they do not want to lose their jobs.[39]

Right down the smokestack, Dr. Washington.

When an argument revolves around issues of race, Republicans go limp. They seem intimidated to the point of paralysis. Why?

As fair-minded and mostly Christian folks, they concede that there is truth in the indictment of America's past. Our fathers did participate in slavery. We did practice segregation. Our treatment of the Indians was not what one should have expected of people to whom the Sermon on the Mount was divine command. But, having internalized a guilt that gnaws at their souls, these Republicans, in their lifelong quest for absolution, are easy prey for confidence men like Jackson and Sharpton who run the Big Sting.

The truth? In the story of slavery and the slave trade, Western Man was among the many villains, but Western Man was also the only hero. For the West did not invent slavery, but it alone abolished slavery. Had it not been for the West, African rulers would still be trafficking in the flesh of their kinsmen. Slaves, after all, were the leading cash crop of the friends of Mansa Musa. In Mauritania and Sudan today, slavery has returned, to the deafening silence of intellectuals who have built careers on the moral shakedown of America and the West. America was a segregated society, but in no other nation do people enjoy greater freedom, opportunity, and prosperity than here in the United States.

The time for apologies is past. But if Middle America believes that capitulations and reparations will buy peace in our time, it deludes itself. If there were no more demands, the race racketeers would have to find a new line of work. But as long as the silent majority keeps acceding to their demands, they will keep on making them. Time to just say no.


THE DEGRADATION OF civil rights and the merger of that movement with the cultural revolution compounds the risks of the balkanization of America. For, where FDR's New Deal coalition was based on economics, the haves versus the have-nots, the new Democratic coalition is based on bloc voting and ethnic politics.

If the party loses its lock on black America, no Democratic lock on the presidency is possible. That is a political fact of life. Thus, Democrats have an immense stake in sustaining the fear and loathing of Republicans among African Americans. In every election of the 1990s, the race card was played, by stoking the fear that either black churches would be burned or black voters disfranchised. In the 2000 election, Mr. Gore went to a black church in Pittsburgh to offer these reflections on his rival:

> When my opponent, Governor Bush, says that he will appoint strict constructionists to the Supreme Court, I often think of the strictly constructionist meaning that was applied when the Constitution was written and how some people were considered three-fifths of a human being.[40]

Mr. Gore was implying that Mr. Bush had no real problem with slavery. Divisive? Yes. But it paid off. African Americans turned out in record numbers in many states and voted eleven to one for Albert Gore. With the White House the prize, why would Democrats give up a race card that is the ace of trumps in urban America? What would Al Sharpton and Jesse Jackson do in a high-stakes poker game where the race card has been dropped from the deck?

The more interesting questions: Why do Republicans continue, election after election, to devote such energy and effort trying to crack the most solid voting bloc the Democratic party has? Why do they not "go hunting where the ducks are"? The Republicans' largest and most loyal voting bloc is America's majority. In 1972, Mr. Nixon won 67 percent of the white vote; in 1984, Mr. Reagan won 64 percent. Mr. Bush won 54 percent, but 60 percent of white males. As whites still cast 82 percent of the ballots, if Republicans can raise their share of that vote from 54 to 60 percent, almost no other votes are needed.

White males are the victims of quotas, affirmative action, set-asides, and reverse discrimination. They are the preferred targets of abuse by academics, journalists, and feminists, as well as the Jacksons, Sharptons, and Bonds. Yet, none of their attackers are beloved of Middle America. If the GOP would come out for an end to racial preferences and a moratorium on immigration, and appeal to the great silent majority, as Democrats appeal to minorities, the party's chances in national elections could not but improve.

One recalls that the first President Bush won the White House by draping the weekend pass Michael Dukakis gave murderer Willie Horton, and his ACLU membership card, around Dukakis's neck. And the first President Bush lost the White House by raising taxes and signing a quota bill—to "reach out" to dissidents who invariably pay Republicans back with a wet mitten across the face.

## THE TWO AMERICAS

When you come to a fork in the road, take it, said Yogi Berra.

The Republican party is at a fork in the road. And the decision it takes will be as fateful as the one it took at the San Francisco Cow Palace in 1964, when the party chose Barry Goldwater in that time when "Bliss was it in that dawn to be alive / To be young very heaven."[41]

As commentators Left and Right are discovering, race and culture are becoming decisive in presidential politics. Blacks, Hispanics, and Jewish Americans voted in landslides for Gore, but his 60 percent vote among white males made Mr. Bush president. A county-by-county electoral map shows America becoming two nations. Al Gore swept the coastal counties of Washington, Oregon, and California, but carried barely a single county east of the coast. Of some 230 counties in Nevada, Utah, Idaho, Wyoming, Nebraska, and Kansas, Gore carried three. Gore did well coming up the Mississippi River

Valley from New Orleans to Baton Rouge, Memphis, St. Louis, the Quad Cites, and St. Paul. But beyond the river cities and their suburbs, Gore was crushed in these mid-American states. As historian Ralph Raico wrote, you can drive across America by almost any route without going through a single county carried by Gore.[42] But it is almost impossible to drive through any state, except Rhode Island, without crossing counties that went for Bush.

What defines the new politics of the twenty-first century? According to the *Washington Post,* it is morality and culture:

> Battles over abortion, gun control and other cultural values are dramatically reshaping the voting behavior of the American electorate, turning long-time working-class white Democrats into Republicans and moving many affluent whites from the GOP to the party of Roosevelt. . . . Racial issues such as busing and affirmative action have pushed blue-collar voters into the GOP, at the same time that cultural issues, especially abortion rights, have built Democratic allegiance among white professionals.[43]

Among Americans who earn fifty thousand dollars a year or more, once-solid Republican voters, Bush's margin was cut to 7 percent. The American Bar Association and American Medical Association were once Republican bastions. No longer. Now they are considered hostile fiefdoms. Of the media, that has long since been true. On election night, writes analyst Terry Teachout, "CNN staffers had to be warned . . . not to cheer when the network's anchors announced that Gore had been declared the winner of a state, lest their cheers be heard by viewers."[44]

But if professional elites are moving left, poor whites are moving to the right. An exchange of electorates is taking place. The *Post's* Tom Edsall discovered that "in nine out of the ten poorest counties in Kentucky . . . places where the Democratic Party of Harry S. Truman ran roughshod over Republican adversaries, George W. Bush won, frequently by margins the mirror image of Gore's in the richest and best educated counties."[45]

Gore lost every income segment of white America, except for those earning under fifteen thousand dollars a year, and he split this vote with Bush forty-nine to forty-six, an astonishing loss of loyalty among poor whites for the party of the people. "The only three issues in my district," an Oklahoman congressman told this writer a few years back, are "God, gays, and guns!"

Race aside, frequency of church attendance has become almost the best indicator of how a person will vote. Those who go to church weekly and more often vote Republican by landslides. Those who attend church rarely or never vote Democratic. Yes, Virginia, we are two countries.

In the 2000 election, the Republican ticket ran away from the issues of race, culture, and life, assuming, correctly, that the hostility to and even detestation of Clinton and Gore would bring social conservatives home. They were right. But the Gore-plus-Nader three-million-vote margin over Bush-Cheney may be the last wake-up call the Republican party will receive.

If Mr. Bush and his White House do not champion the cause of life, of a color-blind society, and of traditional values, those causes will be lost. And if the Republican party refuses, once in power, to offer leadership to moral and cultural conservatives, as well as to economic conservatives, many will give up on the party, and politics as well. For Mr. Bush, the litmus test is the Supreme Court. Nomination of a pro-choice justice would dishearten and demoralize the Right. If the president lets the next seat go to the Souter-Stevens-Ginsberg-Breyer wing of the court, the only argument left for the GOP is that it is the lesser of two evils, and that is not enough. What Joe Louis said of his light heavyweight challenger Billy Conn is true for the president in the culture wars: "He can run, but he can't hide."

———

NO MATTER WHAT "compassionate conservatives" may wish, the culture war and racial conflict are not going away. Too many have a vested interest. African Americans and Hispanics are a fourth of our population. Both vote increasingly as blocs in presidential elections. Our media, too, have a stake in racial conflict. Ratings and the ad dollars that flow from them require conflict, and no conflict—save war itself—is more riveting than racial conflict. The O.J. trial may have divided and polarized America, but it guaranteed a successful year at CNN.

The ballooning budgets of federal agencies—the EEOC, the Civil Rights Commission, the civil rights divisions of Justice, Education, and HHS—require a steady supply of fresh "victims" of racism. The more money these agencies receive, the more violators and victims they must find. By Parkinson's Law, the work expands to fill the time allotted.

Civil rights has also attracted the trial lawyers. A news report that a black customer has been sassed, or a black diner denied service, is a winning lottery ticket. For being slow to serve six black Secret Service agents in Annapolis, Denny's parent company had to pay $54 million to 295,000 plaintiffs and their lawyers, and to sign an agreement with the NAACP to hire more African Americans and patronize more minority-owned suppliers.[46]

Reverend Jackson's 1980s boycott of Anheuser-Busch was resolved so amicably that, by 2000, his sons Yusef and Jonathan were running the largest Anheuser-Busch distributorship in Chicago. The *Chicago Sun-Times* reports that after Jackson "threatened protests" against mergers of GTE and Bell Atlantic, AT&T and CTI, he "changed his tune" when they "donated" to Jackson-led groups and "agreed to [Jackson's] demands by giving contracts to minority business owners—at least some of whom Jackson introduced to the corporate chiefs."[47] Countless are the ways to keep hope alive.

Black employees of the Christian Coalition, who claim they were not invited to a Christmas party and had to serve at an Inaugural dinner rather than sit with other employees, have sued for the damage done their psyches and self-esteem. The sum demanded—$621 million.[48]

Racial racketeering is not going away; indeed, it is going global. In Durban, South Africa, in September 2000, the United Nations hosted a World Conference Against Racism, Racial Discrimination, Xenophobia, and Related Intolerance. Purpose: Extract a formal U.S. apology for "transatlantic slavery" and a commitment to tens of billions in "reparations" to African Americans for this nation's historic "crime against humanity."

Reverend Jackson and his Black Caucus allies had hoped to have Colin Powell on hand to ensure worldwide coverage, as his country was indicted, convicted, denounced, and ordered to make restitution to all descendants of African slaves. The Bush Administration, however, refused its assigned role, Secretary Powell begged off going, and the conference blew up after Arab nations hijacked it and converted it into a drumhead court-martial of Israel for "racism" and "apartheid." The low-level U.S. delegation walked out, but this is not the last Americans will hear of "reparations" for slavery, for the would-be beneficiaries have too large a stake in running the scam.

With the media, the Democratic party, the federal bureaucracy, the trial lawyers, the UN, and the Third World all having huge investments in racial politics, we will endure it until Western nations decide they have had enough and walk away from the game. But that may be too much to expect of an intimidated people.

# A HOUSE DIVIDED

"This used to be a helluva good country. I can't under-
stand what's gone wrong with it."[1]
—Jack Nicholson, 1969
*Easy Rider*

The world is a fine place and worth fighting for.[2]
—Ernest Hemingway, 1940
*For Whom the Bell Tolls*

Civilizations, nations, and states can die many ways. They can be
invaded and put to the sword, as Constantinople was in 1453. They
can be absorbed by empires, as the Greek city-states were by Rome
and the German principalities were by Prussia. Nations can disu-
nite, dissolve, break apart, as Yugoslavia, the USSR, and Czechoslovakia did, though many contend that these were always artificial
nations.

Countries and civilizations can undergo conversions that create a
new people, as happened to Ireland with St. Patrick, to Arabia with
Muhammad. In "Humanism and the New Order," historian Christopher Dawson, seven decades ago, saw this happening to the West:

> For centuries a civilisation will follow the same path, worship-
> ping the same gods, cherishing the same ideas, acknowledging
> the same moral and intellectual standards. And then all at once
> a change will come, the springs of the old life run dry, and

men suddenly awake to a new world, in which the ruling principles of the former age seem to lose their validity and to become inapplicable or meaningless. . . . We seem to be
experiencing something of the kind in Europe to-day.[3]

Civilizations can also fail to reproduce and be overwhelmed by
immigrants indifferent to their culture. "Rome was conquered not by
barbarian invasion from without," wrote Will Durant, "but by barbarian multiplication from within. . . . The rapidly breeding Germans
could not understand the classic culture, did not accept it, did not
transmit it; the rapidly breeding Orientals were mostly of a mind to
destroy that culture; the Romans possessing it, sacrificed it to the
comforts of sterility."[4]

THE WEST IS the most advanced civilization in history and America
the most advanced nation—first in economics, science, technology,
and military power. No superpower rival exists. Europe, Japan, and
America control two-thirds of the world's wealth, income, and productive capacity.

But America and the West face four clear and present dangers.

The first is a dying population. Second is the mass immigration of
peoples of different colors, creeds, and cultures, changing the character of the West forever. The third is the rise to dominance of an
anti-Western culture in the West, deeply hostile to its religions,
traditions, and morality, which has already sundered the West. The
fourth is the breakup of nations and the defection of ruling elites to
a world government whose rise entails the end of nations.

The West does not lack the capacity or power to repel these dangers, but it seems to lack the desire or will to maintain itself as a vital,
separate, unique civilization. As the ex-Trotskyite and geostrategist
James Burnham wrote over a third of a century ago:

I do not know what the cause is of the West's extraordinarily
rapid decline, which is most profoundly shown by the deep-

ening loss, among the leaders of the West, of confidence in themselves and in the unique quality of their own civilization, and by a correlated weakness of the Western will to survive. The cause or causes have something to do, I think, with the decay of religion and with an excess of material luxury; and, I suppose with getting tired, worn out, as all things temporal do.[5]

This struggle to preserve the old creeds, cultures, and countries of the West is the new divide between Left and Right; this struggle will define what it means to be a conservative. This is the cause of the twenty-first century and the agenda of conservatism for the remainder of our lives.

In considering any strategy for the preservation of our culture and country, an assessment of the balance of forces is needed. Not only have the cultural institutions of the West been captured, so, also, have the major corporate centers of power. And just as globalism is the antithesis of patriotism, the transnational corporation is a natural antagonist of tradition. With its adaptability and amorality, it has no roots; it can operate in any system. With efficiency its ruling principle, it has no loyalty to workers and no allegiance to any nation. With share price and stock options its reasons for being, it will sacrifice everything and everyone on the altar of profit. The global capitalist and the true conservative are Cain and Abel. But the growing power of global capitalism cannot be denied. Measured by GDP, fifty-two of the world's one hundred most powerful economies are corporations, and forty-eight are countries.[6]

THE DEMOCRATIC PARTY is a lost cause in the culture war, and many Republicans are reluctant warriors. If a battle impends and losses are anticipated, they will vanish from camp before sunup. In cultural conflict, a Davos Republican is no match for a San Francisco Democrat.

As the cultural revolution took generations to triumph, it will take generations to roll back. And the great battles will not be political, but moral, intellectual, and spiritual. For the adversary is not another party, but another faith, another way of seeing God and man. And the outcome will be less often decided in Congress than in the schools, the media, and the high court. For the prize contested is the souls of the young. "We'll get you through your children," boasted poet Allen Ginsberg in unconscious echo of that other cultural revolutionary, Adolf Hitler: If they do not go with us, it does not matter. We already have their children.[7]

Needed for victory is not only a conservative spirit, to defend what is right about America and the West, but a counterrevolutionary spirit to recapture lost ground. To preserve their rights, and their right to live as they wished, the Founding Fathers had to become rebels. So shall we.

THE "REVOLUTION," WROTE Jean-François Revel, "writes the play in which political leaders act much later."[8] That is what this revolution has been about: capturing the culture, and with it the power to write the play in which the political leaders act.

Regimes not rooted in cultures cannot endure. The Stalinist regimes in the captive nations of Eastern Europe never put down roots in the culture. When the threat of Russian tanks was gone, so were the regimes. Republicans today abandon moral terrain they confidently defended in the Reagan era because they sense the culture has turned hostile. And they may be right. There may be "more of them than there are of us." Thus, conservatives need to make alliances with any who will stand with them. Not every liberal wants to see our civilization end its days in a new Babylonian captivity; not a few "conservatives" have stacked arms in the culture war.

This is the struggle that succeeds the Cold War and will consume the balance of our lives. While none of us may live to see the promised land, ultimately, victory is assured. For we have it on the highest authority that truth crushed to earth shall rise again.

---

OF THE FOUR clear and present dangers, the population crisis of the West is the most immediate, and most dangerous.

History teaches that the correlation between power and population is *not* absolute. A few million British conquered a fourth of the world. Tiny Portugal and Holland seized territory and planted colonies in lands far larger and more populous: Brazil, India, China, Africa, the Indies. But population is a component of power. Soldier for soldier, the Confederacy was the equal of the Union, but there were not enough Confederates, and too many Yankees. France's paranoia over a soaring German population after Versailles proved justified. Hitler's Wehrmacht may have been the superior in arms of the Red Army, but 80 million Germans ruthlessly organized under Hitler could not defeat 197 million Soviets ruthlessly organized under Stalin. A Soviet Union of 290 million could control a world empire. An aging, shrinking, dying Russia of 145 million will be fortunate to hold what it has. Indeed, one is hard-pressed to find in history any example of a family, a tribe, a people, a nation, or a civilization whose population has grown old and whose numbers have begun to shrink that did not have taken from it what it once took from others.

The Death of the West may already be baked in the cake. The baby boom that began in 1946 and ended in 1964 was the largest generation in U.S. history. But it failed to reproduce itself. With its oldest now fifty-five, and its youngest thirty-seven, that generation is about done having children. The eldest have begun to look toward retirement, when families pay down debts, curb spending, and lower consumption.

Japan, where the median age is five years greater than in the United States, hit the wall in 1990. Real estate and equity markets collapsed and have yet to recover. In October 2001, Japanese stocks were 75 percent below their 1989 peak, and Japan's economy was as dormant as her population growth.

Europe's populations have already begun to shrink. With fewer children entering the workforce, and the number of seniors and elderly soaring, Europe must raise taxes and retirement ages and cut benefits to seniors—or import new workers. Europe will try both. As Europeans are forced to work longer for less, to support the idle elderly, generational tensions will increase; and as Arabs and Africans pour in, social tensions will rise. The race riots in the Lancashire mill town of Oldham, and in Leeds, Burnley, and Bradford, the fights between Spaniards and Moroccans in El Ejido, the bloody battles between French and Algerian youth in Paris, and skinhead attacks on immigrants and Turks in Germany are harbingers of the "long hot summers" that are coming to Europe. But should Europe reject immigration, and European women refuse to have children, the Continent will soon stare senescence in the face.

AMERICA FACES THE same questions. If tens of millions of American girls and young women are determined not to have children, or to have no more than one, America either accepts mass immigration or the fate of Japan and Europe. But America has time to act. If Americans wish to preserve their civilization and culture, American women must have more children. While there is no guarantee that government incentives can change the mind-set of women, a profamily, pro-child bias can be built back into national policy. For what is more important than the permanence of the American nation and people?

- The Civil Rights Act should be amended to allow employers to pay higher wages to parents than to single people, to enable one spouse to stay home with infants and toddlers and to be there when the kids come home from school. This should apply to single dads and single moms.
- Instead of a tax deduction for day care, so mothers can return to work, the federal tax credit for each child should be raised to three thousand dollars. This might eliminate federal income taxes for large families as well as poor families. Give women freedom

to choose whether to stay home with their kids—and have more kids. America does not need more workers; America needs more children.

- Employers should be given tax incentives to pay higher wages to parents. We need to revive the idea of the family wage, where a single income is adequate for a secure and comfortable life for a growing family.
- The burden of corporate taxation should be shifted off family businesses and farms onto the larger corporations. As Ronald Reagan used to say, corporations don't pay taxes, people do. Corporations only collect taxes. Let the Fortune 500 do the collecting.
- "Death taxes" should be abolished immediately for family businesses, family farms, and family estates worth under five million dollars.
- If new revenue is needed to pay for these family tax cuts, it can be obtained through taxes on consumption and duties on imports. If America has a crisis, it is certainly not a lack of imported consumer goods down at the mall.

Today, the values of feminism and the counterculture are built into our social policies and tax code. Conservatives should act to remove them. A free society cannot force women to have children, but a healthy society can reward those who preserve it by doing so.

For two decades, Republicans have touted the "supply-side" benefits of cuts in marginal tax rates. They have been proven right. And tax cuts are a positive good. But what is at stake now is far more important than whether our economy grows at 3 or 4 percent. It is the survival of our civilization, culture, and country.

Yet, easing the economic burden of raising children is no substitute for a revival of religious faith. For strong faith and big families go hand in hand. Among white Americans today, it is no surprise where the highest birthrate may be found—in Utah.

## ASSIMILATION

In Madison's notes from the Constitutional Convention, Gouverneur Morris is quoted as saying: "Every society from a great Nation down to a Club has the right of declaring the conditions on which new members should be admitted."⁹ To stem today's invasion of the United States and assimilate our thirty-one million foreign-born, America must, without apology, exercise that right.

• Legal immigration should be rolled back to 250,000 each year. Welfare benefits should be restricted to Americans. Immigration laws should be rewritten to end "chain immigration," where new immigrants are entitled to bring in their extended families. In short, immigration laws should be rewritten, with the emphasis on what is best for America.

• The H-1B program, expanded to benefit Silicon Valley, under which 200,000 professional workers are brought in yearly, should be suspended. In 2000 and 2001, U.S. high-tech workers lost tens of thousands of jobs. College grads cannot find the jobs they thought would be there. To bring in foreign workers to compete with our own jobless citizens is to betray our own workers and their families. We should put Americans first.

• A new amnesty for illegal aliens, as proposed by President Fox, would invite tens of millions more to break America's immigration laws and break into our country in anticipation of yet another amnesty. It would be tantamount to declaring open borders. Opposition to amnesty is an imperative.

• The United States must summon up the moral courage to deport illegal aliens. If there is no sanction for breaking into the United States, what is the sense of having immigration laws? If we turn a blind eye to what is happening on our borders, a huge slice of the Third World will arrive here in the first decades of the twenty-first century. For the word is out that the candy store is open and the cop no longer walks the beat.

• The horrific atrocities at the World Trade Center and Pentagon, the other acts of terrorism that have occurred, should be wake-up calls to this generation of what is at risk in our naive embrace of "open borders." The world is not as we wish it would be, but a world where some regimes and rulers and renegade terrorists bear a murderous hatred of America. And because of our immigration policies, our enemies are already inside the gates. To preserve the security and freedom of our people, we must run them down and remove them from our midst, and protect our borders far better than we have in recent decades. The survival of a free society depends upon it.

• Immigrant children should be immersed in English from the day they enter an American classroom. Most immigrant parents want it for their children; more important, the nation needs it. And immersion works. As the *New York Times* reports:

> Two years after Californians voted to end bilingual education and force a million Spanish-speaking students to immerse themselves in English as if it were a cold bath, those students are improving in reading and other subjects at often striking rates, according to standardized test scores.[10]

Ken Noonan, the founder of the California Association of Bilingual Educators, was among the most vociferous opponents of Proposition 227, whose purpose was to end bilingual education. But, two years after his defeat, Noonan was singing the praises of Proposition 227: "I thought it would hurt kids. The exact reverse occurred, totally unexpected by me. The kids began to learn—not pick up, but learn—formal English, oral and written, far more quickly than I thought they could."[11]

A Californian whose own Mexican mother never learned English, Noonan went on: "You read the research and they tell you it takes seven years. Here are kids within nine months in the first year, and they literally learned to read."[12]

If we are to remain one nation and one people, an end to bilingual education is essential, for two languages means two cultures and eventually two countries. The American people know this. English must become the official language of the American people.

• The Republican party's drive to make Puerto Rico a state should be defeated. Like Cuba and Costa Rica, Puerto Rico is a separate country with its own language, customs, and culture. Her people's right to independence and eventual nationhood should not be taken away.

• The U.S. Border Patrol should get the manpower it needs to police our borders, and Americans alone should decide whether and when our national family should be enlarged. If President Fox wants open borders, let him open up his own border with Guatemala.

• Businesses that repeatedly hire illegal aliens to avoid paying the wages and providing the benefits and protections legislated for American workers should be prosecuted.

• Any expansion of NAFTA should be opposed. As the European Economic Community (EEC) inexorably evolved from a customs union into a political union, a U.S.-Mexico economic union is a fatal step toward political union of the United States and Mexico, i.e., the end of true independence and nationhood. If Mr. Bush is not aware of this, President Fox is. The history and culture of Mexico and of our Southwest are inseparable, but we remain separate and distinct nations—neighbors, not brothers. And as that most American of poets, Robert Frost, wrote, "Good fences make good neighbors." Let us "walk the line / and set the wall between us once again."[13]

## THE SOVEREIGNTY QUESTION

In its agenda for world community, the *Humanist Manifesto* of 1973 was almost prophetic. Americans, it declared, must "transcend the limits of national sovereignty and . . . move toward the building of a

world community. . . . We look to . . . a world order based on transnational federal government."[14] In words that echo Gramsci and *The
Greening of America,* the manifesto rhapsodized:

> The true revolution is occurring. . . . At the present juncture
> of history, commitment to all humankind is the highest com-
> mitment of which we are capable; it transcends the narrow
> allegiances of church, state, party, class, or race in moving to-
> ward a wider vision. . . . What more daring a goal for human-
> kind than for each person to become, in ideal as well as
> practice, a citizen of the world community.[15]

This idea, of an end of nations and the creation of a world government, has been a dream of intellectuals since Kant. Though utopian, it recurs in every generation. It is a Christian heresy. When the
philosophes of the Enlightenment repudiated the church, they needed
a substitute for the church's promise and vision of heaven. So, they
created a new vision of all mankind laboring together to create heaven
here on earth. The trading away of the hereafter for the here-and-
now is the bargain Esau bought into when he sold Jacob his birthright
for a bowl of potage. And the children of the Enlightenment are now
far along with their project. As Christianity dies in the West, the
foundation and first floor of a world government are already in place.

The UN is to be its parliament, with the Security Council its upper
chamber (the veto is to be abolished), and the General Assembly its
lower house. The International Criminal Court, the World Court, and
the World Trade Organization would constitute its judicial branches.
The IMF is its Federal Reserve. The World Bank and its sister development banks are the foreign aid agencies. The UN Food and
Agricultural Organization and the World Health Organization are
among its welfare agencies. The Kyoto Protocol on global warming
creates the global EPA. The model and forerunner is the European
Union, the EU. Strobe Talbott, Clinton's roommate at Oxford and

architect of his Russian policy, in a column a decade ago in *Time,* declared that the twentieth century had "clinch[ed] the case for world government, and described the regime that will rule in the closing decades of the twenty-first century:

> All countries are basically social arrangements. . . . No matter how permanent and even sacred they may seem at any one time, in fact they are all artificial and temporary. . . . Within the next hundred years . . . nationhood as we know it will be obsolete; all states will recognize a single, global authority. A phrase briefly fashionable in the mid-20th century—"citizen of the world"—will have assumed real meaning by the end of the 21st.[16]

In Talbott's vision, the WTO, the IMF, and the World Bank are the "protoministries of trade, finance and development for a united world."[17]

"Are we all clear that we want to build something that can aspire to be a world power, not just a trading bloc but a political entity?" thundered Romano Prodi, president of the European Commission, to the European Parliament in February 2001. "Do we realize that our nation states, taken individually, would find it far more difficult to assert their existence and their identity on the world stage?"[18]

Europe is already face-to-face with the "National Question." Do its great nations—Britain, France, Italy, Germany, Russia—and its ancient states, with their magnificent histories and heritage—Portugal, Spain, Austria, Hungary, Holland, Poland, Greece, all the rest—wish to live on as separate and unique peoples? Do they have the will to endure as who they are? Or are they weary of independence? Would they prefer national euthanasia inside a socialist superstate and a life as permanent dependencies of a Brussels bureaucracy?

The great European civil war lasted from 1914 to 1989. Fascism and Bolshevism were crushed. But that is not the end of history. With the war against International Communism over, a new struggle, against international socialism, has begun. This is the decisive conflict of the twenty-first century. It will determine whether the unique cultures of the West survive or become the subcultures of a multicultural continent. It will determine whether the nations of Europe will survive independent and free, or be converted into provinces of a European superstate where the exercise of their inherent right to preserve their unique identity will be forever outlawed.

Today, the peoples of Europe are being told that decency, justice, and rightful restitution for their past sins require that they throw open their doors and share their national homes with the descendants of those their fathers misruled and persecuted, however many wish to come. Can the nations of Europe resist the nonnegotiable demands of the cultural Marxists? For what is being demanded of them is nothing less than the demographic, national, and cultural suicide of their countries—for the good of mankind.

"Commitment to all humankind is the highest commitment of which we are capable; it transcends the narrow allegiances of church, state, party, class, or race in moving toward a wider vision." So declared the *Humanist Manifesto*. But some of us yet believe our loyalty to our own families, countries, church, and culture comes first. So the lines are drawn in the battle of the century. Patriotism or globalism. Nation-state or New World Order. "Independence Forever!" or world government.

Independence is more precious than power, and countries are worth fighting for. And because men will not give love or loyalty to an EU, a UN, a WTO, or any "international community," the fight for independence forever can be won, if patriots of all nations pull together and do not lose heart. For what James Burnham said of liberalism is true of globalism. "[It] does not offer ordinary men compelling motives for personal suffering, sacrifice and death. . . . [It] proposes a set of pale and bloodless abstractions—pale and bloodless for the very reason that they have no roots in the past, in deep feeling, and in suffering."[19]

Because it is a project of elites, and because its architects are un-known and unloved, globalism will crash on the Great Barrier Reef of patriotism. That is our belief, and in that is our hope.

Nations may break up, some may surrender their sovereignty to vanish inside a European superstate, but people will rebel, as they did against the Soviet empire, and re-create the countries whence they came.

Mr. Gore may have slipped his Kyoto Protocol by customs, Mr. Clinton may have signed us on to the UN International Criminal Court, but Mr. Bush has repudiated Kyoto and the ICC. As for the WTO, it is paralyzed by transatlantic quarrels over U.S. steel tariffs, dumping, and export subsidies, and, outside Davos, its admirers are few. And as the Battle of Seattle showed, the passion and fire, be it laborite, Naderite, or Far Right, were outside the hall in the street.

Europe's peoples are growing wary of the brave new world being prepared for them by the Strobe Talbotts and Romano Prodis. At the EU summit in Nice, the smaller nations balked at new surrenders of national sovereignty. Danes rejected the euro. In March 2001, 77 percent of the Swiss and every single canton voted no in the "Yes to Europe" referendum that would have produced immediate negotia-tions to enter the EU.[20] In some German-speaking cantons, the "no" vote reached 85 percent.[21]

When Ireland ignored an EU directive and cut taxes, Dublin was disciplined. "Sorry," said President Prodi, "but sometimes the teacher has to punish the best pupil."[22] The Irish foreign minister, whose economy was growing at 8 percent, fired back, "Perhaps when other countries in Europe have [Ireland's] sort of success, I will take more cognizance."[23] Irish voters then torpedoed the Nice agreement and EU expansion as a dilution of Dublin's voice in Europe and a threat to Irish sovereignty.

Italians have a new center-right government that means to put Italy first. The German Christian Democrats are increasingly blunt about their desire to maintain their national identity and culture. British Tories went down to defeat, but the causes they espoused—preserving the nation and saving the pound—have majority support. Rising resistance in Europe needs to hear an echo from this side of the Atlantic.

WHEN THE EU expands eastward, the crunch will come. An EU of twenty-five nations cannot be ruled from Brussels, unless Brussels acquires the power the U.S. government wields over the fifty states. As the Cold War against world communism was won, the struggle against global socialism is not lost.

Americans should resist any surrender of sovereignty, no matter which president or party favors it, and align themselves with the patriots of Europe like Margaret Thatcher and the Euroskeptics who are making retention of the British pound the red line of patriotism. For all countries, the choice is coming: between national defiance and national extinction. And we cannot go gentle into that good night.

How can Americans enlist in this battle?

• Oppose new funding to the IMF and World Bank. These agencies have squandered hundreds of billions of tax dollars on loans that would put most bankers in prison. But the IMF now has a golden hook in scores of countries to force them to conform to the dictates of the global elite. That hook needs to be removed.

• Press the president to send the treaty establishing the International Criminal Court that Mr. Clinton signed, and the Kyoto Protocol that Mr. Bush has rejected, to the Senate, with a recommendation that both be voted upon and voted down. Any UN attempt to seize governmental powers should be resisted, especially any taxes for exclusive UN use or any plans for a UN Army.

• America's ultimate goal should be the abolition of the WTO and a return to bilateral trade treaties enforced by the United States and its trade partners, and an end to this international tribunal in which America has one vote and the European Union has fifteen.

• Oppose any expansion of NATO. Once a defensive alliance of free nations to block any invasion of Western Europe by Stalin's empire, NATO has been converted into a neoimperialist bloc, which now asserts a sovereign right to attack and invade small nations like Serbia in the name of democracy and human rights. The Founding Fathers would have been ashamed of what Clinton and Albright did to the Serbs. This small nation did not attack us, did not threaten us, did not seek war with us. Yet, we smashed Serbia as horribly as Hitler had, for defying our demand for an unrestricted right of passage through their land, to tear off the cradle of their country, Kosovo.

• Support a complete withdrawal of U.S. ground forces from Europe and Asia and a review of all treaty guarantees that date back to a Cold War that ended a decade ago. Old allies such as South Korea should begin to provide the troops and pay the costs for their own defense. Every great empire of the last century perished for the same reason. Overextended, each involved itself in wars far beyond the scope of its own vital and national interests. Let us learn from history.

While vigilance against terrorism and a defense against missile attack by rogue nations are national priorities, the best way to avoid any attack on our nation or its armed forces is to get them out of harm's way, by disengaging the United States from ideological, religious, ethnic, historic, or territorial quarrels that are none of America's business.

What happened on September 11, 2001, was a direct consequence of an interventionist U.S. policy in an Islamic world where no threat to our vital interests justifies our massive involvement. We are a republic, not an empire. And until we restore the foreign policy urged upon us by our Founding Fathers—of staying out of other nations' quarrels—we shall know no end of war and no security or peace in our own homeland.

## THE CULTURE WAR

Challenging Prof. Samuel P. Huntington's thesis of a coming "clash of civilizations," James Kurth wrote in *The National Interest* that Huntington's batteries, like the guns of Singapore, are pointed in the wrong direction:

> The real clash of civilizations will not be between the West and one or more of the Rest. It will be between the West and the Post-West within the West itself. This clash has already taken place within the brain of Western civilization, the American intellectual class. It is now spreading from that brain to the body politic.[24]

Exactly. Like colon cancer, the long-term threat to the West lies deep within, and whether the West survives is a question Western peoples will answer. As Pogo said, "We have met the enemy and he is us."

The revolution has thus far triumphed, but its tenure, like that of Danton and Robespierre, may be brief. For the civilization it is creating cannot endure. Like heroin, it gives a good high, but imbibed too deeply, it kills. Six hundred Americans had died of AIDS in 1983 when the author urged the White House to address the medical crisis in a column that closed, "The poor homosexuals; they have declared war on nature and nature is exacting an awful retribution."[25] So it did. Hundreds of thousands have since died. Hundreds of thousands who carry the HIV virus are kept alive only by daily "cocktails" of miracle drugs.

The sexual revolution has begun to devour its children. The statistics on abortion, divorce, collapsing birthrates, single-parent homes, teen suicides, school shootings, drug use, child abuse, spouse abuse, violent crime, incarceration rates, promiscuity, and falling test scores show how this society, in which the cultural revolution is ascendant, is decomposing and dying. Empty nurseries and full waiting rooms outside the psychiatrist's office testify that all is not well. But before this diseased culture runs its course, it may take the West down with it.

WHY CANNOT THE new culture and civilization endure?

First, the elite it has produced is unloved and commands no loyalty. Indeed, it is detested for its intolerance and amorality, and for what it has done to traditional heroes and the old faith. The public jubilation over Mr. Clinton's disgrace in the pardons scandal reflects the public's contempt for the counterculture he came to embody.

Second, the ideology of the revolution clashes with the laws of human nature and nature's God. Thus, this new society is built on sand. Women are not the same as men, and saying so does not make it so. Women are profoundly different, with separate and distinct social roles that are not interchangeable, judicial orders notwithstanding. They cannot live as men do without calamitous consequences for the family, society, and country.

Homosexuality is not redemptive; it is addictive. By the very way in which they define themselves, the homosexuals are killing themselves, physically, morally, and spiritually. So say Augustine, Aquinas, and the Atlanta Center for Disease Control, as well as the Torah, the New Testament, and the Koran. Who says otherwise?

Even a glance at the obituary pages testifies that homosexuality is incompatible with a long life. Like other societies, ours is discovering that before He wrote his commandments in stone, God took the precaution of writing a copy on the human heart. Deny that His laws are binding, rage against them, you still cannot escape the consequences of living outside the laws of nature and of nature's God.

We may indoctrinate children into believing that gender differences exist only in the mind, that all civilizations, cultures, religions, and nations are equal. The world will teach them they were lied to. While our "current relativism asserts the equality of all cultures," writes Kenneth Minogue in *New Criterion,*

> nobody, of course, seriously believes this. Quite apart from technology, the moral inequality of cultures is conspicuous in the position of women in different cultures. It was only the West that abolished slavery. But it is a mark of current decorum—perhaps avoidance of the dreaded "triumphalism"—that we should not proclaim any superiority in European civilization, even though it is the one place the millions want to get into.[26]

In their hearts, who truly believes in the equality of all civilizations, cultures, faiths? Do followers of the Prophet believe Christianity is a religion equal to their own? Did the North American martyrs who died to bring the Catholic faith to the Iroquois believe Indian religions were entitled to equal respect? Did Cortes and Pizarro believe all civilizations were equal when they set out to conquer and convert the Aztecs and Incas? Have all cultures produced equally great works of poetry, prose, painting, sculpture, music, and architecture? Does anyone believe that, or is that just polite prattle at the Metropolitan and the Museum of Modern Art?

Are all nations equal? Why then are the refugees from all over the world fleeing to the West? Are all peoples equal? In America we have equal rights under the law. But the idea of the innate dignity of every human being and of equal justice under law is not a product of China, Japan, Africa, or Arabia. It came out of the West. Is chattel slavery evil? Yes, but which faith first began to teach that, and what nation began the eradication of slavery? Was it not Christianity and the British nation?

Under our First Amendment, all ideas and faiths have an equal right to be heard, but it is illogical and absurd to thereby conclude that all ideas and faiths are equal. All civilizations are not equal. The

West has given the world the best that has been thought and taught. Western civilization and culture are *superior*. One-person, one-vote democracy is not an inviolate principle; it is a utilitarian idea. On a global basis it will not do. With 4 percent of the world's people and 30 percent of its economic wealth and military power, Americans should be the last people on earth to be babbling nonsense about the equality of nations, and the last people to yield an ounce of sovereignty to the Tower of Babel on Turtle Bay.

A world government in which all nations and peoples have an equal voice in determining the destiny of man is absurd. The pilot flies the plane, not the passengers, and parents do not give toddlers a voice and vote in family decisions. This is not a call to arrogance, but to a new moral certitude and self-confidence on the part of those to whom the truth has been given.

In his 1931 essay "A Plea for Intolerance," Bhp. Fulton Sheen deplored that "want of intellectual backbone" that causes the modern preacher "to straddle the ox of truth and the ass of ignorance."[27] Toward some things, Sheen admonished us, moral people must be "intolerant."[28]

> Tolerance applies only to persons, but never to truth . . . or principles. About these things we must be intolerant. . . . Right is right if nobody is right; and wrong is wrong if everybody is wrong. And in this day and age we need, as Mr. Chesterton tells us, "not a Church that is right when the world is right, but a Church that is right when the world is wrong."[29]

The revolution will be short-lived, because the spirit of cynicism it has bred in the young will turn against it. Its icons will be smashed by the barbarians it has spawned. Critical Theory is a game all can play. The politics of personal destruction used on John Tower and Robert Bork are now a weapon in the arsenals of both sides in the culture war. With the revolution in power, the cynical attitude of the sixties slogan—"Don't Trust Anybody over Thirty!"—is easily turned against it. With Western culture, the immune system of our civilization, discredited and damaged, the new America is as defenseless as the old.

When German Panzers were at Moscow's gates, Stalin discovered that few would die for Bolshevism, but her people would fight to stop the rape of Mother Russia. Patriotism saved the motherland, but American patriotism has been subverted by the sappers of the culture war. When Madeleine Albright, William Cohen, and Sandy Berger went to Ohio State to drum up support for renewed bombing of Iraq, they found that the Gen-Xers were no more enthusiastic about Clinton's wars than Bill Clinton and his Woodstock comrades had been to fight "Nixon's war."

"CAN'T WE ALL just get along?" Rodney King plaintively asked as the riots raged in LA, after the cops who had thrashed him were acquitted in Simi Valley. If only we could. But the painful truth is: We cannot "all just get along," because we are going through a civil war of the soul, a clash over who we are, what we believe, what we stand for as a people. It is an irrepressible conflict, for it is about first things. Those who deny that the culture war is at root a religious war have not dug down to its roots. It is self-delusion to believe that there can be a brokered peace. This revolution will quickly violate any armistice we agree upon, for it is about absolute power, and the annihilation of the old America.

Conservatives and traditionalists are called racists, fascists, bigots, extremists, homophobes, and Nazis because to the revolution that is who and what we are. The assaults on our history and heroes are not going to end, because to the cultural revolution that is the way to purify America of a hateful legacy and make her a good nation.

Look at what is being asked of the God-and-country people. Their children are forced to drink from a culture they consider decadent, if not demonic. The government uses their tax dollars to fund what they believe is the slaughter of unborn children. They must send their young to schools they believe imperil their faith. They are told to give up trying to create a godly nation that conforms to biblical law, for that is now forbidden by the Constitution. This is the asking price of peace in the culture war, and, for millions of Christians, the price is too high.

A society steeped in pornography, where homosexual unions are blessed by clergy, and from which all Christian symbols and celebrations have been purged, is one they no longer wish to live in. To the silent majority, government is losing its legitimacy. They have not resisted violently, for they are not violent people. But they are a put-upon people, who have begun to see the government as them, not us, and they are searching for ways to secede from a decadent dominant culture.

In *Gone With the Wind,* a bitter Rhett Butler, patience exhausted, takes his final leave of Tara. A shaken Scarlett cries after him, "But what will I do?" Rhett replies, "Frankly, my dear, I don't give a damn."[30]

Less and less do we Americans seem to give a damn what happens to the other side in the culture war. We just want out of this marriage. We are drifting toward break-point. Has the time come to split the blanket and concede the truth of Dos Passos's verdict, "All right, we are two nations"?[31]

A few years ago, a neoconservative magazine editorialized that you cannot both love your country and loathe its government. But Washington did not hate England when he went to war to overthrow the rule of Parliament and king. Robert E. Lee did not hate the country he had fought for in Mexico; he only wished to be free of its government. Alice Roosevelt and Charles Lindbergh loathed FDR, but they loved America and did not want her dragged into another European bloodbath that they believed was not America's war. A man can love his country and loathe a government led by Mr. Clinton. Millions did.

———

IF AMERICA IS ceasing to be the good country we grew up in, what do we owe the government? The answer lies in Matthew XXII, 21: "Render therefore unto Caesar the things that are Caesar's and to God the things that are God's."[32] Traditionalists should emulate Roman converts. The empire still merited their allegiance, but they came to see the culture as decadent. Escape was essential. So they separated themselves from old comrades and customs and created a new Christian culture in their own families and within the fellowship of the converted. They remained loyal to the Roman Empire, but seceded from its pagan culture.

Secession from this culture can take many forms—from giving up movies and TV, to blacking out channels, to homeschooling, to protesting outside abortion clinics, to moving to a less-polluted environment. The Amish seceded long ago. Orthodox Jews have seceded. Mormons seceded with Brigham Young's trek to the Great Salt Lake. Catholics in the nineteenth century removed their children from public schools to put them in parish schools. In the 1980s, Evangelical and Fundamentalist Christians began to create an alternative culture and parallel institutions—Christian schools, TV shows, magazines, radio stations, networks, bookstores, and publishing houses. Millions of children attend Catholic and Christian schools; over a million are homeschooled. Addressing Catholic traditionalists, *Wanderer* columnist James K. Fitzpatrick writes, "We will have to adjust to life as a subculture with all that implies . . . The alternative is making our peace with the new America being shaped by the Hollywood porn merchants. . . . That surrender is unthinkable."[33]

Adults can secede from the dominant culture by buying books, tapes, and CDs. The local video store may be pushing "adult films," but Blockbuster carries the finest films ever made. What Hollywood produced yesterday is not what Hollywood produces today. The films of yesterday celebrated heroism, honor, and patriotism. *Gladiator, The Patriot,* and *Thirteen Days,* honored and popular films of 2000, were positive films. When, in 1999, the American Film Institute compiled its list of the one hundred Greatest American Movies, only one movie made after 1982 was in the top fifty.[34]

The much-derided 1950s had seven of the top twenty: *On the Waterfront, Singin' in the Rain, Sunset Boulevard, The Bridge on the River Kwai, Some Like It Hot, All About Eve,* and *The African Queen.*[35] Among the other 1950s films in the one hundred greatest: *High Noon, Rear Window, Streetcar Named Desire, From Here to Eternity, Rebel Without a Cause, Vertigo, An American in Paris, Shane, Ben-Hur, Giant, A Place in the Sun,* and *The Searchers.*[36]

In 1998, the Modern Library board offered its selection of the one hundred best novels of the twentieth century. While the counterculture was represented, the list contained four of Conrad's works, including *Lord Jim* and *Heart of Darkness,* Orwell's *Animal Farm* and *1984,* Huxley's *Brave New World,* Koestler's *Darkness at Noon,* Robert Penn Warren's *All the King's Men,* William Golding's *Lord of the Flies,* Walker Percy's *The Moviegoer,* and Kipling's *Kim.*[37] The one hundred nonfiction books had a leftward tilt, but T. S. Eliot, H. L. Mencken, Shelby Foote, Tom Wolfe, Winston Churchill, Paul Fussell, and British war historian John Keegan made the cut.[38]

It would not be difficult for traditionalists to put together a reading course for high school and college students, plus a film library, that would introduce America's young to the best that has been written, spoken, and put on the silver screen. If raw sewage is being dumped in the reservoir, buy bottled water. The rule applies to a polluted culture.

The Internet can put together communities of political and religious belief. Adults can find what they want in biography, history, politics, and news, not only in books but on cable TV. Radio carries trash talk, but also Christian and conservative talk, and classical and popular music, as well as acid rock, hard rock, satanic rock, hip-hop, and gangsta rap.

For children, escape is far more difficult. Hedonism pervades the music they hear, the movies they see, MTV, and prime-time. It is in the magazines and books they read. There is no way out. Perhaps the best parents can do is to inculcate in their children values by which to live and pray these values see them through the Great Dismal Swamp of American popular culture in the twenty-first century.

## POLITICS

But if we can secede from the dominant culture, we cannot escape from politics. To do so is to surrender and permit the cultural revolution to have its way with America. So where do we go from here?

Clearly, the White House wants the cup of culture war to pass away. Mr. Bush said as much when his Florida victory was confirmed:

> I believe things happen for a reason, and I hope the long wait of the last five weeks will heighten a desire to move beyond the bitterness and the partisanship of the recent past. Our nation must rise above a house divided. Americans share hopes and goals and values far more important than any political disagreements.[39]

"Isn't it pretty to think so?" said Jake in the sad final line of *The Sun Also Rises*.[40] But the truth is that America *is* a house divided, and Americans do not "share hopes and goals and values." That is what the culture war is all about. As Chilton Williamson, Jr., writes in *Chronicles,* the revolution is "not willing to live and let live."[41]

> The Old America would deny the New America abortion, gay marriage and certain other demands at war with natural law and traditional morality. The New America would deny the Old anything it finds incompatible with the progressive agenda *du jour*: tobacco, alcohol, fast foods, red meat, keeping caged birds, hunting, rodeos, sport shooting, prayer at football games, hate speech, free speech, freedom of association, four-wheel drive trucks, *guns*.[42]

"Cheyenne, Wyoming, can tolerate the existence of New York City and Los Angeles," writes Williamson, "but L.A. and New York City can't abide knowing that, out there on the steppes and in the mountains of the Great American Desert, the other America is leading an existence that fits its own particular circumstances, customs, and preferences."[43]

The culture war is not going away, because it is not finished with us yet. Eventually, even Mr. Bush, a reluctant warrior, will be dragged in.

There are many things that you can refuse to do with a man. You can refuse to work for him, dine with him, or talk to him. But if he wants to fight, you have got to oblige him. Leaders are paroled from combat in the culture war only by exiting the field or raising a white flag. Since the sixties, no president has been able to escape. Eventually, all had to take sides, and all paid a price.

But until Mr. Bush takes up his post, traditionalists need to take stock of the ground lost. As Dorothy said, "Toto, I don't think we're in Kansas anymore."[44] This is not Ronald Reagan's America. A large slice of America has been Clintonized. "There may be more of them than I thought," said Rush Limbaugh, postelection. Were an election held today between Clinton and Reagan, 90 percent of our cultural elite would forget the pardons and vote for Clinton. Could Reagan carry California today as he did four times? Could a presidential candidate who is pro-life sweep forty-nine states, as Nixon did in 1972 and Reagan did in 1984?

Politics cannot pull the West out of its crisis, for it is not a crisis of material things, but a crisis of the soul. The refusal of Western women to have children, the embrace by Western society of hedonism and materialism—these will not be undone by Tom DeLay, Trent Lott, or Mr. Bush. But politics is not irrelevant. FDR called the presidency "preeminently a place of moral leadership."[45] Steps can be taken to impede the revolution and advance the day when, as with the "evil empire," rollback begins.

• *The Imperial Judiciary.* Reshaping the Supreme Court is crucial to any strategy for victory in the culture war, for the court is the battering ram of revolution. It must be returned to constitutionalism, and the people left alone to create the society they wish to live in and have their children grow up in. If America is still a free land, that is their right. "I have no litmus test" for justices, says President Bush, but conservatives do have a litmus test: no liberal judicial activists need apply. Nominees such as his father's choice, David Souter, or President Ford's choice, John Paul Stevens, would be an irredeemable blunder.

Eventually, the incorporation doctrine, by which all the restrictions imposed on Congress by the Constitution are imposed, through the Fourteenth Amendment, on the states, must be overturned. From *Miranda* to *Roe v. Wade,* this is the authority by which the Court dictates to the nation.

In November of 1996, Fr. Richard John Neuhaus, editor of *First Things,* conducted a symposium, "The End of Democracy? The Judicial Usurpation of Politics." Born out of anger and frustration with recent court rulings, the symposium was based on this proposition:

> The government of the United States of America no
> longer governs by the consent of the governed. . . . The
> question here explored is whether we have reached or
> are reaching the point where conscientious citizens can
> no longer give moral assent to the existing regime.[46]

The authors, wrote Father Neuhaus, "examine possible responses to laws that cannot be obeyed by conscientious citizens." These responses range from "non-compliance to resistance to civil disobedience to morally justified revolution."[47] Among the contributors was Robert Bork, who wrote, "When the VMI decision came down, my wife said the Justices were behaving like 'a

band of outlaws.' . . . An outlaw is a person who coerces others
without warrant in law. That is precisely what a majority of the
present court does."⁴⁸ The former U.S. appellate court judge suggested it may be time that public officials began defying the Supreme Court:

> Perhaps an elected official will one day simply refuse
> to comply with a Supreme Court decision.
>
> That suggestion will be regarded as shocking, but it
> should not be. To the objection that a rejection of a
> court's authority would be civil disobedience, the an-
> swer is that a Supreme Court that issues orders with-
> out authority engages in an equally dangerous form of
> civil disobedience.⁴⁹

Several neoconservatives were shocked by the premise that the
U.S. government was a "regime" that had lost its "legitimacy";
they called the symposium "an outburst of anti-Americanism." A
few resigned from the board of *First Things*. But the symposium
proved beneficial. It moved the issue to a discussion of action.
Given that the court has assumed dictatorial powers over a democratic republic, what do we do about it, besides deplore it?

One answer is to support public officials who are willing to
ignore court orders and pay the price the court imposes. Alabama's Judge Roy Moore, for one, said that the United States
would have to send troops to remove a plaque with the Ten
Commandments from the wall of his courtroom. He would refuse
to take it down, no matter who ordered him.

Another recourse is to demand that members of Congress use
their constitutional power to circumscribe the juridiction of the
Supreme Court and pass legislation that would enable Americans
to recall and fire federal judges by majority vote, as they can in
California. Term limits can be imposed on federal judges by legislation. If there is a will, there is no shortage of constitutional

ways by which a people can recapture their right to rule themselves.

- *Cashier the Old Generals.* During Vietnam, Sen. George Aiken was hailed for his witticism "Let's declare victory and get out."[50] Aiken was urging us to accept defeat and all that meant for the Vietnamese and Cambodians who had put their lives and trust in us. It was Aiken's clever way of saying, "Let's cut and run, and say we won." The humor escaped some of us. Yet the Aiken approach appears to have found favor today with some neoconservatives in the culture war. "I regret to inform Pat Buchanan that those [the culture] wars are over and the left has won," said Irving Kristol after my address to the Houston Convention.[51] Gertrude Himmelfarb (Mrs. Irving Kristol) wrote in *One Nation, Two Cultures:*

> let us be content with the knowledge that the two cultures are living together with some degree of tension and dissension but without civil strife or anarchy. America has a long tradition of tolerance . . . that serves as a mediating force between the two cultures, assuaging tempers and subduing passions, while respecting the very real, very important differences, between them.[52]

Pace Mrs. Kristol, should passions be subdued when a million babies are yearly butchered, when infanticide is legal, when Catholic symbols are desecrated, when children are taught the pleasures of perversion in public schools, when our culture is poisoned and our heroes are dragged through the mud? Should we be "content" with such a situation? Are these the kinds of "differences" we should respect?

After the Nazis marched into Paris without a shot being fired, André Gide wrote: "To come to terms with yesterday's enemy is not cowardice but wisdom, as well as accepting what is inevitable."[53] Gide was wrong.

But if the Kristols take the Aiken line, the neoconservative Norman Podhoretz has sailed for Yalta. In his celebration of himself, *My Love Affair with America,* Podhoretz sees the culture war dissolving into "an as yet unspoken and unratified accommodation between the two sides . . . a *de facto* armistice on the ground."[54] He quotes approvingly one Mark Lilla on the terms of armistice: "Americans . . . see no contradiction in holding down day jobs in the unfettered global marketplace—the Reaganite dream, the Left nightmare—and spending weekends immersed in a moral and cultural universe shaped by the 60s."[55] But the "moral and cultural universe shaped by the 60s" was a sewer.

Podhoretz cites as a role model Huw Wheldon, who ran the BBC Television Service and let writers and producers "get away with using obscene language and filming sexual encounters that approached the level of soft porn."[56] How did Wheldon deal with these debasers of the culture? He cautioned them that their shows might "fail to attract or hold a sizable audience."[57] No wonder we are losing. This is capitulationism in a battle for what T. S. Eliot defined as "that which makes life worth living."[58]

Podhoretz echoes Henry Kissinger's famous line in the final weeks of the Paris negotiations on Vietnam, "Peace is at hand," a phrase even Henry must surely regret. "As the twentieth century approached its end," writes Podhoretz, "I had the impression . . . that some kind of peace was at hand."[59]

Tell it to the Boy Scouts! For such attitudes, neoconservatism has come to be known, in Sam Francis's phrase, as the "harmless persuasion." The Kristols and Podhoretzes are the summertime soldiers of the culture war, but America needs men and women of more kidney, spleen, and heart if the struggle for the soul of America is not to be irretrievably lost.

• *Open Defiance of Political Correctness.* The right response to the intolerant new orthodoxy is defiance, ridicule, and counterattack. Political adversaries who use terms like *Nazi, fascist, anti-Semite, nativist, homophobe, bigot, xenophobe,* and *extremist* have started a fight and should be accommodated.

Courage is contagious, and defiance can lead to a recovery of will. Americans love underdogs, rebels, and fighters, and are fed up with being demonized and dictated to. The old admonition—speak truth to power!—will stand us in good stead.

In 2001, provocative ads were placed in several college newspapers headlined: "Ten Reasons Why Reparations for Slavery Is a Bad Idea—and Racist Too."[60] Placed by David Horowitz, the ads argued that blacks owe America more than America owes to blacks. At Harvard and Columbia, editors refused the ad. At Brown, students seized the first press run. With a few dollars, the emerging moral shakedown was exposed, and the country got a good look at where the true intolerance in America may be found.

• *Countering Hate Crimes Propaganda with Truth.* Rather than just oppose hate crimes laws designed to demonize white males, conservatives should insist that the Justice Department report annually on *all* interracial violent crimes, including gang assaults and gang rapes, by race and victim, and break down all sex crimes against children into the heterosexual and homosexual. If it is true that white males commit a disproportionate share of interracial crimes, we ought to know. If it is untrue, let us find out who does.

Justice should also report on all violent assaults against immigrants and all violent assaults by immigrants. News reports seem to emphasize the former and ignore the latter. Again, let's learn the truth and, as Al Smith said, let's get it out in the open, because "nothing un-American can live in the sunlight."

• *Pro-Life Laws.* Only 17 to 19 percent of Americans favor outlawing all abortions.[61] But the number of those who claim to be "pro-life" has risen from 33 to 43 percent in five years, and 51 percent believe there should be at least some restrictions.[62] This

is enough support to have Congress vote both to outlaw partial–
birth abortion and to ban all abortions of babies who can live
outside the womb. Such a bill could rally the churches that still
consider "life" the paramount issue. Catholic bishops could be
pressed to demand the support of Catholic legislators, including
Senators Dodd, Leahy, Harkin, Daschle, and Kennedy, who need
to be reminded of the words of Pius XI in his 1930 encyclical
*Casti Connubi (On Christian Marriage):*

> Those who hold the reins of government should not
> forget that it is the duty of public authority . . . to de-
> fend the lives of the innocent . . . among whom we
> must mention in the first place infants hidden in the
> mother's womb. And if the public magistrates . . . do
> not defend them, but by their laws and ordinances
> betray them to death at the hands of doctors and oth-
> ers, let them remember that God is the Judge and
> Avenger of innocent blood which cries from earth to
> heaven.[63]

The late pope's words could be read from the pulpit at Sunday
mass the week of the vote.

Since the Supreme Court overturned a Missouri ban on
partial-birth abortions, Congress has been reluctant to enact a
federal ban. But the time has come for Congress and the president to exercise *their* rights under the Constitution, and to lead
the Court back into the narrow stall set aside for it in the Constitution.

• *Citizen Boycotts.* The Montgomery bus boycott marked the birth
of the modern civil rights movement. An NAACP boycott caused
business leaders to plead for the Confederate battle flag to be
removed from atop the capitol in South Carolina. Boycotts can
also be used to punish those who assault traditional values and
serve as recruitment vehicles for a traditionalist coalition.

The Baptist boycott of Disney failed only for a lack of focus. It was a declaration of economic war on a vast and disparate media empire that includes ESPN, ABC, Disney World, the History Channel, and the Anaheim Angels. But this legitimate democratic weapon of consumer boycott can be used to good effect if good folks will focus on a single product of a single advertiser. When Ronald Reagan began the rollback of the Soviet Empire, he did not send NATO's armies crashing into Central Europe; rather, he overran tiny Grenada. A Grenada strategy can work. How? The same way Cesar Chavez won recognition for California farm workers by leading a boycott of table grapes. If traditionalists and Republicans would unite, select a single product being advertised on one particularly offensive TV show with weak ratings, and everyone would boycott that one product, they could force the advertiser to pull his ads. Then follow up on the next product, until no one is willing to pay the cost of advertising on a TV show offensive to so many. If the weapon worked for Cesar Chavez and the NAACP, there is no reason it cannot work for traditionalists.

- *Initiatives and Referenda.* Soon after South Carolina took down the battle flag and Georgia abolished the state flag containing the St. Andrew's Cross came Mississippi's turn. After fumbling the hot potato for months, Mississippi legislators tossed it to the people to decide in a referendum: did they wish to keep the Magnolia State flag with its replica of the Confederate battle flag or reject and replace it? The governor, editorial pages, and business community lined up for abolition of the old flag and Republican senators Trent Lott and Thad Cochran maintained a discreet silence. On April 17, 2001, the people of Mississippi voted sixty-five to thirty-five to keep their 104-year-old flag.[64]

The call of tradition defeated the command of money. Even a few minority counties bravely voted for the old flag. The message: On matters of culture and morality, traditionalists should take decisions away from elected officials and return them to the people. The last best hope of preserving and reviving a Judeo-Christian culture rests with citizens immune to the power of money and unconcerned with media disapproval.

The author of our Constitution believed in the people's right to rule themselves. "As the people are the only legitimate fountain of power," wrote Madison, "it seems strictly consonant to the republican theory to recur to the same original authority whenever it may be necessary to enlarge, diminish or new-model the power of government."[65]

Not all decisions can be taken by popular vote. Not all decisions by the people are going to be warmly received by traditionalists. After all, the adversary culture has made deep inroads. But a referendum is at least a court of final appeal from dictatorial judges and craven legislators.

• *Defunding the Cultural Revolution.* If Republicans could be convinced they had no choice but to fight a cultural war imposed upon them, they could wreak havoc on their tormentors. For the federal government is today the exchequer of the cultural revolution. If a Republican Congress would identify and terminate all discretionary federal funds to organizations like Planned Parenthood and the NAACP, and close down agencies like the Endowments for the Arts and Humanities, the Department of Education, and the Civil Rights Commission, they could demobilize whole armies of their adversaries. Unfortunately, Republicans are fearful of being branded as "divisive."

Nevertheless, some courageous researcher should produce a listing of all institutions with an arm in the federal trough, and the White House and Congress should be asked to defund all of those, Left or Right, that play politics with tax dollars. As Jefferson wrote, "To compel a man to furnish contributions of money for the propagation of opinions which he disbelieves and abhors is sinful and tyrannical."

• Congress should abolish Presidents' Day and restore Washington's Birthday to honor the Father of our Country.

- The California Civil Rights Initiative, which voters passed sixty to forty, outlawed racial discrimination or favoritism by the state government. A congressman should be found to put the language of the CCRI, written by Ward Connerly of the Board of Regents of the University of California, into legislation, and have Congress vote it up or down as the Civil Rights Act of 2003. The wording is clear:

> The state shall not discriminate against, or grant pref-
> erential treatment to, any individual or group, on the
> basis of race, sex, color, ethnicity or national origin in
> the operation of public employment, public education,
> or public contracting.[66]

Asked his view of this statement, Sen. Joseph Lieberman, Mr. Gore's vice presidential nominee, responded, "I can't see how I can be opposed to it. . . . It is basically a statement of American values . . . and says we shouldn't discriminate in favor of somebody based on the group they represent."[67] Indeed, the words define a color-blind society. If Congress cannot accept this language, which is in the spirit of the Civil Rights Act of 1964, we need a new Congress.

- *Devolution.* In Britain, devolution meant the transfer of power from the Parliament in London to Scotland, Wales, and Ulster. And devolution may be the salvation of traditionalism.

Among the historic victories of secular humanism was the Supreme Court's expulsion of all vestiges of Christianity from the public schools. As the near-monopoly over the education of America's children by public schools no longer serves America's majority, that monopoly should be broken up. School boards, principals, and teachers should be granted independence and freedom to decide what children are taught, what books are used, what holidays are observed, what the character of the school shall be. Parents should be allowed to direct the tax dollars for their children's education to schools, public or private, secular or religious, of their own choosing. Tax credits are preferable to vouchers that can serve as the camel's nose of intrusive government in religious schools. Let the public schools reflect the diversity of our people, which would mean all boys' schools, all girls' schools, and co-ed schools that mirror the religious and cultural values of the parents whose children attend them.

If one school wishes to celebrate Hanukkah, another Christmas, another Kwanzaa, let freedom ring and conformity disappear. Let the local community decide, by democratic vote. We are a disparate people who disagree on almost everything. Let those differences be reflected in our schools. Cracking the education monopoly is far more vital to the health of our society than breaking up any monopoly Bill Gates ever had on computer software.

Regrettably, both parties are moving toward nationalization. When Mr. Clinton is calling for school uniforms, and Mr. Bush talks about how to raise the test scores of third graders, we are going the wrong way.

• *Censorship.* In *Slouching Toward Gomorrah,* Robert Bork raises an issue whose time has come, given the squalid, degraded "art" being pushed in the face of the American people. Must we tolerate this filth in the name of the First Amendment? Writes Bork:

> We seem too timid to state that Mapplethorpe's and Serrano's pictures should not be shown in public, whoever pays for them. We are going to have to overcome that timidity if our culture is not to decline further still. . . . The photographs would be just as offensive if their display were financed by a scatterbrained billionaire.[68]

Where state censorship is not permitted, the moral censorship of a community is imperative. The nation needs a Supreme Court that understands that the Constitution permits states and communities to establish and enforce standards of decency. It is absurd, writes Jacques Barzun, that nations "deplore violence and sexual promiscuity among the young, but pornography and violence in films and books, shops and clubs, on television and the Internet, and in the lyrics of pop music cannot be suppressed, in the interests of the 'free market of ideas.' "[69]

"When people accept futility and the absurd as normal, the culture is decadent," the historian adds.[70] Detoxification of America's culture is far more important than any absolutist interpretation of the First Amendment.

• *Teaching History.* America's young have an astonishing ignorance of American history. Tests confirm it. This is both a tragedy and a danger. If the Supreme Court will not permit the immersion of children in their religious faith in public schools, it cannot forbid the immersion of children in their country's past. Parents and teachers should ensure that American history is taught every school year, and every book from which it is taught should be read by parents to ensure it includes the best of what Americans have said and done through the centuries. No nation has a history to rival ours. Peoples all over the world know this; so should Americans. Almost any child who is steeped in American history will emerge a patriot.

A White House Conference on American history should be called by President Bush to honor and hear our finest historians. Purpose: To call national attention to the scandalous history deficit among America's young, and to encourage the reading and teaching of American history in every school year and throughout a lifetime. The History Project should have the urgency of President Eisenhower's call for a new emphasis on science and physical fitness after the Soviets woke up our generation with Sputnik.

A National History Bee on the lines of our National Spelling Bee could draw scores of thousands of children into a deeper study of their nation's past. The more a child learns of American history, the better he or she will be able to give the lie to those who make war on America's past. As important, the door to the past can be opened to these children for a lifetime. It is a magnificent and marvelous world to visit and explore.

AFTER THE BRITISH defeat at Saratoga, a friend wrote to Adam Smith that the loss of the American colonies must devastate Britain. Smith wrote back, "There is a great deal of ruin in a nation."[71] What Smith meant was that great nations endure defeats, even amputations, and go on. Many of her finest hours, from Trafalgar and Waterloo to Dunkirk and the Battle of Britain, lay ahead of Britain and her empire in 1777.

But what are the prospects for a renaissance of the West?

Candor compels one to admit the prognosis is not good. Western Man may be living out the final act of a tragedy that began five centuries ago. Then, Christendom, though split by a schism between the Orthodox and Roman churches, and shattered by the Reformation, burst out of Europe to conquer the world. But with the eighteenth century came a far more radical challenge from within, not only to the authority of Rome, but to Christianity itself and the cultural and political order to which it had given birth. "Ecrasez l'infame!" Voltaire signed off his letters: "Wipe out the infamous thing!"—the church.[72] "Mankind will not be free until the last king is strangled with the entrails of the last priest," declared Diderot.[73] "Mankind was born free but everywhere he is in chains," said Rousseau.[74]

France rose up and followed the scribblers. The monarchy came crashing down. Louis XVI, Marie Antoinette, and the aristocrats went to the guillotine. The church was dispossessed and looted. Reason triumphed over faith and produced the September massacres, the Terror, Robespierre and the dictatorship, Bonaparte and the empire, and a quarter century of European wars from which France never recovered her unity or primacy.

Then came Darwin to explain that we are all products of evolution, not creation, Marx to declare religion the "opium of the people," and Nietzsche with the courage to take the thread of the argument to its logical end: "God is dead . . . and we have killed him."[75] And if God is dead, said Alyosha in *The Brothers Karamazov*, all things are permissible. And if God is dead, logic leads us to another conclusion: Christianity is a fraud to empower a class of clerical parasites and merits swift eradication for its centuries of deceit and crimes against human dignity and progress. Then, once Christianity is abolished, we can follow science and reason and create the best of all possible worlds here on earth, the only world we shall ever know.

But if Christianity gave birth to the West and undergirds its moral and political order, can the West survive the death of Christianity? Will Durant could find "no significant example in history, before our time, of a society successfully maintaining moral life without the aid of religion."[76] In Belloc's epigram: "The Faith is Europe. Europe is the Faith."[77] But if that faith is dying, what is the belief system, what is the unifying principle, what is the source of moral authority that holds the West together? What makes the West unique? What are the ties that bind?

Some say racial solidarity. But the past five hundred years have been an endless chronicle of European peoples slaughtering one another, with World Wars I and II as climax to the horrors. And during that past half-millennium, the great enemies of Western faith, culture, and civilization have come out of the West. Moreover, America is a multiethnic, multiracial nation today, and the nations of Europe will be tomorrow.

Lincoln spoke of a people held together by the "mystic chords of memory."[78] But ask English, French, or Poles if they share "mystic chords of memory" with Germans and Russians. When Americans recall their history, some find it glorious; others find it villainous and shameful. And as America and Europe open their doors to millions from countries and continents Americans and Europeans once subjugated and colonized, the mystic chords of memory are as likely to divide us as to unite us.

Democracy appears to be the great unifying idea agreed upon. Democracy, free markets, American values—this is what we stand for and will fight for. But this will not do. Most Americans could not care less how other nations govern themselves. A common belief in democracy is too weak a reed to support the solidarity of the West. It is an intellectual concept that does not engage the heart. Men will fight for family, friends, faith, freedom, and country—but democracy? When George Bush said that, while floating off a Japanese island, after being shot down and losing his copilot, his thoughts turned to "the separation of church and state," people howled. If, tomorrow, the government of India, France, Italy, or Brazil fell to a military coup, how many Americans would think it was a matter worth rectifying at the cost of thousands of American lives?

Democracy is not enough. Yeats was right: once faith goes, "Things fall apart, the centre will not hold."[79] So it may be that the time of the West has come, as it does for every civilization, that the Death of the West is ordained, and that there is no sense prescribing new drugs or recommending painful new treatments, for the patient is dying and nothing can be done. Absent a revival of faith or a great awakening, Western men and women may simply live out their lives until they are so few they do not matter.

GROWING UP, ONE *knew* the Cold War could be won. While few realized how weak the other side was, how the ruthlessness of its rulers masked the hollowness of its system, and even fewer anticipated the sudden and total crash that came in 1989, still, we believed we could win, if we had the will, the perseverance, and the leadership to endure.

But the cultural revolutionaries are succeeding where the Leninists failed. Communism ceased making converts in the West two generations before it fell. The cultural revolution is making converts even now. And democracy alone cannot defeat it, for democracy is defenseless against an ideology that has as its end the transformation of democracy by a new elite, a new faith, and a new order. Indeed, democracy facilitates the revolution, as its exploiters and enemies like Marcuse realized. Hitler showed what pathetic resistance democracy offers to True Believers who can convert the masses to be rid of it. This is what Eliot meant when he wrote in 1939:

> The term "democracy," as I have said again and again, does not contain enough positive content to stand alone against the forces you dislike—it can easily be transformed by them. If you will not have God (and He is a jealous God), you should pay your respects to Hitler and Stalin.[80]

Once an ideology takes hold of a society, only a superior force or a superior ideology can exorcise it. To defeat a faith you must have a faith. What, other than Christianity, is the West's alternative faith? Again, Eliot: "As political philosophy derives its sanction from ethics, and ethics from the truth of religion, it is only by returning to the eternal source of truth that we can hope for any social organization which will not, to its ultimate destruction, ignore some essential aspect of reality."[81]

But if Christianity has lost its appeal and Christianity "is not an option," the revolution will accelerate until we hit the retaining wall of reality. Perhaps Cyril Connolly was right when he wrote, half a century ago, "It is closing time in the gardens of the West."[82]

America is a paradox. She remains the greatest nation on earth, the land of opportunity, possessed of a vitality and energy unlike those of any other nation. We are the most blessed people on earth. Our science, technology, and medicine are the envy of mankind. Some of us are alive today only because of surgical procedures, medical devices, and miracle drugs that did not exist when we were young. We have so much to be thankful for, and we all owe America. And while no one can deny the coarseness of her manners, the decadence of her culture, or the sickness in her soul, America is still a country worth fighting for and the last best hope of earth.

Seated on his coffin in the wagon carrying him through the Virginia countryside to his place of execution, the old abolitionist John Brown was heard to say softly, "This is a beautiful country."[83] And so it is. And that is why we must never stop trying to take her back.

# AFTERWORD

Since *The Death of the West* was published in January 2002, the four threats to the survival of Western civilization that it identified—Third World immigrant invasions, the dying out of European peoples, the menace of multiculturalism, the rise of a world socialist superstate—have become headline issues from Melbourne to Moscow. These mega-issues will dominate our lives as totally as did the Cold War, and how we manage them will determine whether America and the West survive.

Yet, the spring of 2002 showed us how far Western politicians were out of touch with the people. Across Europe, parties of the populist Right again and again stunned the establishment. In the first round of the French elections, Jean-Marie Le Pen humiliated Socialist Prime Minister Lionel Jospin and eliminated him from the run-off. In the climate of hysteria and hate that followed Le Pen's showing, Dutch leader Pim Fortuyn, who had campaigned for a moratorium on immigration into Holland, the most densely populated country in Europe, was assassinated. His party went on to win a place in the new government.

When a cargo ship laden with 900 Kurdish asylum seekers landed in Sicily before Easter, the Italian government declared a state of emergency. "Police searches are needed otherwise we will be thrown out of our own country by the massive arrival of clandestine immigrants," declared Prime Minister Silvio Berlusconi. "If we don't use force to to stop them," said coalition partner Umberto Bossi of the Northern League, "the hordes will arrive and rub out all they find, imposing their own rules and religions."

British Tory Iaian Duncan Smith now says of illegal aliens, "not one . . . should be allowed to set foot in Britain." Even Labour has gotten the message. "We're not advocating a 'Fortress Europe,' " says Tony Blair, "but what we are saying is there's got to be some order and some rules brought into the system."

According to the *Guardian*, Blair's government is considering using the Royal Navy to intercept refugee traffickers in the Mediterranean and the Royal Air Force transport planes for mass deportations. Those 20 percent showings by the far right British National Party in some working-class towns in the Midlands appear to have concentrated British political minds wonderfully.

As I also wrote in these pages, the exploding birthrate among Arab peoples, especially Palestinians, has created an existential crisis for Israel, compounded by the suicide bombers of Hamas. Paul Kennedy, who has written of the fall of nations, looked at the same demographic data as did I and wondered aloud whether the Jewish state can survive through the mid-century.

In Australia, Prime Minister John Howard was a lost candidate until he took a tough stand against the boatloads of aliens crashing into his country's north coast. When he turned them back, he was reelected. In May, Japan's Health Minister Chikara Sakaguchi warned that the nation's 127 million people in the Home Islands will begin shrinking by 2008. If our birth rate is not turned around, Sakaguchi warned, "the Japanese race will become extinct." Recent figures showed that the number of Japanese children under 15 has now fallen for the twenty-first straight year.

In the United States, President Bush's call upon Congress to grant amnesty to illegal aliens from Mexico created a firestorm that shook the White House, as did the revelation that his INS had granted a student visa to Muhammad Atta, six months after he crashed that hijacked airliner into the World Trade Center.

Also in May, a study of census data for Southern California by the *Los Angeles Times* found that the mass migration of the 1990s, legal and illegal, from south of the border, had sent poverty rates soaring 28 to 68 percent in Los Angeles and its neighboring counties. Only 44 percent of the 9.5 million people living in giant Los Angeles County now speak English as their first language in their own homes.

Economically, America is becoming two nations. Socially, culturally, ethnically, we are becoming, two, three, many nations which have less and less in common with one another. Around kitchen tables and on bar stools, in restaurants and locker rooms, these issues are endlessly argued. But the modern inquisition of Political Correctness dictates that politicians remain silent, or be read out of the company of decent men.

Yet if we do not discuss them, we will not deal with them, and if we do not deal with them, our civilization will die and our country is going to come apart, and we will lose the last best hope of earth. As Bishop Butler said: "Things and actions are what they are, and their consequences will be what they will be; why then should we desire to be deceived?"

Within days of publication, *The Death of the West* was a national bestseller. Within weeks, contracts had been signed to have it published abroad in Russian, Chinese, and Spanish. The American people who love their country and cherish this greatest of all civilizations want these issues addressed, and it is time our elites addressed them. For, if they do not, then, as Lincoln warned, this, too, shall pass away. And we cannot let that happen.

—PATRICK J. BUCHANAN
June 1, 2002

# ACKNOWLEDGMENTS

As has been my custom after campaigns, in November of 2000, I retired to my basement office to read, reflect, and write. This book is a by-product of that sabbatical. Without the support of my wife, Shelley, in the periods of transition and new beginnings that follow those campaigns, it could not have been done.

I also want to express my gratitude, yet again, to my friend, editor, and agent, Fredi Friedman, for her loyalty and unindulgent editing. This is the fourth book of mine that Fredi has chaperoned through to publication. My thanks also to Tom Dunne, my editor and publisher at St. Martin's Press, for his confidence and assistance and Sean Desmond, who saw the text through from word processor to the printed page.

Five friends were kind enough to read the text and to urge cuts, alterations, and additions, many of which were made: Sam Francis, Bill Lind, Scott McConnell, Bill Hawkins, and Allan Ryskind. Also, I must thank Kara Hopkins, my intrepid researcher, who dug up quotes I could only recall from memory, and mined new facts, arguments, and ideas out of books I had not before read. Without her assistance, this work would not be as complete or as persuasive as I hope it is. Finally, my thanks to Joseph Chamie at the UN Population Division for his friendly and swift response to all my requests.

# NOTES

## Introduction

1. "Bush Promotes Agenda for Improving America's Readiness," PR Newswire, May 30, 2000, p. 1.

2. Thomas Edsall, "Political Party Is No Longer Dictated by Class Status; Sex, Religion, Lifestyle Temper Education, Income," *Washington Post,* November 9, 2000, p. A37.

3. Michael Barone, "The 49 Percent Nation," *National Journal,* June 9, 2001, p. 1,715.

4. Terry Teachout, "Republican Nation, Democratic Nation?" *Commentary,* January 2001, p. 25.

5. "Text of Bush's Inaugural Speech," Associated Press, January 20, 2001.

6. Joseph A. D'Agostino and Timothy Carney, "Congressmen: Illegals Here to Stay," *Human Events,* April 2, 2001, p. 3.

7. Arthur M. Schlesinger, Jr., *The Disuniting of America: Reflections on a Multicultural Society* (New York: W. W. Norton & Company, 1992), p. 32.

8. "Transcript of Clinton Remarks at Portland State Commencement," U.S. Newswire, June 15, 1998.

9. Jacques Barzun, *From Dawn to Decadence: 500 Years of Western Cultural Life* (New York: HarperCollins Publishers, 2000), p. 774.

10. Ibid.

11. "Remarks by the President and President-Elect Fox of Mexico at Press Availability," *Federal Document Clearinghouse Federal Department and Agency Documents,* August 24, 2000.

12. Edmund Burke, *Reflections on the Revolution in France* (New Rochelle, N.Y.: Arlington House), p. 91.

13. Hagop Jack Touryantz, "Multifaceted Problems in Multiethnic States: Ethnic

Homogeneity Through Population Exchange," *Armenian Reporter,* March 20, 1999, p. 4.

14. Teachout, p. 29.

15. Donald M. Rothberg, "Bush's One-Time Primary Challenger Endorses President, Blasts Democrats," Associated Press, August 17, 1992.

16. United Nations Secretariat, Department of Economic and Social Affairs, Population Division, *World Population Prospects: The 1998 Revision. Vol. 1: Comprehensive Tables,* November 24, 1998, pp. 100, 118, 152, 158, 164, 182, 202, 224, 240, 258, 268, 338, 350, 352, 366, 368, 376.

17. Gustave Le Bon, *The Crowd* (New York: The Viking Press, 1960), p. 13.

## Chapter One: Endangered Species

Author's Note: Unless otherwise specified, all the statistics in this chapter were published by the Population Division of the United Nations in *World Population Prospects: The 2000 Revision, Highlights,* released on February 28, 2001, *Replacement Migration: Is It a Solution to Declining and Ageing Populations?,* released March 21, 2000, or *World Population Prospects: The 1998 Revision, Vol. 1.* All remaining figures that are not otherwise specified are from the *New York Times 2001 Almanac.*

1. *London Times,* January 16, 2000. http://www.childrenforthefuture.org/fertility%20rate%20by%20education.htm

2. Peter F. Drucker, *Management Challenges for the 21st Century* (New York: HarperBusiness, 1999), p. 44.

3. Population Division, Department of Economic and Social Affairs, United Nations, *World Population Prospects: The 2000 Revision, Highlights,* February 28, 2001, p. 1.

4. Joe Woodard, "Look Out Below!: The Plummeting Birth Rate Will Have a Profound Impact on Boomers as Well as Gen-Xers in the Next Century," *Calgary Herald,* September 12, 1999, p. A12.

5. Ben Wattenberg, "Trés Gray: The Birth Dearth in Europe," *Intellectualcapital.com,* January 24, 1999.

6. Cheryl Stonehouse, "A Taxing Time for the Village with No Babies," *Express,* November 26, 1999.

7. James K. Robinson and Walter B. Rideout, eds., *A College Book of Modern Verse* (Evanston, Ill.: Row, Peterson and Company, 1960), p. 370.

8. Count Harry Kessler, *Walter Rathenau: His Life and Work* (New York: Howard Fertig, 1969), p. 271.

9. Alistair Horne, *To Lose a Battle: France 1940* (Boston: Little, Brown & Co., 1969), p. 10.

10. Joseph Chamie, director, United Nations Population Division, "Letter to Author," January 17, 2001.

11. Toby Helm, "Stoiber Pins Poll Hopes on Cash for Babies Plan," *Daily Telegraph,* January 3, 2001, p. 17.

12. Ellen Hale, "Graying of Europe Has Economies in Jeopardy," *USA Today,* December 22, 2000, p. A14.

13. Ibid.

14. Nicholas Eberstadt, "The Population Implosion," *Wall Street Journal,* October 16, 1997, p. A22.

15. Gregg Easterbrook, "Overpopulation Is No Problem—in the Long Run," *New Republic,* October 11, 1999, p. 22.

16. "The Rise of the Only Child," *Newsweek,* April 23, 2001, p. 50.

17. Ibid.

18. Hale, p. A14.

19. Ibid.

20. Jonathan Steele, "Europe Confronts the Unthinkable," *Manchester Guardian Weekly,* November 8, 2000, p. 14.

21. Jonathan Steele, "The New Migration: Affluent, Controversial," *Guardian,* October 30, 2000, p. 17.

22. Michael Specter, "The Baby Bust,"*New York Times,* July 10, 1998, p. A1.

23. Amelia Gentleman, "Wanted: More Russian Babies to Rescue a Fast Dying Nation," *London Observer,* December 31, 2000; Robert Leqvold, "Russia's Uninformed Foreign Policy," *Foreign Affairs,* September/October 2001, p. 63.

24. Julia Duin, "Former Abortion Providers Find Peace, Solace in Therapy: Many See Religion as Integral to Change," *Washington Times,* February 22, 2001, p. A2.

25. Gentleman, "Wanted: More Babies to Rescue a Fast Dying Nation."

26. Chamie, "Letter to Author."

27. Paul Craig Roberts, "Hearing the Bell Toll," *Washington Times,* December 10, 2000, p. B4.

28. Anthony Browne, "UK Whites Will Be Minority by 2100," *London Observer,* September 2, 2000.

29. Anthony Browne, "Focus: Race and Population: The Last Days of a White World," *Observer,* September 3, 2000, p. 17.

30. "British Birth Rate Drops to Record Low," *Xinhua News Agency,* May 10, 2001.

31. Peggy Orenstein, "Parasites in Prêt-a-Porter," *Sunday New York Times,* Section 6, p. 31.

32. Ibid.

33. Ben Wattenberg, "Counting Change in Euroland," *Washington Times,* January 28, 1999, p. A18.

34. "Remarks by Mother Teresa of Calcutta, India, National Prayer Breakfast, Washington Hilton, Washington, D.C.," *Federal News Service,* February 3, 1994.

35. "Joan Ganz Cooney: Creator of 'Seasame Street,' " *Fort Worth Star Telegram,* September 26, 2000, p. 1.

*Chapter Two: Where Have All the Children Gone?*

1. Ben J. Wattenberg, *The Real America* (Garden City, N.Y: Doubleday & Company, 1974), p. 158.

2. Ibid., p. 159.

3. Ibid.

4. Allan Carlson, "The Natural Family Faces a New World Order: The Case of Population," *The Family in America,* The Howard Center for Family, Religion, and Society, October 1999, p. 4.

5. Ibid., p. 5.

6. James Kurth, "The American Way of Victory," *National Interest,* Summer 2000, p. 5.

7. Theodore Caplow, Louis Hicks, and Ben J. Wattenberg, *The First Measured Century* (Washington, D.C.: AEI Press, 2001), p. 38.

8. Eleanor Mills, "Too Busy to Have a Baby," *Spectator,* September 16, 2000.

9. Ibid.

10. Ibid.

11. Allan Carlson, "The Changing Face of the American Family," *The Family in America,* The Howard Center for Family, Religion, and Society, January 2001, p. 2.

12. Ibid.

13. Friedrich Engels, *The Origin of the Family, Private Property, and the State* (New York: International Publishers, Inc., 1972), p. 137.

14. Carlson, "The Changing Face of the American Family," p. 2.

15. Ibid.

16. Ibid., p. 3.

17. Ibid.

18. Ibid., p. 4.

19. Ibid., p. 5.

20. H. Arthur Scott Trask, "The Rise and Fall of Orestes Brownson," *Southern Partisan,* Summer 2001, p. 25

21. Father C. John McCloskey, "Book Review: American Abundance," http://www.catholicity.com/cathedral/mccloskey/kudlow.html

22. Christopher Cerf and Victory Navasky. *The Experts Speak: The Definitive Compendium of Authoritative Misinformation* (New York: Pantheon Books, 1984), p. 299.

23. Jacqueline R. Kasun, "Population Control Today—and Tomorrow?" *The World and I,* No. 6, Vol. 16, p. 50.

24. Ibid.

25. Ibid.

26. Joseph Collison, "Weaving the Tangled Web," *New Oxford Review,* January 2001, p. 16.

27. George Grant, *Grand Illusions* (Brentwood, Tenn.: Wolgemuth & Hyatt, 1988), p. 59.

28. Andrea Dworkin, *Pornography: Men Possessing Women* (New York: G. P. Putnam's Sons, 1981), p. 9.

29. Kathleen Parker, "Moms Need to Admit Dad Isn't Disposable," *Orlando Sentinel,* November 6, 1996, p. E1.

30. Robin Morgan, ed., *Sisterhood Is Powerful* (New York: Random House, 1970), p. 573.

31. Valerie Solanis, *SCUM Manifesto* (London: Phoenix Press, 1968), p. 1.

32. Fr. Ted Colleton, "Family Is Key to Social Integration," *Interim,* May 1998, p. 1.

33. Vivian Gornick, *Daily Illini,* April 25, 1981.

34. Lynn Langway and Nancy Cooper, "Steinem at 50: Gloria in Excelsis," *Newsweek,* June 4, 1984, p. 27.

35. Paul Greenberg, "American Satire, from Bland to Worse," *Chicago Tribune,* November 18, 1991, p. 19.

36. Bonnie Angelo, "The Pain of Being Black," *Time,* May 22, 1989, p. 120.

37. Stephen Chapman, "Concern for Family Provokes Backlash from Feminists," *Chicago Tribune,* July 24, 1994, p. 3.

38. Wade Horn, "Supporting Men as Dads Can Benefit Everyone," *Washington Times,* February 8, 2000, p. E2.

39. Caplow, Hicks, and Wattenberg, p. 72.

40. Eric Schmitt, "For First Time, Nuclear Families Drop Below 25% of Households," *New York Times,* May 15, 2001, p. A1.

41. Katarina Runske, *Empty Hearts and Empty Houses* (Britain: Family Publications, 1990), p. 21.

42. Rudyard Kipling, "Gods of the Copybook Headings," 1919. http://www.kipling.org.uk/poems_copybook.htm

43. David A. Noebel, *The Legacy of John Lennon: Charming or Harming a Generation?* (Nashville, Tenn.: Thomas Nelson, 1982), p. 53.

44. Ibid.

45. Ron Lesthaeghe, "A Century of Demographic and Cultural Change in Western Europe: An Exploration of Underlying Dimensions," *Population and Development Review,* Fall 1983, p. 429.

46. *Humanae Vitae: Encyclical of Pope Paul VI on the Regulation of Birth,* July 25,1968. http://www.vatican.va/holy_father/paul_vi/en . . . /hf_p-vi_enc_25071968_humanae-vitae_en.htm

47. "Gay Times," *Washington Times,* July 28, 2000, p. A2.

48. John Leo, "Have It Your Way Is the New Moral Order," *Conservative Chronicle,* August 15, 2001, p. 6

49. J. M. and M. J. Cohen, eds., *The New Penguin Dictionary of Quotations* (London: Penguin Books, 1992), p. 314.

50. Will Durant, *Caesar and Christ* (New York: Simon & Schuster, 1944), p. 666.

51. Ibid.

52. Ibid.

53. Ibid.

54. Robert Debs Heinl, Jr., *Dictionary of Military and Naval Quotations* (Annapolis, Md.: United States Naval Institute, 1966), p. 317.

## Chapter Three: Catechism of a Revolution

1. C. S. Lewis, *God in the Dock: Essays on Theology and Ethics,* Walter Hooper, ed. (Grand Rapids, Mich.: William B. Eerdmans Publishing Company, 1972), p. 220.

2. American Humanist Association, *Humanist Manifesto II,* 1973. http://www.humanist.net/documents/manifesto2.html

3. Robert Nisbet, *Prejudices: A Philosophical Dictionary* (Cambridge, Mass.: Harvard University Press, 1982), p. 101.

4. Phyllis Schlafly, "Secular Humanists Give Dunphy Another Platform," *Education Reporter,* November 1995. http://eagleforum.org/educate/1995/nov95/dunphy.html

5. Percy Bysshe Shelley, "A Defense of Poetry," *Selected Poetry and Prose,* Kenneth Neill Cameron, ed. (New York: Rinehart & Company 1958), p. 490.

6. John Lennon, "Imagine," *Imagine* (1971). http://beatleslyrics.tripod.com/lennon/imagine.htm

7. David A. Noebel, *The Legacy of John Lennon: Charming or Harming a Generation?* (Nashville, Tenn.: Thomas Nelson, 1982), p. 11.

8. Ibid., p. 47.

9. Joan Acocella, "The Hunger Artist: Is There Anything Susan Sontag Doesn't Want to Know?" *New Yorker,* March 6, 2000, p. 68.

10. Susan Sontag, *Partisan Review,* Winter 1967, p. 57.

11. Myron Magnet, *The Dream and the Nightmare* (New York: William Morrow and Company, Inc., 1993), p. 203.

12. Camille O. Cosby, "America Taught My Son's Killer to Hate Blacks," *USA Today,* July 8, 1998, p. 15A.

13. "Unrelenting Hostility," *Washington Times,* October 8, 1998, p. A2.

14. Magnet, p. 207.

15. Magnet, p. 205.

16. "How Minorities Are Damaged," *Newsday,* September 10, 1989, p. 1.

17. James K. Robinson and Walter B. Rideout, eds., *A College Book of Modern Verse* (Evanston, Ill.: Row, Peterson and Company, 1960), p. 354.

18. Allan Bloom, *The Closing of the American Mind* (New York: Simon & Schuster, 1987), p. 56.

19. Carol Innerst, "Multiculturalists Push Their Agenda; Want 'Far Right' School Board Ousted," *Washington Times,* August 10, 1994, p. A4.

20. Ibid.

21. Larry Rohter, "Battle over Patriotism Curriculum," *New York Times,* May 15, 1994, p. 22.

22. Ibid.

23. Ibid.

24. Ibid.

25. Ike Flores, "Board Demands Schools Teach American Superiority, Teachers Say Bias," Associated Press, May 25, 1994.

26. Ibid.

27. Ibid.

28. Ike Flores, "Candidates Who Backed 'Cultural Superiority' Defeated at Polls," Associated Press, October 7, 1994.

29. Ronald Radosh, "Mumia and the Historians," *FrontPageMag.com,* February 2, 2001.

30. Thomas Jefferson, "Letter to John Adams," October 28, 1813, in Albert Fried, *The Essential Jefferson* (New York: Collier Books, 1963), p. 517.

31. Lewis Carroll, *Alice's Adventures in Wonderland* (Franklin Center, Pa.: The Franklin Library, 1980), pp. 30–31.

32. David Dennett, *Darwin's Dangerous Idea: Evolution and the Meaning of Life* (New York: Touchstone Books, 1995), p. 516.

33. Ibid.

34. David A. Lieb, "Two Men Accused of Murder, Rape of 13-Year-Old Boy," Associated Press, November 2, 1999.

35. L. Brent Bozell III, "No Media Spotlight on Sex Killing of Boy," *Washington Times,* November 2, 1999, p. A14.

36. Andrew Sullivan, "The Death of Jesse Dirkhising," *Pittsburgh-Post Gazette,* April 1, 2001, p. E1.

37. Frank Morriss, "Compassion and Forgiveness Do Not Negate Justice," *Wanderer,* January 4, 2001, p. 4.

38. David Horowitz, "Racial Witch-Hunt," *Salon.com,* January 22, 2001.

39. William J. Bennett, *Index of Leading Cultural Indicators* (New York: Broadway Books, 1999), p. 17.

40. William Wilbanks, "Frequency and Nature of Interracial Crimes," submitted for publication to *Justice Professional,* November 2, 1990, pp. 2–9.

41. Robert Stacy McCain, "Hate Crimes Not Big Problem in Race Relations, Study Finds; Black-on-White Crime More Frequent and More Damaging," *Washington Times,* June 1, 1999, p. A2.

42. John Woods, "Race and Criminal Cowardice," *Right Now!,* October 2000, p. 11.

43. McCain, p. A2.

44. Ibid.

## Chapter Four: Four Who Made a Revolution

1. Michael Loewy, *Georg Lukács from Romanticism to Bolshevism* (Patrick Caniller, Translator (London: NLB, 1979), p. 112. Cited by Raymond V. Raehn, "The Historical Roots of Political Correctness," The Free Congress Research and Education Foundation.

2. "We Won't Be Slaves to Enemies of the Truth," *Milwaukee Journal Sentinel,* October 3, 1999, p. 5.

3. Barbara Tuchman, *The Proud Tower: A Portrait of the World Before the War: 1890–1914* (New York: Ballantine Books, 1993), p. 462.

4. Loewy, p. 93.

5. Ibid., p. 151.

6. Gerald L. Atkinson, "What Is the Frankfurt School?" August 1, 1999, p. 2. http://www.newtotalitarians.com/FrankfurtSchool.html

7. Arnold Beichman, "In Search of Civil Society," *Washington Times,* February 3, 1993, p. G4.

8. Charles A. Reich, *The Greening of America* (New York: Bantam Books, 1971), p. 2.

9. John Fonte, "Why There Is a Culture War," *Policy Review,* December 2000 and January 2001, p. 17.

10. "Transcript #2077: War Powers Debate," *The MacNeil/Lehrer NewsHour,* September 13, 1983.

11. Raehn, p. 2.

12. Reich, p. 148.

13. Ibid.

14. Charles J. Sykes, *A Nation of Victims* (New York: St. Martin's Press, 1992), p. 54.

15. Ibid.

16. Patrick J. Buchanan, "Americans Need Not Fear United Germany," *Toronto Star,* October 16, 1989, p. A18.

17. Stephen Goode, "Radical Leftovers," *Insight on the News,* November 22, 1999, p. 10.

18. Sykes, p. 54.

19. Christopher Lasch, *The True and Only Heaven: Progress and Its Critics* (New York: W. W. Norton & Company, 1991), p. 447.

20. Jim Nelson Black, *When Nations Die* (Wheaton, Ill.: Tyndale House Publishers, 1994), p. 77.

21. William Lind, "Turn Off, Tune Out, Drop Out: A Cultural Conservative's Strategy for the 21st Century," *Against the Grain,* Free Congress Foundation, Washington, D.C., 1998.

22. Fonte, p. 16.

23. Reich, p. 276.

24. William Lind, "Origins of Political Correctness," Address to Accuracy in Academia's Annual Summer Conference, George Washington University, July 10, 1998.

25. John Leo, "Where Double Standards Are Accepted," *Washington Times,* August 5, 2000, p. A12.

26. Herbert Marcuse, *The Carnivorous Society*; cited by Raehn, p. 3.

27. Roger Kimball, *The Long March* (San Francisco, Calif.: Encounter Books, 2000), p. 15.

28. "Declaration by the Pontifical Council for the Family on Decrease of Fertility in the World," February 27, 1998, p. 3.

29. John Burgess, "Remembering Wren," *Washington Post,* June 14, 1998, p. E1.

30. Gertrude Himmelfarb, "Two Nations or Two Cultures? Party Differences Not as Stark as Cultural Differences," *Commentary,* January 1, 2000, p. 29.

31. F. O. Matthiessen, ed., *The Oxford Book of American Verse* (New York: Oxford University Press, 1950), p. 415.

32. Peter Hitchens, *The Abolition of Britain* (San Francisco, Calif.: Encounter Books, 2000), p. viii.

33. Ibid., p. 3.

34. Linda Massarella, "Angry Pope Slams Rome's Gay Fiesta as a Bitter 'Insult,'" *New York Post,* July 10, 2000, p. 20.

35. Ibid.

36. Patrick J. Buchanan, "Dehumanization of Dissent," *Washington Times,* February 8, 1999, p. A16.

37. Lionel Van Deerlin, "The Dynasty of Huey Long," *San Diego Union-Tribune,* February 28, 1985, p. B1.

38. Julien Benda, *La Trahison des Clercs: The Treason of the Intellectuals* (New York: W. W. Norton & Company, 1969).

39. Broadcast of American Dissident Voices, "The NEA's Anti-American Agenda Threatens Our Nation," March 13, 1993.

40. Walter Adolphe Roberts, "Birth Control and the Revolution," *Birth Control Review,* June 1917, p. 7.

41. Robert Nisbet, *Prejudices: A Philosophical Dictionary* (Cambridge, Mass.: Harvard University Press, 1981), p. 22.

42. Travis LeBlanc, "Western World Not Doomed After All," *University Wire,* November 3, 1997.

43. Eric Hoffer, *First Things, Last Things* (New York: Harper & Row, 1971), p. 71.

44. Laurence Barrett, "Can the Right Survive Success?" *Time,* March 19, 1990, p. 16.

45. Ibid.

46. James F. Cooper, "The Right Agenda: Recapture the Culture," *American Arts Quarterly,* Spring/Summer 1990, p. 3.

47. Ibid.

48. Ibid.

49. Ibid.

## *Chapter Five: The Coming Great Migrations*

1. Robert J. Samuelson, "The Specter of Global Aging," *Washington Post,* February 28, 2001, p. A25.

2. Population Division, Department of Economic and Social Affairs, United Nations Secretariat, *Replacement Migration: Is It a Solution to Declining and Ageing Populations?* March 21, 2000, p. I39.

3. Ibid., p. 137.

4. Peter G. Peterson, *Gray Dawn: How the Coming Age Wave Will Transform America and the World* (New York: Times Books, 1999), p. 18.

5. "The Population Vacuum: Though Humanity Is Imploding, Demographers Refuse to Urge Women to Have More Babies," *Report Newsmagazine,* June 5, 2000, p. 43.

6. Jonathan Steele, "The New Migration: Affluent, Controversial," *Guardian,* October 30, 2000, p. 17.

7. London Observer Service, "British Whites to Be Minority by Year 2100," *Houston Chronicle,* October 8, 2000, p. 34.

8. Roger Cohen, "Illegal Migration Increases Sharply in European Union," *New York Times,* December 25, 2000, p. A1.

9. Molly Moore, "Smuggling of Humans into Europe Is Surging," *Washington Post,* May 28, 2001, p. 1.

10. Nicholas Eberstadt, "The Population Implosion," *Wall Street Journal,* October 16, 1997, p. 22.

11. Steele, p. 17.

12. Roger Cohen, "From Germany's East to West, Conservatives Try to Span Gulf," *New York Times,* June 1, 2001, p. A1.

13. Ibid., pp. A1, A8.

14. John O'Mahony, "A People Skating on Thin Ice," *Guardian,* February 3, 2001, p. 1.

15. Ibid.

16. Robert Cortell, "Islands of Contention," *Financial Times,* August 27, 2001, p.10.

17. "The Population Vacuum: Though Humanity Is Imploding, Demographers Refuse to Urge Women to Have More Babies," p. 43.

18. Sarah Karush, "Government Seeking Ways to Overcome Roots of Low Birth Rate," Associated Press, May 6, 2001.

19. Ibid.

20. Patrick J. Buchanan, "America Loses an Opportunity, and Russia as Ally," *Augusta Chronicle,* February 19, 1998, p. A4.

21. Thomas Babbington Macaulay, *Lays of Ancient Rome,* Horatius, xxvii.

22. American Humanist Association, *Humanist Manifesto II,* 1973. http://www.humanist.net/documents/manifesto2.html

23. Nat Hentoff, "Expanding the Culture of Death," *San Diego Union-Tribune,* January 1, 2001, p. B6.

24. Rita Marker, "Dutch Parliament Votes to Legalize Euthanasia," *International Anti-Euthanasia Task Force Update,* Fall 2000, p. 2.

25. Ibid., p. 3.

26. Ibid.

27. "Netherlands Parliament Legalizes Euthanasia," www.euthanasia.com, November 2000.

28. Marker, p. 3.

29. Licia Corbella, "Euthanasia Law an Open Door to 'Evil,' " *London Free Press,* April 24, 2001, p.A8.

30. Philip Pullella, "Pope Christmas Speech Laments 'Culture of Death,' " Reuters, December 25, 2000.

31. Ibid.

32. Hentoff, p. B6.

33. Marker, p. 7.

34. Marker, p. 8.

35. John Jacobs, "Richard Lamm's Hard Choices," *Sacramento Bee,* July 11, 1996, p. B6.

36. Paula Span, "Philosophy of Death; Bioethicist Peter Singer's Views on Euthanasia Foment Debate," *Washington Post,* December 9, 1999, p. C1.

37. Jacqueline R. Kasun, "Population Control Today—and Tomorrow?" *The World and I,* No. 6, Vol. 16, June 1, 2001, p. 50.

38. Wesley J. Smith, "Peter Singer Gets a Chair," *FrontPageMag.com,* October 22, 1998, p. 4.

39. P. J. King, "Lessons from History: Euthanasia in Nazi Germany," *Pregnantpause.org,* September 9, 2000.

40. Ibid.

41. Ibid.

42. Walker Percy, *The Thanatos Syndrome* (New York: Farrar, Straus Giroux, 1987), p. 360.

43. Terence Kealey, "Don't Blame Eugenics, Blame Politics," *Spectator,* March 17, 2001, p. 10.

44. Dorothy Thompson, "Review of *Mein Kampf,*" from Adolf Hitler, *Mein Kampf* (New York: Reynal & Hitchcock, 1939), Introduction.

45. Kealey, ibid.

46. "Nazi Euthanasia," *The History Place: World War Two in Europe*. http://www.historyplace.com/worldwar2/timeline/euthanasia.htm

47. Ibid.

48. Kasun, op. cit.

49. John W. Wright, ed., *The New York Times Almanac: The Almanac of Record* (New York: Penguin Reference Books, 2000), pp. 470–72.

50. Warren H. Carroll, *The Building of Christendom: A History of Christendom*, vol. 2 (Front Royal, Va.: Christendom College Press, 1987), p. 280.

51. Barry Bearak, "Over World Protests, Taliban Are Destroying Ancient Buddhas," *New York Times*, March 4, 2001, p. 10.

52. William Wallace, "Europe, the Necessary Power," *Foreign Affairs*, May/June 2001, p. 24.

53. Ibid.

54. J. C. Willke, "Global Population: A Reality?" *Life Issues Connector*, January 1998. http://www.lifeissues.org/connector/98jan.html

55. Otto Scott, "The Shape of Events," Speech to the 15th Annual Meeting of the Committee for Monetary Research and Education, November 6, 1989. http://www.fortfreedom.org/h18.htm

56. Roland H. Bainton, *The Horizon History of Christianity* (New York: American Heritage Publishing, 1964), p. 143.

57. Thomas Hobbes, *Leviathan*, Michael Oakeshott, ed. (New York: Macmillan Publishing Company, 1962), p. 80.

## Chapter Six: La Reconquista

1. *Excelsior*, Mexico City, 1982. http://www.americanpatrol.org/ADS/Reconquista Reelectio970719.html

2. Walter A. McDougall, *Promised Land, Crusader State: The American Encounter with the World Since 1776* (New York: Houghton Mifflin, 1997), p. 131.

3. Lewis Lapham, "God's Gunboats," *Harper's Magazine*, February 1993, p. 10.

4. Joseph A. D'Agostino, "Government Deports Only About 1% of Illegal Aliens," *Human Events*, March 23, 2001. http://www.humaneventsonline.com/articles/03-26-01/dagostino.html

5. Glenn Garvin, "Loco, Completamente Loco: The Many Failures of Bilingual Education," *Reason Online*, January 1998, p. 19.

6. Bill Baskervill, "Eugenics Gone but Effects Linger," Associated Press, March 13, 2000.

7. Samuel P. Huntington, "Reconsidering Immigration: Is Mexico a Special Case?" *Center for Immigration Studies Backgrounder*, November 2000, p. 5.

8. Ibid.

9. Ibid.

10. Adam C. Kolasinski, "How Republicans Can Approach the Minority Vote," *FrontPageMag.com*, January 26, 2001, p. 2.

11. Ben Wattenberg, *The First Universal Nation: Leading Indicators and Ideas About the Surge of America in the 1990s* (New York: The Free Press, 1991).

12. Samuel P. Huntington, *The Clash of Civilizations* (New York: Simon & Schuster, 1996), p. 305.

13. Tamsin Carlisle and Joel Baglole, "In Western Canada, a Rising Sense of Grievance," *Wall Street Journal,* March 20, 2001.

14. George Szamuely, "Mexican Merger: United We Fall," Antiwar.com, August 31, 2000. http://www.antiwar.com/szamuely/sz083100.html

15. OECD, "GDP Per Capita, 1999." http://www.oecd.org/std/gdpperca.html

16. Patrick J. Buchanan, "Anti-Americanism in L.A.," *New York Post,* March 7, 1998, p. 13.

17. Lynda Gorov, "A War of Words in Texas Town: Government's Spanish-Only Policy Ignites Controversy," *Boston Globe,* August 28, 1999, p. A16.

18. S. U. Mahesh, "Lawmaker Suggests Racism to Blame After New State Name Axed," *Albuquerque Journal,* February 14, 2001, p. A6.

19. Samuel Francis, "Multiculturalists Preach Hatred of Whites and America," *Las Vegas Review-Journal,* February 27, 1998, p. 17B.

20. "Professor Predicts Hispanic Homeland," Associated Press, February 1, 2000.

21. "Immigration: Threatening the Bonds of Our Union," produced by American Patrol. http://www.americanpatrol.org/_SPECIAL/transcript3.html

22. Ibid.

23. Alan and Suzanne Nevling, "Mexico's Plans for Its Newest Colony: Inevitable Response to U.S. Abdication," *savetheusa.net*, July 11, 2000.

24. Sam Howe Verhovek, "Torn Between Nations, Mexican-Americans Can Have Both," *New York Times,* April 14, 1998, p. A12.

25. Ed Mendel, "Speaker-elect Product of Humble Past, Fiery Ascent," *San Diego Union-Tribune,* February 13, 1998, p. 13.

26. James Lubinskas, "Expressions of Ethnic Animosity," *FrontPageMag.com,* November 24, 1999. www.frontPageMag.com/archives/racerelations/lubinskas11-24-99.htm

27. Sam Dillon, "Mexico Woos U.S. Mexicans, Proposing Dual Nationality," *New York Times,* December 10, 1995, p. 16.

28. El Plan Espiritual de Aztlan, http://www.panam.edu/orgs/MEChA/aztlan.html

29. Ibid.

30. Ibid.

31. Ibid.

32. Ibid.

33. Ibid.

34. Movimento Estudiantil Chicano de Aztlan, National Constitution. http://www.panam.edu/orgs/MEChA/aztlan.html

35. Mark Levin, *FrontPageMag.com*, March 10, 2000. http://frontPageMag.com/archives/leftism/levin03-10-00p.htm.

36. Linda Wertheimer, "Mexico and the United States Agree the Problem of Accidental Border Incursions Must Be Dealt With," *All Things Considered,* March 31, 2000.

37. Robert Collier, "NAFTA Gives Mexicans New Reasons to Leave Home," *San Francisco Chronicle,* October 15, 1998, p. A11.

38. "An Unlikely Mexican Foreign Minister," *New York Times,* May 12, 2001, p. A26. Jorge Castaneda, "Ferocious Differences: Differences Between Mexico and the U.S.," *Atlantic Monthly,* July, 1995, p. 68.

39. San Quinones, "Mexico to Give Survival Kits to Border Jumpers," *San Francisco Chronicle,* May 17, 2001. www.sfgate.com/cgibin/article.cgi?file

40. William H. Frey. "Regional Shifts in America's Voting-Aged Population: What Do They Mean for National Politics?" Population Studies Center, 2001, p. 1.

41. Ken Ringle, "Ellis Island, the Half-Open Door; For a Nation That Struggled to Make Room in Its Heart, a New Monument to Immigrants," *Washington Post,* September 7, 1990, p. B1.

42. Arthur M. Schlesinger, Jr., *The Disuniting of America: Reflections on a Multicultural Society* (New York: W. W. Norton & Company, 1992), p. 118.

43. Carol Morello, "Living in Fear on the Border: Little Desert Town Is New Immigration Battleground," *USA Today,* July 21, 1999, p. 1A.

44. Nancy San Martin, "Unwelcomed Visitors: Arizonans Angry over Flood of Immigrants They Accuse of Damaging Their Property," *Dallas Morning News,* April 25, 1999, p. 53A.

45. Jonathan Aitken, *Nixon: A Life* (Washington, D.C.: Regnery Publishing, 1993), pp. 247–48.

46. George Will, "Blaming the Voters," *Washington Post,* September 24, 2000, p. B7.

47. Jim Yardley, "Non-Hispanic Whites May Soon Be a Minority in Texas," *New York Times,* March 25, 2001, p. A22.

48. Ibid.

49. Todd J. Gillman, "Latinos in U.S. Grow Diverse," *Dallas Morning News,* May 10, 2001, p. 7A.

50. Peter Brimelow, "Time to Rethink Immigration?" *National Review,* June 22, 1992. http://www.vdare.com/time_to_rethink.htm.

51. Stephen Glover, "Are the Tories the Stupid Party Again?" *Daily Mail,* December 5, 2000, p. 13.

52. Laura Parker, "U.S. Hispanics' Youth Assures More Growth," *USA Today,* May 10, 2001, p. 3A.

53. Walter V. Robinson, "Immigrant Voter Surge Seen Aiding Gore," *Boston Globe,* November 4, 2000, p. A1.

54. Ibid.

55. Ibid.

56. Ibid.

57. Ibid.

58. Ron Unz, "California and the End of White America," *Commentary,* November 1, 1999, p. 17.

59. George Borjas and Lynette Hilton, "Immigration and the Welfare State, Working Paper Series #5372," National Bureau of Economic Research, December 1995. http://www.fairus.org/html/04105611.htm

60. Dr. Donald Huddle, "The Net Costs of Immigration: The Facts, the Trends, and the Critics," Rice University, October 22, 1996. http://www.fairus.org/html/04105611.htm

61. Maria L. LaGanga, "California Grows to 33.9 Million, Reflecting Increased Diversity," *Los Angeles Times,* March 30, 2001, p. 1.

62. Robin Fields, "White Exodus Attributed to Economic Slump," *Los Angeles Times,* March 31, 2001, p. 22.

63. "California Census Confirms Whites Are in Minority," *New York Times,* March 30, 2001, p. 1.

64. Ibid.

65. Ken Ward, "The Double-Talk About Diversity," *Las Vegas Review-Journal,* October 11, 2000, p. 9B.

66. Georgie Anne Geyer, "Creative Politics on Alien Conflict," *Washington Times,* August 22, 1999, p. B4.

67. Charley Reese, "Truth Is, George W. Is No Match for Gore in Gaffe Department," *Orlando Sentinel,* November 16, 1999, p. A12.

68. Steven A. Camarota, "Immigrants in the United States, 2000: A Snapshot of America's Foreign-Born Population," *Center for Immigration Studies Backgrounder,* January 2001, p. 7.

69. D'Agostino, ibid.

70. U.S. Census Bureau, "The Foreign-Born Population in the United States," January 2001, p. 4.

71. Ibid., p. 5.

72. Ibid., p. 6.

73. Federation for American Immigration Reform, "Issue Brief: Immigrants on Welfare," June 1999, p. 1.

74. Federation for American Immigration Reform, "Issue Brief: Immigrants and the Economy," April 1999, p. 1.

75. Federation for American Immigration Reform, "Issue Brief: Government Studies on Criminal Aliens," April 1996, p. 2.

76. Federation for American Immigration Reform, "Issue Brief: Criminal Aliens," December 1998, p. 1.

77. Ibid., p. 2.

78. "Business Sets Strategies for Legislation and the 2002 Congressional Races," *Wall Street Journal,* May 18, 2001, p. 1.

79. Ibid.

80. Werner Sollors, *Beyond Ethnicity* (New York: Oxford University Press, 1986), p. 4.

81. Dan Schweikert, "Cultural Wars: A General Ignorance of Language, Logic, and Philosophy," *ENewsViews,* June 27, 1999, p. 1.

82. John Jay, *The Federalist, No. 2,* October 31, 1787.

83. Will Herberg, *Protestant, Catholic, Jew: An Essay in American Religious Sociology* (Chicago: University of Chicago Press), 1983 reprint.

84. Jeff Jacoby, "The Role of Religion in Government: Invoking Jesus at the Inauguration," *Boston Globe,* February 1, 2001, p. A15.

85. Ibid.

86. "Text of Bush's Inaugural Speech," Associated Press, January 20, 2001.

87. Schlesinger, p. 134.

88. John Stuart Mill, *Considerations on Represenative Government* (London: Everyman, 1993), p. 233

## Chapter Seven: The War Against the Past

1. Otto Scott, "The Shape of Events," Speech to the 15th Annual Meeting of the Committee for Monetary Research and Education, November 6, 1989. http://www.fortfreedom.org/h18.htm

2. "Prepared Text of President Reagan's Farewell Address to the Nation," Associated Press, January 12, 1989.

3. George Orwell, *1984* (New York: Signet Classics, 1961), p. 32.

4. Marvin Seid, "Stories That Shaped the Century; Cold War First Turned Hot in Korea," *Los Angeles Times,* November 6, 1999, p. B4.

5. Karen Turni, "Scholars Fighting Battle of Myths," *Times Picayune,* January 9, 1994, p. A1.

6. Luke 17:2, *Holy Bible,* King James Version.

7. Arthur M. Schlesinger, Jr., *The Disuniting of America* (New York: W. W. Norton & Company, 1992), p. 52.

8. Ibid.

9. Mike Feinsilber, "499 Years Later, His Reputation Is as Tattered as His Sails," Associated Press, October 7, 1991.

10. Elisabeth Hickey, "500 Years After Discovery/Encounter, Columbus Is Up for Bashing," *Washington Times,* September 8, 1991, p. D4.

11. Lynda Hurst, "The First Immigrant," *Toronto Star,* October 12, 1991, p. D1.

12. Barbara Vobejda, "Which Legacy? Explorer's Image Changes with the Times," *Washington Post,* October 11, 1992, p. A1.

13. George Szamuely, "The Real Shame of the West," *American Outlook,* Winter 1999, p. 69.

14. John Noble Wilford, "Discovering Columbus," *New York Times Magazine,* August 11, 1992, p. 25.

15. Carmen Radedaugh, "Berkeley Holiday Honors Indigenous People," *University Wire,* October 10, 2000.

16. Robert Mercer Taliaferro Hunter, "Origin of the Late War," *Southern Historical Society Papers, vol. 1,* January 1876. http://www.civilwarhome.com/warorigin.htm

17. Robert Novak, *Completing the Revolution* (New York: The Free Press, 2000), p. 62.

18. Theodore Caplow, Louis Hicks, and Ben J. Wattenberg, *The First Measured Century* (Washington, D.C.: AEI Press, 2001), pp. 210–11.

19. Ibid.

20. David A. Yeagley, *FrontPageMag.com,* May 18, 2001.

21. Ibid.

22. James Verniere, "War Is Mel; Say You Want a Revolution?" *Boston Herald,* June 28, 2000, p. 51.

23. Ann Hornaday, "Freedom from Logic Defeats 'The Patriot,'" *Baltimore Sun,* June 28, 2000, p. E1.

24. Jam! Showbiz/Sun Wire, "Spike Lee Blasts 'Patriot' over Slavery," *Ottawa Sun,* July 7, 2000, p. 28.

25. Jonathan Foreman, "The Nazis, er, the Redcoats Are Coming!" *Salon.com,* July 3, 2000. http://www.salonmag.com/ent/movies/feature/2000/07/03/patriot/

26. Ibid.

27. Ibid.

28. Ibid.

29. Ibid.

30. Ibid.

31. Kevin Sack, "Un-Naming Names; Today's Battles Topple Yesterday's Heroes," *New York Times,* November 17, 1997, p. 5.

32. "Will State Dems Back Declaration?" *Wisconsin State Journal,* December 28, 2000, A1.

33. Andrea Billups, "Black Legislators Stall Bill on Independence Pledge," *Washington Times,* March 1, 2000, p. A3.

34. Florida American Indian Movement, "Press Release: Florida AIM Rejects Desperate Compromise to Keep Hitler Prototype in Springtime Tallahassee Parade," March 7, 2000.

35. "Indians Target Highway Named After Jackson," *Middle American News,* June 2001, p. 7.

36. Michael Rust, "Remembering Faces of Heroism," *Insight on the News,* July 19, 1999, p. 47.

37. "Schools Aren't Eager to Give Up Indian Nicknames, Tradition," Associated Press, April 19, 2001.

38. John Cummins, "Taking the Offensive Against Indian Nicknames," *Salt Lake Tribune,* August 6, 1994, p. A13.

39. Brian Bergstein, "Statue of Flag-Planting Mayor Causes Decade of Controversy in San Jose," Associated Press, October 15, 2000.

40. Peter Guinta, "The Flap About Ponce," *St. Augustine Record,* October 22, 2000, p. A12.

41. Elizabeth Kiggen Miller, "Anti-Bias Task Force Says No to a Pilgrim," *New York Times,* October 10, 1999, p. 16.

42. Ibid.

43. Bob Lewis, "Ex-Confederate Capital Still Struggles with Questions of Race," Associated Press, July 19, 2000.

44. Ralph Z. Hallow, "New DNC Chairman Enters Ring Swinging," *Washington Times,* February 4, 2001, p. A1.

45. Christy Hoppe, "Confederate Plaques Are Taken Down; Governor's Office Makes Quiet Change at Courts," *Dallas Morning News,* June 13, 2000, p. 1A.

46. "Florida Capitol Retires Confederate Flag," Associated Press, February 12, 2001.

47. Emily Wagster, "Confederate Emblem to Stay on Flag," Associated Press, April 18, 2001.

48. Randy Kraft, "Harpers Ferry History Involves Much More than John Brown," *Morning Call* (Allentown), March 28, 1998; Otto Scott, *The Secret Six: John Brown and the Abolitionist Movement* (New York: Times Books, 1979), pp. 288–91.

49. Steve Vogel, "New Controversy Under Old Banner; Prisoners' Descendants Want Confederate Flag in Cemetery," *Washington Post,* October 18, 2000, p. B1.

50. Fern Shen, "Group Rebels over Recall of Auto Tags; Confederate Flag Logo at Center of Maryland Fight," *Washington Post,* January 4, 1997, p. B1.

51. David L. Greene, "Civil War Buff Stands His Ground as Antietam Proposal Draws Fire," *Baltimore Sun,* September 24, 2000, p. 1B.

52. "Plan to Change City's Confederate Park into Cancer Memorial Draws Complaints," Associated Press, May 10, 1999.

53. Jack Hurst, *Nathan Bedford Forrest: A Biography* (New York: Vintage Books, 1994), p. 361.

54. Ibid., p. 385.

55. Ibid.

56. Walter Williams, "Overlooked Black Confederates," *Washington Times,* January 31, 2000, p. A13.

57. Stephen Dinan, "Gilmore Surrenders Virginia's Heritage," *Washington Times,* March 21, 2001, p. A1.

58. R. H. Melton, "Va. Scraps Tribute to Confederacy," *Washington Post,* March 21, 2001, p. A1.

59. Ibid.

60. Ibid.

61. "Carry Me Back, RIP," *Richmond Times Dispatch,* February 26, 1997, A12.

62. Justin Kaplan, "Selling 'Huck Finn' Down the River," *New York Times,* March 10, 1996, p. 27.

63. Linda Grant, "In Search of Harper Lee," *Independent,* December 15, 1991, p. 36.

64. Rod Dreher, "Banning Flannery; Down and Out in Louisiana," *Weekly Standard,* September 11, 2000, p. 33.

65. Ibid.

66. Ibid.

67. Ibid.

68. Ibid.

69. Ibid.

70. "African-American Lawyers Criticize Rehnquist for Singing 'Dixie,' " Associated Press, August 12, 1999.

71. Ibid.

72. Craig Timberg, "Rehnquist's Inclusion of 'Dixie' Strikes a Sour Note," *Washington Post,* July 22, 1999, p. B1.

73. Ibid.

74. Robert Stacy McCain, "Black Leaders Refuse to Pledge Allegiance to Flag; Call Stars and Stripes Symbol of Slavery," *Washington Times,* June 22, 1001, p. A1.

75. Ibid.

76. Paul Kelso, "Mayor Attacks Generals in Battle of Trafalgar Square," *Guardian,* October 20, 2000.

77. Ibid.

78. Gregory M. Grant, "What If It Becomes Desert Sword?" *Chicago Tribune,* September 20, 1990, p. 29.

79. Otto Scott, "The War Against the Past," *Compass,* October 1, 2000, p. 11.

80. "Super Bowl Closer After Arizona Vote," *USA Today,* November 5, 1992, p. 1C.

81. Orwell, p. 217.

82. Wilbert Bryant, Secretary of Education, "The Necessity of Civic Education," Speech to South Brunswick High School, Southport, North Carolina, November 10, 1998. http://www.seced.state.va.us/speechfiles/vetspch-web.htm

83. Scott, "The Shape of Events," op. cit.

84. Hugh Dellios, "Battle over History May Itself Prove Historic," *Chicago Tribune,* October 30, 1994, p. 1.

85. Vaishali Honawar, "Early Grades to 'Simplify' History; Keller, Pocahontas Replace Southern Generals in Lessons," *Washington Times,* December 31, 2000, p. A10.

86. Scott Veale, "History 101: Snoop Doggy Roosevelt," *New York Times,* July 2, 2000, p. 7.

87. Ibid.

88. Phil Kent, "The Tragic Decline of U.S. College Education," *Augusta Chronicle,* April 7, 1996, p. A4.

89. Ibid.

90. Andrea Billups, "History a Mystery to Collegians," *Washington Times,* February 21, 2000, p. A3.

91. Arthur Schlesinger, Jr., "Speaking Up," *Los Angeles Times,* February 7, 1992, p. B2.

92. John Leo, "The National Museums of PC," *U.S. News & World Report,* October 10, 1994, p. 21.

93. Tom Wolfe, "The Tyranny of Theory," *Guardian,* July 8, 2000, p. 1.

## *Chapter Eight: De-Christianizing America*

1. *The Oxford Dictionary of Quotations* (London: Oxford University Press, second edition, 1966), p. 381.

2. Russell Kirk, *Eliot and His Age* (Peru, Ill: Sugden, 1971), p. 390.

3. Lawrence Auster, "Scam Artists or Victims? The Hasidic Defendants of New Square," *NewsMax.com,* January 31, 2001, p. 1.

4. Sarah Karush, "Couple with 16 Kids, and Counting, Defies Russia's Population Trend," Associated Press, April 28, 2001.

5. Peter Ford, "Churches on Wane in Europe," *Christian Science Monitor,* October 25, 1999, p. 1.

6. "Has Christianity Lost Its Identity in Europe?" *Classical Christian News,* October 8, 1999. http://www.prayerbook.ca/pblam699.htm

7. Ibid.

8. Nadia Rybarova, "Czech President Vaclav Havel: Man May Have Lost God," Associated Press, September 4, 1997.

9. Ibid.

10. Larry Witham, " 'Christian Nation' Now Fighting Words; Fordice Fumbles in PC Territory," *Washington Times,* November 23, 1992, p. A1.

11. Gary DeMar, *America's Christian History: The Untold Story* (Atlanta: American Vision, 1995), pp. 51–58.

12. Ibid., p. 1.

13. Ibid., p. 12.

14. Ibid., p. 3.

15. Ibid., p. 11.

16. Ibid., p. 2.

17. Ibid.

18. Ibid., p. 11.

19. Ibid., p. 3.

20. "Excerpts from Supreme Court Opinions on Prayer," *New York Times,* June 20, 2000, p. A22.

21. Marina Zogbi, "Marilyn Manson—a Controversial Conversation with the Irreverent Reverend," *Metal Edge,* July 1996. http://www.cfnweb.com/manson/press/me796.htm

22. Charles Lane, "High Court Lets Ruling on Church, State Stand," *Washington Post,* May 30, 2001, p. A3.

23. American Humanist Association, *Humanist Manifesto II,* 1973. http://humanist.net/documents/manifesto2.html

24. Ibid.

25. Ibid.

26. Ibid.

27. Ibid.

28. Ibid.

29. Ibid.

30. Jim Nelson Black, *When Nations Die* (Wheaton, Ill.: Tyndale House Publishers, 1994), p. xix.

31. C. S. Lewis, *God in the Dock: Essays on Theology and Ethics,* Walter Hooper, ed. (Grand Rapids, Mich.: William B. Eerdmans Publishing Company, 1972), p. 262.

32. "ACLU Asks Judge to Reel in Republic's Fish Symbol," Associated Press, May 6, 1999.

33. Bishop Norman McFarland, "A July 4 Meditation on the Faith of the Founders: One Nation Under God," *Orange County Register,* July 2, 1995, p. J1.

34. *Richmond Newspapers, Inc., et al., Appellants v. Commonwealth of Virginia et al.,* 448 U.S. 555, No. 79–243, Supreme Court of the United States, Concurring Opinion. Argued February 19, 1980. Decided July 2, 1980.

35. J. William J. Brennan, Jr., "To the Text and Teaching Symposium," Georgetown University, Washington, D.C., October 12, 1985. http://www.politics.pomona.edu/dml/LabBrennan.htm

36. William J. Quirk and R. Randall Bridwell, *Judicial Dictatorship* (New Brunswick N.J.: Transaction Publishers, 1995), p. xiii.

37. The Gallup Organization, Princeton, N.J., Poll taken August 12–13, 1997. http://www.gallup.com/poll/indicators/indreligion.asp

38. Christie Storm, "Communities of Faith," *Arkansas Democrat-Gazette,* October 30, 1999, p. H2.

39. Theodore Caplow, Louis Hicks, and Ben J. Wattenberg, *The First Measured Century: An Illustrated Guide to Trends in America, 1900–2000* (Washington, D.C.: AEI Press, 2001), p. 117.

40. Ibid., p. 116.

41. Fulton J. Sheen, "A Plea for Intolerance," 1931.

42. Patricia Rice, "Singing Out: Revisions Steal Poetry, Meaning from Hymns, Professor Says," *St. Louis Post-Dispatch*, June 21, 1997, p. 31.

43. Marjorie Hyer, "Discord on Hymn Changes; United Methodists Aim to Delete Sexism, Racism from Songs," *Washington Post*, March 1, 1986, p. B6.

44. Ibid.

45. John H. Adams, "Inclusive Language for God Is 'Battleground' in PCUSA," *Layman Online*, October 24, 2000. http://www.layman.org/layman/news-from-pcusa/inclusive-language-is-battleground.htm

46. "Debating Baptismal Language," *The Christian Century*, September 27, 1995, p. 880.

47. Sen. Robert Byrd, "Polytheism in Modern Garb," Speech to Senate, July 22, 1992. http://www.senate.gov/~byrd/speech-polytheism.htm

48. Richard N. Ostling, "O God Our [Mother and] Father; New Translations Seek to Rid Bible of 'Male Bias,'" *Time*, October 24, 1983, p. 56.

49. Michael Nelson, "Language Revision Sings; Methodist Hymnal Shows Amazing Grace in Rooting Out Hints of Sexism, Racism," *Commercial Appeal*, September 29, 1991, p. B6.

50. "Quotes from Nontheists." http://memberstripod.com/~Rhatheist/quotes.html

51. Patrick J. Buchanan, "Yes, Mario, There Is a Culture War," *Chicago Tribune*, September 14, 1992, p. 17.

52. David A. Noebel, *The Legacy of John Lennon: Charming or Harming a Generation?* (Nashville, Tenn.: Thomas Nelson, 1982), p. 38.

53. Ibid., p. 39.

54. "In the Bosom of Jesus: Yo Mama's Last Supper," *Nation*, May 28, 2001, p. 30.

55. Elizabeth Bumiller, "Affronted by Nude Last Supper, Giuliani Calls for Decency Panel," *New York Times*, February 16, 2001, p. A1.

56. Michael Janofsky, "Uproar over Virgin Mary in a Two-Piece Swimsuit," *New York Times*, March 31, 2001, p. A11.

57. Ibid.

58. Ibid.

59. Justin Bachman, "Critics Say King Heirs Are Selling Out His Image," Associated Press, March 30, 2001.

60. James F. Cooper, "The Right Agenda: Recapture the Culture," *American Arts Quarterly*, Spring/Summer 1990, p. 3.

61. Ibid.

62. Jay Lindsay, "Christian Group Says Tufts Decision to Cut Funding Threatens Religious Freedom," Associated Press, May 3, 2000.

63. Charles Socarides, "How America Went Gay," *America*, November 18, 1995, p. 20.

64. Ibid.

65. Ibid.

66. Ibid.

67. Harry V. Jaffa, *Homosexuality and Natural Law* (Montclair, Cal.: Claremont Institute for the Study of Statesmanship and Political Philosophy, 1990), p. 31.

68. Martin Luther King, Jr., "Letter from a Birmingham Jail," April 16, 1963. http://www.tcf.ua.edu/courses/Jbutler/T112/King-BirminghamJail.htm

69. George Washington, "Farewell Address," Philadelphia, Penn., September 17, 1796. http://www.virginia.edu/gwpapers/farewell/transcript/html

70. David Limbaugh, "On a Mission for Marriage," *Creators Syndicate,* September 7, 2000.

71. William J. Bennett, *Index of Leading Cultural Indicators* (New York: Broadway Books, 2000), p. 48.

72. Caplow et al., p. 70.

73. Bennett, p. 145.

74. Bennett, p. 52.

75. Bennett, p. 69.

76. Bennett, p. 27.

77. Bennett, p. 35.

78. Bennett, pp. 50, 27.

79. Anthony Harrigan, "The New Anti-Civilization," *Chronicles,* June 2001, p. 44.

80. Jim Nelson Black, *When Nations Die* (Wheaton, Ill.: Tyndale House Publishers, 1994), p. 8.

81. Ruth Gledhill, "Christianity Almost Beaten Says Cardinal," *London Times,* September 6, 2001.

82. Bruce Frohnen, "T. S. Eliot on the Necessity of Christian Culture," Witherspoon Lectures, Family Research Council. http://www.frc.org/papers/witherspoon/index.cfm?get=WT01&arc=yes

83. Russell Kirk, *Eliot and His Age* (New York: Random House, 1971), p. 324.

84. Boy Scouts of America, *Handbook for Boys* (Boyscouts of America, 1911), p. 215.

85. Jeffrie A. Herrman, "BSA Supports Spiritual Direction in Life," *Sun-Sentinel,* October 16, 2000, p. 25A.

86. Boy Scouts of America, "Position Statement on Homosexuality and the BSA," February 15, 1991. http://www.religioustolerance.org/bsa_0.htm

87. Peter Ferrara, "The Battle over the Boy Scouts," *Weekly Standard,* June 11, 2001, p. 21.

88. Transcript, "Should the ACLU Defend NAMBLA?" *The O'Reilly Factor,* January 2, 2001; Bill O'Reilly, "Corrupters Setting the Standards," *Washington Times,* May 21, 2001, p. A16.

89. Superior Court of New Jersey, Appellate Division, A-2427-95T3, *James Dale v. Boy Scouts of America,* Argued December 8, 1997, Decided March 2, 1998. http://diana.law.yale.edu/Diana/db/4298-36.html

90. "Spielberg to Quit Boy Scouts Board," Associated Press, April 17, 2001.

91. Valerie Richardson, "Democratic Delegates Boo the Boy Scouts of America," *Washington Times,* August 18, 2000, p. A1.

92. Nat Hentoff, "Scouts Honor? '60 Minutes' Coverage Biased and Unfair," *Washington Times,* April 16, 2001, p. A17.

93. Ibid.

94. T. S. Eliot, "Notes Towards the Definition of Culture," *Christianity and Culture* (New York: Harcourt, Brace, 1967), p. 200.

## Chapter Nine: Intimidated Majority

1. James Lubinskas, *FrontPageMag.com*. http://www.FrontPageMag./RaceRelations/lubinskas11-24-99.htm

2. Roger Kimball, *The Long March* (San Francisco: Encounter Books, 2000), pp. 274–75.

3. Transcript. "Larry King Live," *CNN*, August 4, 2000.

4. "Taking Stock," *Nationalreview.com*, November 15, 2000. http://www.nationalreview.com/daily/nr111500.shtml

5. Jim Abrams, "Armey Expresses Concern About 'Racial McCarthyism,'" Associated Press, February 23, 2001.

6. Ibid.

7. Ibid.

8. Ibid.

9. Joseph D'Agostino and Timothy Carney, "Congressmen: Illegals Here to Stay," *Human Events*, April 2, 2001, p. 3.

10. "Transcript of Clinton Remarks at Portland State University Commencement," U.S. Newswire, June 15, 1998.

11. Peter Brimelow, *Alien Nation: Common Sense About America's Immigration Disaster* (New York: Random House, 1995), p. 233.

12. Henrik Bering, "Denmark, the Euro, and Fear of the Foreign," *Policy Review*, December 2000, p. 6.

13. Ibid.

14. James Burnham, *Suicide of the West* (New York: The John Day Company, 1964), p. 26.

15. Richard Weaver, *The Southern Tradition at Bay: A History of Post-Bellum Thought* (New Rochelle, N.Y.: Arlington House, 1968), p. 18.

16. George F. Will, "A Summons to Gratitude," *Newsweek*, August 17, 1998, p. 70.

17. Lionel Trilling, *Liberal Imagination: Essays on Literature and Society* (New York: Harcourt Brace, 1979 reprint), intro.

18. Crane Britton, *Anatomy of Revolution* (New York: Vintage Books, 1952), p. 45.

19. Adolf Hitler, *Mein Kampf* (New York: CPA Books, 2000), p. 191.

20. "Be Not Afraid; Justice Thomas on Courage and Civic Principles," *Washington Times*, February 15, 2001, p. A17.

21. Ibid.

22. Ibid.

23. Samuel Francis, *Revolution from the Middle* (Raleigh, N.C.: Middle American Press, 1997), p. 174.

24. Ibid.

25. Transcript, "This Week with David Brinkley," *ABC*, July 2, 1995.

26. Transcript, "Hannity and Colmes," *FOX NEWS*, December 20, 2000.

27. Steve Miller and Jerry Seper, "NAACP Tax Exempt Status Questioned; Critics Say Group Oversteps Bounds with Democratic Leanings," *Washington Times*, February 6, 2001, p. A1.

28. Richard Lezin Jones, "Georgia Is the Latest Battlefield in the Stars and Bars War," *Knight Ridder News Service,* February 6, 2001.

29. Richard Lowry, " 'Conservative' and 'Racist': The Ashcroft Nomination and the Left's Foulest Card," *National Review,* February 5, 2000, p. 2.

30. John Sawyer, "Bush Says Scrutiny of Missouri Voters Validates Ashcroft," *St. Louis Post Dispatch,* January 14, 2001, p. A1.

31. David Garrow, *Bearing the Cross* (New York: William Morrow & Company, 1999), p. 351.

32. James K. Robinson and Walter P. Rideout, eds., *A College Book of Modern Verse* (Evanston, Illinois: Row, Peterson, and Company, 1960), p. 549.

33. Joan Acocella, "The Hunger Artist: Is There Anything Susan Sontag Doesn't Want to Know?" *The New Yorker,* March 6, 2000, p. 68.

34. Tom Wolfe, "The Tyranny of Theory," *Guardian,* July 8, 2000, p. 1.

35. Ibid.

36. Dinesh D'Souza, "Racism Is Not the Problem: Why Martin Luther King Got It Half Right," Accuracy in Academia Address, Georgetown University, 1999. http://www.conservativeuniversity.org/lecturehall/index.htm

37. Paul Craig Roberts and Lawrence M. Stratton, Jr., "Color Code," *National Review,* March 20, 1995, p. 48.

38. Barbara Tuchman, Conservativeforum.org. http://www.conservativeforum.org/authquot.asp?ID-622

39. Walter Williams, "Scholastic Expectations," *Washington Times,* November 18, 2000, p. A12.

40. Walter Williams, "Race Hustling Chorus," *Washington Times,* December 22, 2000, p. A20.

41. Stephen Gill, "The French Revolution: A Tale of Two Cities," *Independent,* June 14, 1989.

42. Chilton Williamson, "Democracy and the Art of Handloading," *Chronicles,* February 2001.

43. Thomas Edsall, "Voter Values Determine Political Affiliation," *Washington Post,* March 26, 2001, p. A1.

44. Terry Teachout, "Republican Nation, Democratic Nation?" *Commentary,* January 2001, p. 25.

45. Edsall, op. cit.

46. Amy Martinez, "Fighting Discrimination with What Business Fears: Big-Dollar Lawsuits," Cox *News Service,* March 4, 2001.

47. "The Truth About Jesse," *New York Post,* April 1, 2001, p. 52.

48. "Black Employees Sue Christian Coalition," *Washington Times,* February 24, 2001, p. A2.

## Chapter Ten: A House Divided

1. Michael Blowen, "Jack Nicholson Roles Often Contradict His Life," *Des Moines Register,* April 30, 1998, p. 3.

2. J. Donald Adams, "Worth Fighting For," *New York Times,* October 6, 1996, p. 55.

3. Francis Beauchesne Thornton, ed., *Return to Tradition* (Fort Collins, Colo.: Roman Catholic Books), p. 304.

4. Will Durant, *Caesar and Christ* (New York: Simon & Schuster, 1944), p. 666.

5. James Burnham, *Suicide of the West* (New York: The John Day Company, 1964), p. 301.

6. Donna Nebenzahl, "Why the Globalization Pot Is About to Boil," *Gazette,* April 2, 2001, p. E4.

7. Norman Podhoretz, "My War with Allen Ginsberg," *Commentary,* August 1997. http://www.commentarymagazine.com/9708/norman.html

8. Roger Kimball, *The Long March: How the Cultural Revolution of the 1960s Changed America* (San Francisco: Encounter Books, 2000), p. 8.

9. Madison Grant and Charles Stewart Davison, *The Founders of the Republic on Immigration, Naturalization, and Aliens* (New York: Charles Scribner's Sons, 1928), p. iv.

10. Jacques Steinberg, "Test Scores Rise, Surprising Critics of Bilingual Ban," *New York Times,* August 20, 2000, p. 1.

11. Ibid.

12. Ibid.

13. *The New Oxford Book of American Verse,* Richard Ellmann, ed. (New York: Oxford University Press, 1976), pp. 395–96.

14. American Humanist Association, *Humanist Manifesto II,* 1973. http://humanist.net/documents/manifesto2.html

15. Ibid.

16. Strobe Talbott, "America Abroad; The Birth of the Global Nation," *Time,* July 20, 1992, p. 70.

17. Ibid.

18. Michael Mann, "Prodi Urges Fundamental Debate on Future of EU," *Financial Times,* February 14, 2001, p. 1.

19. Samuel Francis, *Thinkers of Our Time* (London: The Claridge Press, 1999), p. 102.

20. Peter Capella, "Swiss Decide Against Joining EU," *Manchester Guardian Weekly,* March 14, 2001, p. 5.

21. Ibid.

22. Mann, p. 1.

23. Ibid.

24. James Kurth, "The American Way of Victory," *National Interest,* Summer 2000, p. 5.

25. Patrick J. Buchanan, "Nature's Retribution," *New York Post,* February 24, 1983.

26. Kenneth Minogue, "How Civilizations Fail," *New Criterion,* April 2001. http://www.newcriterion.com/archive/19/apr01/minogue.htm

27. Fulton J. Sheen, "A Plea for Intolerance," 1931.

28. Ibid.

29. Ibid.

30. *Gone With the Wind,* Metro-Goldwyn-Mayer, 1939.

31. Terry Teachout, "Republican Nation, Democratic Nation?" *Commentary,* January 2001, p. 25.

32. Matthew 22:21, *Holy Bible,* King James Version.

33. James K. Fitzpatrick, "More of Them," *Wanderer,* December 7, 2000.

34. "100 Greatest Movies," American Film Institute. http://www.afioline.org:82/100movies/100list.asp

35. Ibid.

36. Ibid.

37. "100 Best Novels," Modern Library Board. http://www.randomhouse.com/modernlibrary/100best/novels.html

38. "100 Best Nonfiction," Modern Library Board. http://www.randomhouse.com/modernlibrary/100best/

39. "President-elect Bush's Victory Speech," *Facts on File,* December 13, 2000, p. 951A1.

40. Ernest Hemingway, *The Sun Also Rises* (New York: Scribner and Sons, 1996), p. 222.

41. Chilton Williamson, Jr., "Democracy and the Art of Handloading," *Chronicles,* February 2001.

42. Ibid.

43. Ibid.

44. *The Wizard of Oz,* Metro-Goldwyn-Mayer, 1939.

45. James MacGregor Burns, *Roosevelt: The Lion and the Fox* (New York: Harcourt, Brace, and World, 1956), p. 151.

46. Richard John Neuhaus, *The End of Democracy?: The Celebrated First Things Debate with Arguments Pro and Con and "The Anatomy of a Controversy"* (Dallas: Spence Publishing, 1997), pp. 5, 3.

47. Ibid., p. 7.

48. Ibid., p. 16.

49. Ibid., p. 17.

50. Alan Wolfe, "Oh, Those Beltway Innocents," *New York Times,* August 30, 1998, p. 13.

51. Irving Kristol, "Family Values: Not a Political Issue," *Wall Street Journal,* December 7, 1992, p. A14.

52. Gertrude Himmelfarb, *One Nation, Two Cultures* (New York: Alfred A. Knopf, 1999), p. 146.

53. Hilton Kramer and Roger Kimball, eds., *The Future of the European Past* (Chicago: Ivan R. Dee, 1996), p. 7.

54. Norman Podhoretz, *My Love Affair with America: The Cautionary Tale of a Cheerful Conservative* (New York: The Free Press, 2000), pp. 215, 218.

55. Ibid., p. 218.

56. Ibid., p. 217.

57. Ibid.

58. T. S. Eliot, *Christianity and Culture* (New York: Harcourt Brace Jovanovich, 1968), p. 100.

59. Podhoretz, p. 220.

60. Jonathan Alter, "Where PC Meets Free Speech," *Newsweek,* April 2, 2001, p. 31.

61. Don Feder, "Planned Parenthood Demands a Recount," *Jewish World Review,* December 28, 2000.

62. Ibid.

63. Anne Fremantle, *The Papal Encyclicals* (New York: G. P. Putnam's Sons, 1956), p. 241.

64. Emily Wagster, "Mississippi Flag Vote Falls Largely Along Racial Lines," Associated Press, April 21, 2001.

65. James Madison, "The Federalist 49: Method of Guarding Against the Encroachments of Any One Department of Government by Appealing to the People Through a Convention," February 2, 1788.

66. John Fonte, "Why There Is a Culture War," *Policy Review,* December 2000 and January 2001, p. 21.

67. Ibid.

68. "Yo Philistines," *Washington Times,* February 21, 2001, p. A16.

69. Roger Kimball, "Closing Time? Jacques Barzun on Western Culture," *New Criterion,* June 2000. http://www.newcriterion.com/archive/18/jun00/barzun.htm

70. Ibid.

71. Herbert Stein, "Herb Stein's Unfamiliar Quotations," *Slate Magazine,* May 15, 1997.

72. Richard John Neuhaus, "Lord Acton, Cardinal Newman, and How to Be Ahead of Your Time," *First Things: A Monthly Journal of Religion and Public Life,* August 1, 2000, p. 77.

73. Pat Donnelly, "Know Your Diderot," *Gazette,* August 13, 1991, p. E1.

74. George Walden, "Coasting on Dead Men's Ideas," *Evening Standard,* February 12, 2001, p. 54.

75. Tirdad Derakhshani, "At God's Funeral, Biographer Describes 'Killers' of the Deity," *Arizona Republic,* August 29, 1999, p. E12.

76. Jim Nelson Black, *When Nations Die* (Wheaton, Ill.: Tyndale House Publishers, 1994), p. 9.

77. John Senior, *The Death of Christian Culture* (New Rochelle, N.Y.: Arlington House Publishers, 1978), p. 7.

78. Abraham Lincoln, "First Inaugural Address," Washington, D.C., March 4, 1861. http://libertyonline.hypermall.com/Lincoln/lincoln-1.html

79. James K. Robinson and Walter B. Rideout, eds., *The College Book of Modern Verse* (Evanston, Ill.: Row, Peterson and Company, 1960), p. 65.

80. Eliot, p. 50.

81. Ibid.

82. Kimball. http://www.newcriterion.com/archive/18/jun00/barzun.htm

83. David Ramsey, "John Brown's Body Still Draws Americans to Ponder His Legacy," *Houston Chronicle,* September 27, 1998, p. A38.

# INDEX